Adventures in Coaching

Benjamin Dowman

Adventures in Coaching

Unlocking the power of personal and business
coaching through a captivating story

Benjamin Dowman

NICHOLAS BREALEY
PUBLISHING

London • Boston

First published in Great Britain by Nicholas Brealey Publishing in 2020
An imprint of John Murray Press
A division of Hodder & Stoughton Ltd,
An Hachette UK company

1

The acknowledgments on p. 225 constitute an extension of this copyright page.

A CIP catalogue record for this title is available from the British Library

Trade Paperback ISBN 9781529365832
eBook ISBN 9781529365849

Typeset by Cenveo® Publisher Services.

Printed and bound in Great Britain by Clays Ltd, Elcograf S.p.A.

John Murray Press policy is to use papers that are natural, renewable and recyclable products
and made from wood grown in sustainable forests. The logging and manufacturing processes
are expected to conform to the environmental regulations of the country of origin.

John Murray Press
Carmelite House
50 Victoria Embankment
London EC4Y 0DZ

Nicholas Brealey Publishing
Hachette Book Group
Market Place, Center 53, State Street
Boston, MA 02109, USA

www.nicholasbrealey.com

Contents

About the Author

Ben Dowman is a coach, facilitator, psychologist, and leadership consultant and has worked within personal and organisational development for 20 years, both nationally and internationally. He runs his own business, Irrational Coaching, where he offers individual and executive coaching, coach training and NLP training.

His past clients include O2, NHS, Network Rail, The Law Society, Lloyds Bank, Airbus Group, Vodafone, Rothschild and The UK Royal Air Force and he has previously worked at the University of Cumbria as a Lecturer in Coaching and Mentoring.

Ben lives in the English Lake District and loves the outdoors, notably, cycling up steep hills, lake swimming and climbing vertical rock.

CHAPTER 1

A Guide to the Wonderland
That is Coaching

AN INTRODUCTION TO THE STYLE, FORMAT AND
CONTENT OF THIS BOOK

● ● ●

When we begin coaching we enter a fantasy world, a journey into a wonderland called 'the other person'. It is like the world we know but different; at times it may parallel our own reality and at others it is unrecognizable. When the director of a large organization tells me she wants to do the best she can, we are in territory I can personally relate to. When she describes how she gets up at 5am every day to check and double-check emails and papers before sending them because she is frightened of being considered an imposter, then I feel we have entered into a different reality. A daily experience for her, but to me an invention of her mind that seems hard to comprehend. Yet, comprehend I must, and in order to work with my client effectively, I must step out of the wonderland that is my own reality and be willing to step into hers.

As a coach it is a great privilege and responsibility to be invited into other people's worlds and to be able to offer the skills of enquiry, observation and challenge to help them. While many of the problems we experience in life and work may have commonalities, they are also uniquely individual, shaped by each of our life experiences, thoughts and feelings. Each time I begin working with a client I remind myself that their internal reality may not follow the same rules as mine, and, as such, it is a fantasy wonderland where I don't know where anything will lead. I don't know what is solid and what is fragile. I don't know where there might be historic sites and monuments to past troubles and I don't know where in this wonderland there might be great resources and undiscovered potential.

Coaching isn't just full of wonder because of our clients' challenges. The resolution of problems and the solutions for improvement sometimes follow unexpected and illogical paths. A line of questioning about practical solutions is often unproductive until we examine a client's imaginations and unpick their beliefs and perceptions about what is happening. We must resolve the internal reality before external progress can be made. Sometimes clients suggest solutions which will surely perpetuate their problem or simply create a new one. Only when we take what seems like a fantastical approach and examine the problem at a different level do we find a way forward.

As you read this book I hope you will gain insights into your own reality and you will learn skills to enhance your coaching conversations, as well as ... hang on a minute, 'What's that, Alice?'

'It's a book about me, too – make sure you say it's about *me*.'

'Yes, I will.'

The book is also about Alice, the star of the story and her own journey as she learns about coaching.

'And it's about the characters I meet – make sure you mention Rita and Ronald.'

'But, Alice, Rita is a turtle and Ronald is a fish. It might be too early to introduce talking animals, this is a serious book.'

'Well, you made them all up and brought them to life. That whole ant-rope-stuff-thingy. Don't pretend you didn't write this.'

'Anthropomorphism, Alice. And, good point, I did do that.'

'Anyway, people will soon forget that the animals are talking. Just tell them.'

'Alice, why don't you introduce some of the characters in the story?'

'Right then, I will. First, there's the Caterpillar – I never did find out his name. Then there's Rita – she's a turtle, although I thought she was a tortoise at first and she didn't like that. She is a-ma-zing – she knows everything about coaching and taught me so much. Ronald was my fellow student – he's a manager for a company that makes bikes and Rita taught us both how to coach other people. Oh, and he's a fish, did I mention that? Then there's Christina – she's a ladybird who I coached about her interview technique. Hugo is a chimpanzee – he had some social anxiety and Rita coached him; I learned loads from watching her work. Reynard is a fox who we met when we got sent to the Doghouse. I didn't do anything bad, I promise. And there's Tad – he's a frog. I don't know what to say about him – his songs were good but he was a bit crazy.'

'I think that will do for starters, Alice; I want to keep a few surprises. Let's tell people what they're going to learn about.'

And, since in coaching we often start by identifying a goal, it seems appropriate to ask you what your goals are for reading this book. You might like to consider:

- What do *you* want to learn about with regard to coaching?
- What questions do you have about coaching that you would like answered?
- What would make this a really worthwhile read for you?

Of course, you might not know. If you're new to coaching and want to understand more about what it is, how it works and what the key skills are, then the earlier chapters will be of great interest to you in setting the scene. If you're experienced in coaching, then the first chapters may be revision of key ideas before we progress on to more advanced coaching concepts. The latter chapters introduce some more complex ideas and consider some of the entanglements that coaches and their clients can experience.

'Ben, I think you should also explain why you've written this book.'

'Good suggestion, Alice. I think there are two questions: first, why write about coaching? And second, why write *this* book?'

Why write about coaching? I care about coaching because I believe that the skills and attitudes of a coach are increasingly important. In the world of business, pressures seem only to increase as change happens faster, and I worry that the skills of enquiry and listening are being forgotten. The resulting problems become more protracted and conflicts harder to resolve. The single-minded heroic leader is a thing of the past, and today's leaders must use a blend of styles and approaches if they are to be successful. In wider society we observe increasing polarization and conflict, and I think it unlikely that this will be resolved by each side pushing harder against the other. The ability to listen and acknowledge the views of another, to question and seek to understand, even when these views are different from our own, is central to integration and unity. These may seem like lofty ideals, but I believe that the fundamental skills of a coach have a great deal to offer.

In writing about coaching, I refer to three things: first, working and operating as a coach and offering your services to help clients; second, the leadership style of coaching and the application of coaching skills to managers, business owners and leaders; and third, the attitudes and skills of asking questions, exploring ideas and listening which apply to our everyday conversations, whoever they might be with.

'Wow, Ben, that's a bit heavy. It sounds like you think coaching is going to save the world.'

'Do you think so, Alice? Well, I can assure you I don't and it won't, but I do think the skillset has some important applications which I want to share with people.'

The second question: *why write this book?* There are a couple of reasons. First, most books about coaching are textbooks or manuals.

'BORING! Textbooks remind me of school. Boring. Boring. Boring.'

'You're not a fan of textbooks then, Alice? Personally, I have read some very well-written textbooks about coaching, but sometimes reading a textbook can be hard work. I want to write something fun and engaging that makes learning easy. Furthermore, I want to make the complex ideas in coaching accessible and easier to understand with examples that bring them to life.'

In fact, now might be a good time to map out some of the key ideas in the coming chapters.

Chapter 2 introduces what coaching is and why the approach might be used. My own definition is that coaching unlocks potential, increases flexibility, gives options and develops the individual.

Unlocking potential means helping someone become aware of limiting patterns of thinking, feeling, communicating and behaving, so they are unencumbered and free to utilize and discover their full potential. Sometimes these limitations are rooted in past experiences that may require some examination, but, more often than not, once a person becomes aware of their own internal processes of thinking and feeling, they can begin to work with them. Increasing flexibility and giving options applies behaviourally as well as in thinking and feeling. If a person always has the same feeling in response to something, they have very little choice in how they behave. Coaching can explore and highlight new ways of behaving and bring new perspectives that change thoughts and feelings. Developing the individual refers to the bigger picture of helping someone increase self-awareness and expand their emotional and behavioural range. This may have benefits above and beyond the focus of the coaching and help the person as an individual not just in regard to the specific coaching issue.

Chapter 3 starts with the essential coaching skill of listening, something which a lot of us are not as good at as we think we are.

'Actually, Ben, I read that, in a survey, nearly everyone said their listening skills were above average.'

'Um, well, yes, Alice. Like I said.'

Chapter 3 also explores asking questions, the difference between open and closed questions, and, since coaching is primarily about open questions, what makes a good open question.

'And I get to sing a song while the Frog plays the mandolin.'

'Yes, well remembered, Alice, I'm glad you mentioned that.'

'Shall I sing it again now? It might make a nice introduction.'

'I love your enthusiasm, Alice, but I think we should save it for Chapter 3. People will enjoy it more then. Look, in the meantime, why don't you talk about what else is coming in the book?'

'I'd rather sing a song, Ben, but OK. Chapter 4 is where I meet Ronald and do some coaching with him. He finds it really helpful and becomes curious about learning coaching himself, so I invite him to join Rita and me in learning some more. Chapter 5 is really good because I set Rita and Ronald a really difficult riddle. I ask them: 'What has fewer holes the more holes you make in it?'

'That's a really difficult riddle, Alice. But it's not the main focus of Chapter 5, is it?'

'You're always so serious, Ben, you need to smile more. I'm going to find you a fun poem.'

Alice does rather like poetry and from time to time she recites some verse, although she does tend to get the words wrong.

'I don't get the words *wrong*; I improve them and make them relevant to the subject matter.'

'That's right, Alice, sorry. Is it all right if I continue explaining the book while you find your poem?'

She's gone. Chapter 5 then. As well as Alice's riddle about holes, the chapter introduces the GROW coaching model which provides a structure for how to have a coaching conversation from start to finish. There are plenty of example questions for you to use. In writing this book I've selected the GROW framework because it's simple but effective; there are only four stages to remember and it provides plenty of scope for different applications.

In Chapter 6 Alice puts the GROW framework into practice and there is an example of a coaching conversation. Over the last 15 years

I have had hundreds of coaching conversations and I've noticed patterns in the way clients describe the problems and challenges they face. None of the coaching examples in this book are based on any single coaching client I've worked with but are an amalgamation of coaching work that relates to that issue. I've attempted to make each character's answers as realistic as possible based on my own experience. Chapter 6 also examines the differences between coaching and other approaches: mentoring, teaching, counselling and therapy. When people begin learning coaching I've noticed there is sometimes confusion about the differences and overlaps. All of these approaches are valuable ways to work, but I think it's helpful to be clear about what coaching is and what it isn't.

Chapter 7 introduces the concept of a map of the world, the idea that we each have our own version of reality that is constructed inside of us. We might think that our experience of the world is how it actually is, but in fact our perceptions are shaped by our own thoughts, feelings, beliefs, values and previous experiences. This concept is important in coaching, as it is often useful for coaches to consider how our clients frame their challenges or problems. The separation of these things is essential, and one of our main roles in coaching is to ask questions that enable the client to separate their thoughts about a situation from the actual situation.

Chapter 8 introduces the learning ladder and the four stages that we each progress through when learning something new. These are unconsciously unskilled, consciously unskilled, consciously skilled and unconsciously skilled.

'And we go to the beach.'

'Alice, you're back! I was just introducing the learning ladder.'

'I couldn't find the poem, Ben, so I'm going to do it from memory.'

She's standing up. Here we go.

> 'Smiling is contagious,
> It spreads from me to you,
> A turtle smiled at me today,
> And taught me something new.
>
> I discovered things I didn't know,
> And realized I'm not skilled,
> But because of this I'm keen to learn,
> And my experience will build.

Each time I learn I start to smile,
While I practise something new,
I realized learning can be fun,
And now coaching is what I do.

When you're learning, pause awhile,
And allow yourself some grins,
Knowledge and skills will make you smile,
As your expertise begins.*

'Brilliant, Alice. I don't know how you do that.'

'I'm not sure I remembered it completely correctly.'

'Well, it's a lovely poem. I'm outlining what's coming in the book. I'll carry on, shall I?'

She's muttering to herself. I think she's trying to remember the original poem.

Let's continue.

Chapter 9 is a coaching example with a client who has social anxiety. This is an example of where an issue occurs within the client's own thinking and feeling, within their map of the world. Since the problem exists within the client's own thinking and feeling, that is where we must work to transform and find a way forward. Too often I see coaches attempting 'practical' solutions to issues which are unlikely to be resolved that way. These so-called 'practical' solutions tend to address the symptom of the problem rather than the cause. For instance, in the Chapter 9 example our client, Hugo, has some social anxiety and difficulty talking to new people. A practical suggestion might be to go with a friend for some support or have a drink to relax. These may or may not help but only address the symptom of the problem.

Chapter 10 discusses implementing coaching as a manager and considers its place within organizations. More and more leaders and managers are recognizing the benefits of using a coaching approach as part of conversations with their team, colleagues, customers and suppliers. In this chapter we consider how best to incorporate a coaching approach and how to make it work effectively. The commencement of any coaching

---

*The poem Alice recites here is inspired by *Smiling is Infectious*, a poem which has been attributed to Spike Milligan.

is particularly important, and we examine the contracting conversation and how to ensure clarity about roles, responsibilities and expectations.

In Chapter 11 there is consideration of the dynamics that can exist within a coaching relationship and the entanglements that can arise without clear boundaries. What happens when the coach becomes embroiled in wanting their client to resolve something, either because the coach cares deeply and wants to help or because the coach's own ego requires a 'successful' outcome. Building on this, we ask: when is helping not really helping? And how do we recognize when a coaching conversation may be disempowering a client? All this really raises the question: how do we as coaches empower clients and foster self-reliance instead of dependence?

Chapter 12 is an example of a difficult coaching conversation where a client seems to be resistant to acknowledging their own part in the problem and reluctant to address it. This can happen for many reasons: a lack of awareness of their own part in it; being unwilling to lose a benefit that having the problem gives them, or not having the energy or resources to really face up to it. Whatever the reason, this chapter shows how this issue might be addressed.

In Chapter 13 we consider the importance of rapport with a client. Given how essential rapport is for coaching, it may seem strange that I wait until this point to introduce it. Often, rapport is discussed at the beginning of coaching training and is considered one of the simpler skills to learn. However, in my experience, it all too often gets forgotten subsequently as more complex coaching skills are covered. This is a pity, since in my opinion creating deep rapport with a client by entering into and working with their map of the world is an advanced skill that requires mastery.

'Like Mrs Parker at school saying that science is the only real subject and art is a waste of time.'

'What do you mean, Alice?'

'Well, Rita said there's a big difference between agreeing with someone and accepting that something is true for them in their world. I think Mrs Parker is wrong, but if I was coaching her I'd acknowledge and work with her map of the world.'

'Great description, Alice.'

'She is wrong, though.'

'Of course! And you make a good point. As a coach, the way that we challenge a client's thinking and feeling is by working with it not against it.'

As well as rapport, Chapter 13 also discusses so-called 'client resistance' within coaching. I don't think such a thing really exists intrinsically in the client; rather, resistance is a response to something the coach is doing (or not doing). Usually, resistance appears when a coach has insufficient rapport and is seeking to impose their own map of the world on to their client.

Chapter 14 introduces feedback and examines how it is used in coaching. Giving feedback as a manager is different from giving feedback as a coach. We begin by examining how a coaching style might be employed for managerial feedback and then how it is different in coaching. Feedback in coaching literally means feeding back observations to the client and bringing things to the client's attention when it would be useful – for example, when a client says certain words, when a client changes their body language or tone in response to something, or when the coach notices a pattern of behaviour or thinking. All of these things can be useful to raise a client's self-awareness.

In Chapter 15 there is a coaching conversation through which we explore conflict. Most of us will experience difficulties in our relationships either at work or in our personal lives and it is a common coaching issue. This chapter demonstrates one useful tool for bringing insight and awareness to the dynamics of a conflict which can help a client make progress.

Chapter 16 reflects on this coaching conversation with a more detailed explanation of perceptual positions and we explore the three different positions from which we can perceive something.

1st Position is YOU, feeling how you feel and knowing your own reality, your thoughts, beliefs, values, goals and needs. 1st Position is essential for a strong sense of knowing yourself and your boundaries. 2nd Position is that of the OTHER person, experiencing the other's point of view, their feelings, thoughts, values and beliefs. 3rd Position is that of a detached OBSERVER, someone who is outside the specific context or relationship. It is an objective perspective, standing back from the situation and seeing the bigger picture. It can be very helpful for looking at the wider consequences for everyone involved and detaching from the emotion of the situation.

Chapter 17 introduces the idea of supervision. This could be considered coaching for the coach. There are a number of aspects to supervision which include exploring different approaches to use within coaching, developing skills and considering strategies that would help a particular client, and identifying when a coach's own feelings and thinking might be unduly impacting the coaching. It's also about coach development.

In Chapter 18 we consider how a solution can become the problem. When a person faces a difficulty or challenge, there are times when their own attempt at a solution creates a new problem that perpetuates the initial difficulty. One example of this might be 'burying your head in the sand', a phrase we often use when someone ignores a situation or denies its existence. This is an attempt at a solution: by ignoring or denying a problem, the person detaches and has less contact with the difficulty and they may actually feel better. However, denying the existence of the problem makes it hard to resolve (unless it just goes away on its own, which is often what someone hopes for) because a refusal to look at it includes rejecting opportunities for solutions.

The way forward in such situations is often to examine the problem at a different level.

'If you want to cycle faster, you can either pedal quicker or change gear and pedal at the same rate.'

'I think you might need to explain that, Alice.'

'Ben, it's what Rita taught us. There are different levels of change. A first-order change is change within the situation as it is, like going faster by pedalling quicker. A second-order change is changing the definition of the problem or the construction of it – that's like changing into a new gear.'

'Well explained, Alice. Perhaps I should let you finish this introduction.'

'We haven't mentioned cake yet, Ben; that's one of my favourite things. And space rockets, too. Oh, you've got that look in your eye ... Perhaps I should talk about the next chapter. In Chapter 19 Rita introduced two advanced concepts which were fascinating. The first is called Project Perception – or is it Project Your Perception? No, it's not that. What's it called, Ben?'

'Projection is Perception, Alice. Projection happens when we see attributes that we possess showing up in other people. We can only do so because, at some level, we possess these characteristics ourselves. If we didn't, then we would be unable see them in others. What we perceive is what we project as being present in others.'

'Oh yes, that's it, Ben! What I remember is that in coaching, we need to be careful that the observations and answers our client gives are not projections from ourselves but are indeed what our client means. Otherwise we won't really be working with their map of the world and it will be our own instead.'

'Exactly Alice. What is the second concept in the chapter?'

'It's that the beliefs we hold about our client can have a significant impact on the coaching. Rita told us about some research with schoolteachers that showed how their views of their students made a difference to the performance of the students. It makes me wonder whether the reason I'm not very good at science is because Mrs Parker thinks I'm not.'

'Well, possibly, Alice. Perhaps we should talk more about that. It's certainly true that our views of others impact how we interpret their behaviour and respond to them. Do you remember the helpful "beliefs" in the chapter?'

'Oh yes, I like these. Rita explained she wasn't saying they're true, but that it might be helpful to act as if they are. I like that. The first is that people make the best choice they can at the time. Each of us makes the best choice we can, given the map of the world that we have. Sometimes a choice may be not be good or have negative consequences, but on some level it seems the best way forward.

'The second idea is that people are not their behaviours. Rita explained that we have a bias towards identifying people with the behaviours they display. There's something called attribution theory which is concerned with how we explain actions and behaviour. The most common error is that we attribute the behaviour of other people to something about them whereas we attribute our own behaviour to the environment or situation we're in.'

'Very good, Alice! I'm impressed.'

'The third idea is that we already have all the resources we need, or we can create them. This is the idea that there are no un-resourceful people, only un-resourceful states of mind. We are more than our problems, and we have, within us, the answers and solutions to life's challenges or we can learn how to deal with them.

'How did I do, Ben? Can I talk about cake and space rockets now?'

'Brilliant, Alice! That's a great summary. And, yes, why don't you talk about cake and space rockets? In fact, better still why don't we start at the beginning. Take us back where this all began.'

'You mean when I was ill?'

'Yes, the very beginning, Alice.'

'OK, Ben, here we go then ...'

CHAPTER 2

The Turtle and the Caterpillar

WHAT IS COACHING AND WHY IS IT USED?

● ● ●

It was the second week of the school holidays and Alice was bored and fed up. No sooner had term finished than she was ill with the flu and had spent a week in bed thinking about all the fun her friends were having while she stayed at home. She occasionally read some poetry and dreamed of going on a space rocket, but it was lonely being at home and she was sick of being sick. Each morning she hoped she would be feeling better and able to have fun with her friends. Finally, on Thursday morning Alice woke up and concluded that she might be improving. 'Why, perhaps you'll be able to go for a walk today,' she said to herself encouragingly.

Her father came into her room, gave her a kiss and said, 'Morning, Alice,' while touching her forehead to check her temperature.

'I'm feeling better,' Alice said.

'You're still very warm, darling,' he said, 'I don't think you're right yet. I'm not sure what to do today, I have to go to work and I don't want to leave you here on your own.'

'I'll be all right, Dad,' Alice murmured as she closed her eyes and drifted back to sleep.

It was a disturbed, fitful sleep, and she tossed and turned, waking occasionally. Eventually she woke properly and discovered she felt much better. Something still wasn't quite right, but she had more energy and felt like getting up for the first time in nearly two weeks.

'What are you feeling now?' she asked herself.

Her temperature was gone but there was something strange she couldn't identify. She remembered the feeling of excitement from waking up on her birthday and she was certain this was different. She'd felt anxious before she'd gone to tell Mr Jones next door that she'd accidentally broken a pane of glass in his greenhouse but it wasn't that either. 'Alice, this feeling is undoubtedly something different,' she said to herself in conclusion.

Alice listened carefully to the crunch of her toast as she ate breakfast, but it sounded normal. She checked her fingers and toes and all were present and correct as they should be. She tasted the cup of coffee on the table and it had the same disgusting bitter taste that made her mouth turn itself upside down. Despite this normalness of things, she had a growing anticipation that something was going to happen and she knew from past experience that such 'somethings' were usually wild and adventurous.

'Perhaps you should go for a walk,' she said to herself. 'Some fresh air will do you good.'

The sun was already shining when she stepped outside, and the birds were singing their normal song. Alice walked along the path that led down through the wood to the river. She paused when the path met the riverbank and where the water was at its widest, and she watched the water bubbling and swirling over the pebbles and rocks. She continued her stroll, engrossed in the playfulness of the water, and didn't spot the man until she was standing in front of him. At least, she thought it was a man, because he was dressed in a smart suit and sitting on a bench underneath the tree. When she looked closer, she jumped backwards in shock.

'Why that's not a man at all,' she said to herself. 'Alice,' she added in a concerned voice, 'I think you've eaten something strange.' Sitting on the bench was a very large caterpillar who was indeed wearing a suit. The caterpillar was bending forwards with his head in two pairs of hands. Alice thought he looked rather unhappy.

'Not that you know the difference between a happy caterpillar and an unhappy caterpillar,' she said to herself somewhat tersely. 'Alice, this is what you get for not paying attention at school – if you'd studied more, you might recognize how he feels.' She tried to remember if they had covered the emotions of caterpillars in school, but her mind was blank. 'Oh dear, oh dear,' she said, continuing with her self-reprimand, 'you can't remember anything, can you?'

Looking more closely, Alice noticed that the caterpillar was wearing a dark-blue suit with a pink tie, a brown belt and several pairs of brown shoes to match.

'Very unusual,' said Alice to herself. 'I don't see many suits on this walk, but then I don't see many giant caterpillars either ... Really, Alice, you *ought* to be much more surprised at seeing a giant caterpillar. You see suits most days when your father goes to work but you *don't* – she emphasized this word strongly to herself – 'see giant caterpillars.'

Her thoughts were interrupted by the Caterpillar slowly raising his head. (We'll give 'caterpillar' a capital *C* from now on, as Alice never knew him by any other name, and he was after all a very particular kind of caterpillar.)

'Hello,' said Alice.

The Caterpillar didn't respond.

'Hello,' said Alice again, 'lovely morning.' Her mother had taught her to always say something cheery.

The Caterpillar looked up, stared at Alice – or, more accurately, seemed to stare through Alice, and then put his head back in several of his hands.

'How odd,' thought Alice, 'he doesn't seem to see me. I wonder if I've become invisible. Maybe that's what the strange feeling was.'

'Alice, you've become invisible,' she announced to herself. 'What fun you can have.' She began to think about all the tricks she could play. For a start, she could take cookies from the tray after her mum had baked them and she could also take chips from her dad's plate at dinner and he wouldn't see.

'It's not a lovely morning,' proclaimed the Caterpillar, interrupting Alice's conversation with herself, 'it's a really terrible one.'

Alice looked around to see who he was talking to; if she was invisible, then it obviously wasn't her. But there was no one else in sight. Furthermore, his response appeared to be a reply to her greeting. Maybe she was invisible but she could still be heard – that would make more sense. Perhaps she had become a voice without a body.

'That would be interesting,' she said to herself. 'Why, I can play some tricks on Lorina at last.' She imagined running up to her sister and screaming in her ear without her expecting it. She thought about school, 'Why, Alice! You can shout out all the answers and the teacher can't tell you to wait and put your hand up,' she said to herself gleefully.

Then the Caterpillar looked at her.

Right at her.

'It's a terrible morning,' he repeated.

'Are you talking to me?' said Alice.

'Of course,' replied the Caterpillar, his brow furrowing.

'Then in that case you're right,' agreed Alice. 'It *is* a terrible morning. I thought I'd become invisible, but now it transpires I'm not.'

The Caterpillar looked at her strangely. There was a long pause during which Alice wondered if perhaps she should enquire as to what exactly was so terrible about his morning, if only to keep the conversation going.

'What's so terrible about this morning?' she said.

He looked at her. 'You wouldn't understand.'

Alice thought he was probably right. She knew very little about the occupations of people who wore suits, but she remembered that her father always told her to try to help someone if they were in need.

'You're right,' she said, 'I probably won't understand, but why don't you tell me anyway? I'll see if I can help.'

'I don't know what to do,' began the Caterpillar. 'I'm stuck. I've got a really good job, it pays well and, although the hours are quite long, my boss is friendly and my colleagues are nice. The thing is, though, I hate it. I hate the work – it's boring and meaningless. I sit in meetings and we talk about business development and sales funnels and I can't see the point of it all.'

'Oh, I see,' said Alice, which was about all she could muster in response. She wasn't quite sure she did see at all. In fact, she wasn't sure what business development was. She did know what a funnel was, though – it was the thing her father used when he poured his home-made wine into bottles. Maybe she could help in that area. This might be tricky, though, as she was no expert in wine making or business development.

Before she could say anything else the Caterpillar continued, 'I could leave and get another job. I've got plenty of skills, but any job I get would be the same and I'll have to do that for another 30 years until I retire.'

Alice thought hard about what advice she could give.

And then thought some more.

And then some more.

Fortunately, the Caterpillar seemed so preoccupied with his own thoughts that he didn't seem to notice Alice thinking. Finally, she realized that she didn't have any advice to dispense. None. Perhaps some problems were just too big to help with. How on earth could she possibly fix the situation the poor Caterpillar was in when she knew nothing about it?

As she turned away and prepared to creep back along the path, Alice found her way blocked. She gasped at a huge tortoise in front of her. It was extremely large and was wearing a red hat, a purple dress, spectacles and lipstick. 'Oh dear,' thought Alice, 'I knew it was going to be a strange day.'

'Excuse me,' said Alice in her politest tone, 'please can I pass?'

'Aren't you going to help the poor man first?' retorted the Tortoise.

'Oh dear,' thought Alice again. 'A talking tortoise wearing a dress, spectacles and lipstick. This is getting very silly. Please can this stop and everything go back to normal?'

'Well ...' probed the Tortoise, 'aren't you?'

'To be honest, I don't know what to do,' said Alice, 'I don't know much about wine making or business development so I can't give him any advice.'

'Who said you had to give him advice?' queried the Tortoise.

'Well, he says he doesn't know what to do with his job and ... and my father says you should always try to help people,' stammered Alice, beginning to wish she hadn't gone for a walk at all.

'Indeed, helping people is a generous and kind thing to do, but you don't know what *kind* of help the fellow needs.'

Alice kept quiet.

'Let me explain,' continued the Tortoise, 'First, it's easy to assume that when someone is upset or in difficulty they want help. It's painful to watch another person or animal suffering and our desire is often to help alleviate that. But we have to be careful that our "helping" does not take away that person's own power to help themselves. If each time someone has a difficulty, we solve it for them or fix the situation, then they won't learn how to help themselves. In fact, they just learn that if they have a problem, all they have to do is come to us for it to be fixed. This means that we are forever solving their problems, which can be very time consuming and tiring for us. It also makes them reliant and not able to develop their own skills, abilities and confidence.

'Second, if a person does want help then we ought to consider what form that help takes. There is a proverb in the turtle world that says, "Give a turtle an insect and you feed him for a day. Teach a turtle how to catch insects and you feed him for life." You might have heard it?' The Tortoise looked at Alice enquiringly.

Alice thought she had heard something like it and nodded. In truth, she was wondering whether her interlocutor was a tortoise or a turtle and what the difference was. 'A tortoise is a turtle, but a turtle isn't a tortoise,' she said to herself, remembering a lesson from school. 'Or is it the other way around? A turtle is a tortoise, but a tortoise isn't a turtle. A tortoise is a turtle, a turtle is a tortoise, a tortoise is a turtle, a turtle is a tortoise.' Alice tried to decide which sounded best but wasn't quite sure.

The Tortoise looked at her. 'Are you listening, dear?'

'Yes,' Alice replied. 'Well, no, not exactly. I was just wondering whether you're a tortoise or a turtle?'

'Well, I never, the cheek of it!' said the Turtle. 'How about if I asked you whether you're a boy or a girl?'

'I'm a girl,' said Alice meekly, looking down at her dress. 'Isn't it obvious?'

'I would have thought it was obvious that I'm a turtle.'

'Yes, it is,' said Alice. 'Please forgive me. I've had a very strange morning so far and I'm not quite myself today.'

'Well, who are you then?' asked the Turtle.

'That is a very good question indeed,' Alice replied. 'I thought I was invisible but it's apparent that I'm not. Right now, I don't know who I am. I'm rather confused. Do you think perhaps you could repeat that proverb again? I'm afraid I wasn't listening fully.'

'"Give a turtle an insect and you feed him for a day. Teach a turtle how to catch insects and you feed him for life." *Coach* a turtle how to think and you empower him for life.'

'I'm not sure I understand,' Alice said, still feeling confused.

'Well, what if, instead of *telling* the man what to do, you helped him work it out for himself?'

'But, how would I do that?' Alice replied, thinking to herself all the while that the 'man' was, in fact, a caterpillar.

'How do *you* think you could do it?' asked the Turtle earnestly.

Alice pondered for a moment: what could she do if she didn't *tell* the Caterpillar to do something? She remembered a situation where she herself hadn't known what to do. She'd been lost in a forest and there had been a cat in a tree. A grinning Cheshire Cat. She had asked the cat which way she should go and the cat had replied that it depended on where she wanted to get to. The cat hadn't given her an answer because it didn't know where she wanted to go. Maybe she couldn't help the Caterpillar because she didn't know what he wanted. Perhaps she needed to ask him something.

'I could ask him a question,' said Alice at long last.

'An excellent idea,' said the Turtle, clapping two flippers together. 'And what are you going to ask him?'

'I'm going to ask him what he wants,' said Alice, feeling better and turning round to face the Caterpillar again. It seemed that no time had passed at all and he was still sitting with his head in his hands.

'I understand what you've said about feeling stuck in your job,' Alice began, 'and you hate the job you've got with the wine business, but I can't help wondering what you want?'

The Caterpillar looked at her. 'I've told you. I don't want to be stuck in this job I hate.'

Alice thought about this and decided that he hadn't really answered her question. 'Actually, I think you've told me what you *don't* want. You don't want to be stuck in this job you hate. But you haven't told me what you *do* want. I'm interested in what you actually want instead.'

The Caterpillar looked at her again as the statement began to slowly register.

'Let me put it a different way,' said Alice, although she felt as though it wasn't really her saying the words and it sounded like the Turtle's voice in her head, 'what do you want from your work?'

'I don't really know,' said the Caterpillar.

'Well, if you did know, what would you say?' Alice heard herself reply.

'Well, I'd say I want to be stimulated and I want to do something that makes a difference,' said the Caterpillar, sitting up for the first time.

'What else?' said Alice's mouth, even though she wasn't sure it was really her speaking.

'I want to be paid enough that I can do the things I want, I want some flexibility in when I work, and I want to work with good colleagues.'

'Excellent,' said Alice, 'that's a good start. Which of those things do you currently have?'

'I'm paid enough and I have good colleagues. But I don't feel stimulated and I don't feel I make a difference and I don't have much flexibility.'

'Right, so you want to feel stimulated, to have more flexibility, and to make a difference,' said Alice.

'Yes, I suppose that's right – that's what I want,' said the Caterpillar, brightening up. 'You know, I never really thought about it that way. Thank you, that's most helpful.'

'We're not finished yet,' Alice heard herself say. This was most disconcerting, as she was absolutely sure she wasn't having the thoughts that would instruct her mouth to speak but the words were coming out anyway. Before she had time to consider this further, her mouth added, 'What does making a difference mean to you?'

'Very good question,' said the Caterpillar. 'A very good question indeed.'

Alice began to wonder if perhaps she had instructed her mouth to say that after all and whether, in fact, she was really rather good at this sort of conversation. She was about to congratulate herself on her hidden talents when she realized the Caterpillar had stood up and was now staring intently at her.

'I want to make a difference to people who are trying to start their careers,' he said.

'People who are trying to start their careers?' repeated Alice.

'Yes,' said the Caterpillar. 'You know, you've just given me an idea. Thank you so much!'

At this point he turned and set off, walking briskly while talking to himself.

Alice wasn't quite sure what the idea she'd given him was, but she shouted after him, 'You're welcome!' anyway.

'What a strange morning this has been,' she said to herself. 'I've met a turtle that talks and wears spectacles and lipstick, and I've just helped a caterpillar with his funnels and business.' She could just about handle the talking turtle but she was very confused about the conversation with the Caterpillar. She knew she hadn't told him what to do or suggested any ideas, but he seemed to no longer be upset about his situation and appeared to know what he was going to do. 'Curiouser and curiouser,' she thought.

Alice hadn't noticed that the Turtle had moved until she turned around and saw it shuffling along the grass.

'Excuse me,' she said and began walking after it. The Turtle didn't seem to hear, so she picked up her pace until she drew level with it. 'Excuse me,' she repeated.

'Yes?' replied the Turtle.

'I have a question. I'm confused about what just happened. I didn't give the Caterpillar in the suit any advice or tell him what to do. Yet, somehow he seemed to work out a way forward.'

'You are correct,' the Turtle murmured, 'Hmm ... how best to explain it? Have you ever heard of coaching?'

'Yes, of course,' said Alice. She quickly began thinking about what might night be. She'd been *on* a coach once when her class went to the Natural History Museum and had eaten so many pear drops that she'd been sick from too much sugar. Was that something to do with coaching?

'Well,' she said, 'to be honest I'm not sure. Can you remind me?'

'Coaching is a way of working with someone to help them find solutions for challenges or problems they face or to help them improve the way they do things.'

'Yes,' said Alice, glad that she hadn't mentioned the school trip or the pear drops, 'It sounds very interesting.'

'Why don't you sit for a moment?' said the Turtle, point to a nearby patch of grass. 'Coaching unlocks potential, increases flexibility, gives options and develops the individual. It's a way of working with someone that empowers them to take ownership of their own learning, problem solving and development.'

'What does "unlocks potential" mean?' Alice asked. 'it sounds very grand.'

'My own belief is that we each have a great deal of potential that is unrealized, budding capacity that could be accessible to us but which we haven't or can't make use of. Unlocking potential means helping someone discover and deal with barriers to their potential whether these be in their work, relationships, sport, art or any other aspect of life.'

Alice looked confused. 'What kind of barriers are you talking about?'

The Turtle continued: 'They might be patterns of thinking, feeling, communicating or behaving that are limiting in some way. Perhaps a person doesn't believe it's possible for them to improve or learn something. Maybe whenever they want to perform they feel anxious or self-conscious, or whenever they try to communicate an idea they struggle to articulate it properly. Maybe they behave in ways that have unhelpful consequences but they can't seem to change that. Sometimes these limitations are rooted in past experiences that may require some examination, but more often than not, once a person becomes aware of their own internal processes of thinking and feeling, they can begin to work with them.'

'That makes sense,' Alice said. 'I have a talent for remembering poetry and reciting it, but whenever I want to perform I get really nervous and forget the words. I'm sure I could be good at it but something gets in the way.'

'Unfulfilled potential can take many forms,' the Turtle nodded, 'and each of us might be curious about what is possible if we can fulfil it.'

'Can you say more about increasing flexibility and giving options?' Alice asked.

'Increasing flexibility and giving options applies to thinking, feeling and behaviour. If a person always has the same feeling in response to something, they have very little choice in how they behave. Coaching can explore and highlight new ways of behaving and bring new perspectives that change thoughts and feelings. When a person can evaluate their own thinking and feeling they have greater freedom to behave and communicate in different ways.'

'And what about developing the individual – what you do mean by that?' Alice quizzed.

The Turtle continued: 'Developing the individual refers to the bigger picture of helping someone increase self-awareness and expand their emotional and behavioural range. This may have benefits above and beyond the focus of the coaching and help the person in their life, not just in regard to the specific coaching issue.'

'Coaching sounds really fascinating,' Alice said, 'although I'm not 100 per cent sure I know what it all means yet. It sounds great in theory, but I'm not quite sure *how* I would do it.'

'Well, the final part of my definition of coaching was "a way of working with someone that empowers them to take ownership of their own learning, problem solving and development". This way of working with someone isn't teaching. Teachers, who are very important by the way ...' – at this point the Turtle looked pointedly at Alice – 'typically impart information to the learner. The teacher is more knowledgeable than the learner, and usually describes and demonstrates what is to be learned. Coaching takes a different approach and the person being coached is often the most knowledgeable about the situation or topic.

The coach takes the role of helping the person increase their awareness, think differently and come up with their own answers.'

'Yes, I see,' said Alice, 'I was just wondering about that. Can you say a bit more about it? I'm still a bit confused about how I was able to help the Caterpillar in the suit without teaching him anything or telling him what to do.'

'With pleasure, my dear. Why don't you make yourself comfortable?' said the Turtle.

CHAPTER 3

Rita and the Frog

LISTENING AND EFFECTIVE QUESTIONING

● ● ●

'Well,' said the Turtle, 'where to begin? A starting point to understand coaching would be to consider that in any interaction we can be in one of two modes. We can be either telling or asking, also called advocating or enquiring, pushing or pulling. Of course, in reality, our conversations usually involve some of each, but if we imagine a continuum with "tell" at one end and "ask" at the other, then, for a given interaction, our own involvement will be somewhere along this. If we've just given a speech, we will be wholly at the "tell" end. If we've just asked about a friend's holiday and listened for 15 minutes, we will be at the "ask" end. Coaching sits very much at the "ask" end of the continuum; it's a process where we ask questions of someone else.'

Alice nodded and thought about Mr Hawkins, the Maths teacher at school. He asked lots of difficult questions like 'What is six times eight?' and she didn't always get the answer right.

'Is it like at school when the teacher asks questions?' Alice quizzed.

'It depends on the teacher,' the Turtle said. 'The purpose of questions in coaching is to get the other person to think about something. It's not about a right or wrong answer. It might not even be about the answer at all. It might be about what the person has to think about in order to answer the question. For example, if I ask you what you want instead of what you don't want, it changes the direction of your thinking and your orientation with regard to the situation.'

'Oh yes,' said Alice, 'if you don't know where you want to go, then it doesn't matter much which direction you head in. I learned that from a cat once.'

'Indeed,' continued the Turtle, 'it's very hard to make progress without knowing what you're trying to achieve or where you want to get to. If you only want to get away from somewhere or something, then there may be lots of possibilities, but they might not be what you want.'

'If you don't know where you are going, any road will get you there,' said Alice.

'Exactly,' nodded the Turtle. At least, Alice noticed a small movement of the Turtle's head which she concluded was intended to be an indication of agreement.

'Coaching is about more than asking questions, though,' continued the Turtle. 'A coach will have many other skills. For example, what do you think you need to do in order to ask good questions, Alice?'

'How do you know my name?' said Alice. 'And what's *your* name?'

'My name is Rita,' said the Turtle, ignoring Alice's first question.

Rita! thought Alice. What a strange name for a turtle! Although, in many ways, Rita was the least strange part of a talking turtle that wore spectacles and lipstick.

'So, what do you think you need to do in order to ask good questions, Alice?'

'A list of good questions?' Alice replied.

'Suppose you did have a list of good questions, how would you know which one to ask?'

'It would depend on what the person I'm talking with had said.'

'Exactly,' replied Rita. 'And what would you need to be doing while the person is talking?'

'Listening,' answered Alice.

'Indeed,' Rita continued, 'although listening is often much harder in practice than we expect.'

'What do you mean?' said Alice, somewhat puzzled.

'One way to think about listening is of it having four different levels,' Rita explained as she began to draw a triangle in the earth with her paw.

'Is that a spaceship?' asked Alice, 'I love spaceships.'

'It's not,' Rita said, 'but did you know that my grandfather was one of the first turtles to go into space?'

'Your grandfather? Into space?' Alice looked skywards. 'Really?'

'Really!' said Rita. 'Look it up. In 1968, the Soviet Union sent the *Zond 5* spacecraft to circle the moon. My grandfather was a scientist and was one of the turtles on board.'

Alice made a mental note to look that up when she got home. It sounded a bit far-fetched.

Rita's drawing was finished, and Alice found herself looking at a pyramid in the earth that was divided into four layers.

'Have you ever been in a conversation where you were thinking about something else while the person was talking?' asked Rita.

Alice thought about some of the conversations when her Auntie Rose came to stay. Her auntie would talk about lots of things Alice didn't understand. Alice would smile and nod while thinking about things that were much more interesting, like cake, board games and whether ladybirds had individual names and, if they did, what the most common ladybird name would be.

Alice nodded.

'We could call that *superficial listening* – it's the first level,' said Rita. 'Superficial listening is where the person might appear to be listening on the outside but is really thinking about something else entirely and hardly paying attention to the speaker at all. It can be very useful, particularly at my sister's birthday parties,' added Rita with a wink. 'The problem is that sometimes people aren't aware that their attention has drifted and that they are no longer listening, so they don't even know what they've missed.

'The second level of listening is called *conversational listening*. This is often characterized by people sharing experiences or stories with each other. One person talks about a situation which reminds the listener of their own experience or something similar that happened to them. That person then replies with their own story or parallel situation.'

'I remember telling my sister about a tea party I'd attended with the Mad Hatter and the March Hare,' said Alice, 'and when I finished she immediately told me about her friend's birthday party where there was an inflatable bouncy castle.'

'Yes, that's conversational listening,' said Rita with a smile.

'The third level of listening is called *attentive listening*. This is where the listener is really paying attention not only to *what* is being said but *how* it's being said, too.'

Alice noticed that Rita put particular emphasis on the word 'how' when she said this, but Rita continued before she could think any more about it.

'Attentive listening is where the listener may observe their own thoughts, memories or feelings and may note these while bringing their attention back to the person talking. They will be listening to the content of what is being said, the facts, feelings and descriptions, and also the voice of the speaker, the facial expressions and body language.'

'When you said "how it's being said" you put particular emphasis on the word "how",' Alice observed.

'Well noticed,' said Rita. 'The "how" of someone describing something is often the richest source of information. We might be interested in the language they use, what words they choose to use as well as the tone and volume, the expression on their face, pauses and their body language in general.'

'Why is that so useful?' asked Alice. 'Isn't what they say just as important?'

'It depends. One of the goals of coaching is to help raise awareness within the person being coached. One way we achieve this is by noticing things that they themselves may not be conscious of and using such observations as a starting point for exploration. The way that a person describes something might give clues to their internal processing, perhaps feelings or thoughts that are not being expressed or of which they are not fully conscious. It might show what internal rules or beliefs a person has or what is important to them.'

'It really sounds like you think this is important,' said Alice.

'It's essential,' continued Rita, 'although we are almost straying into the fourth level of listening – *empathic listening*. This sort of listening has been described as almost telepathic, although it's not, of course. It is about establishing a deep level of rapport with the speaker which can lead to an intuitive sense of the person and clear insights into what they are saying. It's unusual to encounter empathic listening in everyday interactions.'

Alice looked across at Rita, a large turtle who was wearing what could best be described as cherry-coloured lipstick and black fashionable spectacles and who was instructing her in the art of listening and coaching. Not for the first time she reflected that, of all the things that had happened or been discussed that morning, empathic listening was far from being the most unusual. Alice could see that Rita really meant what she was saying because she spoke with a certain deliberateness that suggested she knew a great deal about the subject. Alice wondered how Rita had come to know such things and how she had come to be talking to her this morning.

'How do you know all this?' enquired Alice.

'Good question,' Rita replied, 'and before I answer that, it's worth pointing out that questions are also an important element of the coaching approach. Do you know the two simple ways to classify questions?'

'No.'

'Well, do you know what a *closed question* is?'

'Yes,' said Alice. She thought about the sweet shop that was sometimes closed when she went there for pear drops. She couldn't see how that related to questions, though. 'No,' she finally admitted thoughtfully.

'A closed question is one where the answer is a single word or a short phrase, like "Do you understand?" or "Did you have a good day?" A typical answer to a closed question might be "Yes" or "No", but any question that elicits a single-word or simple answer could be considered closed, for example "How old are you?" or "What street do you live on?" Closed questions are useful when it's important to confirm something and tend to close a conversation down. I often use them at my sister's parties,' said Rita with a smirk on her face.

Alice was beginning to wonder about Rita's sister and her birthday parties and who went to them. Or maybe Rita was just mad as a hatter.

'Do closed questions make sense now?' asked Rita.

'Yes,' said Alice, smiling.

'The other type of questions are *open questions*. What do you think they are, Alice?'

Alice thought about this. If closed questions tended to close things down, then it followed that open questions would open things up. An open question would invite the person being asked the question to explore ideas, thoughts or feelings and there could be any number of potential answers.

'I think an open question would invite someone to participate and be involved in the conversation and would stimulate thoughts, ideas and feelings.'

'Exactly,' said Rita, 'and why would that be useful in a coaching conversation?'

'If coaching is about helping someone find their own answers, solutions or insights, then open questions would encourage potentially new ways of thinking and feeling which would support this,' Alice replied, thinking to herself that she sounded awfully grown up.

In fact, she wondered if she had grown up this morning and whether she was now taller. Her feet still seemed to be the usual distance away. Alice remembered when she'd grown very tall and big once before, so tall and big in fact that she couldn't fit into the room she was in. She hadn't had a birthday then or got any older, though. 'If you can grow bigger without getting any older, then it follows that you can get older without getting any bigger,' she said to herself. 'Perhaps I've grown up and become an adult this morning.'

'Mind you,' Alice continued to herself, 'you're going to have to behave differently now if you're an adult. No more being silly and messing around, no more silly songs and poems. It's very serious being an adult you know ...'. She almost immediately corrected herself: 'But I do like songs and poems. Why, I would recite one now if I had some accompaniment.'

No sooner had the thought entered her mind than Alice heard the distant twinkle of a musical instrument.

'Can you hear that?' she said to Rita.

'Yes, dear, it sounds like a banjo. I wonder where it's coming from.'

The two of them looked up to see a large lily leaf floating down the river. Perched on the leaf was a bright-green frog holding a mandolin. He was strumming contentedly and singing softly to himself.

Alice cleared her throat and stood up.

The Frog looked up and halted his strumming as he noticed the pair on the bank. He paused for a moment before starting a new tune.

'The Owl and the Pussy-cat went to sea,' he began melodiously.

Alice cleared her throat again and drew herself up to her full height. The Frog paused again.

Alice started to sing and the Frog began to accompany her:

> 'The Owl and the Pussy-cat went to see
>   If solutions or outcomes they could find,
> They needed a coach but there was none to approach,
>   So the ideas remained undefined.

The Owl made some notes on a nearby stone,
  And sang to a small mandolin,
"O Pussy! I'll give you advice of my own,
  And tell you how you can begin,
    Begin,
    Begin!
I'll tell you how you can begin!"

Pussy said to the Owl, "Your advice is foul!
  Instead you must question me now!
I must be asked, if I'm going to learn fast:
  With questions like what, when and how."
The Owl tried questions to say, for a year and a day,
  And learned how to listen as well,
For each thought that he sought
  There was a question to ask and not tell,
    Not tell,
    Not tell,
There was a question to ask and not tell.

The questions were great and Pussy answered them straight,
  With ideas that started to grow.
The ideas were so clever, the Owl said, 'Never ever
  Will I tell and not ask what you know.'
They questioned for days and explored other ways,
  To try out this whole new approach:
And each day in this way, their problems were nay,
  And they started to think like a coach,
    A coach,
    A coach.
They started to think like a coach.'

'Superb!' said the Frog, clapping his webbed hands together in a strange slapping sound. 'Superb!'

'A lovely rendition,' added Rita, 'and a version I've not heard before. What a talent you have, Alice.'

'Thank you, both,' said Alice with a small curtsy. 'I'm not entirely sure I remembered it correctly. I think I got one or two of the words wrong, but I don't suppose it matters that much.'

'I think I like your version even more,' said Rita, waving goodbye to the Frog as his lily leaf drifted past.

The leaf drifted out of sight, and Alice heard the strumming begin again as she turned her attention back to Rita.

'I've completely forgotten what we were discussing,' she said. 'What were you saying?'

'We were talking about open questions,' Rita reminded her.

'Yes!' said Alice. 'What else can you tell me?'

'Open questions are great because they leave maximum room for the person answering them to think for themselves, and in a coaching situation that is very desirable. Some open questions are better than others, though, and there are several criteria that make a good open question.

'For example, let's imagine someone being coached who says, "I want to improve my presentation skills," and let's consider the following questions:

- "What are some of the ways you think you could improve your presentation skills and what are your reasons and motivations for wanting to do so?"
- "OK, what about them?"
- "What books have you read about presentation skills?"

'What do you think about the first question Alice?'

Alice couldn't remember it. Something about motivations. Oh dear, she thought. 'I can't remember it,' she said out loud, sheepishly.

'Exactly,' said Rita. 'It's too complicated and too long; the person listening has to spend time trying to understand the question instead of thinking about it. A good open question is easy to understand. What about the second question?'

Alice remembered this one but wasn't quite sure what it was asking. It sounded a bit vague. 'I remember this one,' she said, 'but I don't really know what is being asked.'

'Indeed,' nodded Rita. 'The purpose of the question is very unclear. It seems rather casual and doesn't build on anything the person has already said. A good open question is one that is easy to understand *and* has a purpose.'

'Right,' said Alice, 'easy to understand and has a purpose.'

'Of course, sometimes the purpose might be to explore something in a very open way but even then the second question sounds rather non-specific. What about the third question?'

'Well, it's easy to understand,' said Alice, 'and it has a purpose. It seems like a bit of a jump to go from the initial statement to asking about books, though.'

'Yes,' agreed Rita, 'it seems as though the coach is choosing to follow one quite specific avenue of questioning that doesn't appear to be led by anything the person being coached has said. The coach seems to be dictating the direction of the conversation and potentially excluding many other possibilities. A good open question is easy to understand, has a purpose and influences the direction of someone's thinking without dictating it.'

Alice understood. There seemed to be a bit more to asking questions than she had previously been aware of and it was fascinating to analyse this in depth. To be honest, she wasn't quite sure that she would remember it all! And there was one other thing that she had noticed.

'I notice that your questions include the same words used in the original statement. "I want to improve my presentation skills" was what was said and the follow-up questions included the words "presentation skills". Have you deliberately used the same words the speaker used?'

'Very well noticed,' acknowledged Rita, 'it is indeed deliberate. And to answer that we have to stop for a moment to consider words and their meanings ... Come over here to the river,' she added, ambling slowly towards the water.

Alice followed her to the river, and they both looked into the moving water as their reflections looked back at them.

Rita's reflection began to speak. 'Words are labels. They are not the thing themselves.'

'What do you mean?' quizzed Alice.

'Well, have you ever put a cat in your ear?'

'Don't be silly,' Alice said, 'I wouldn't be able to hear anything if I did that.'

'True,' said Rita, 'but what I'm really asking is whether it would be possible to put a cat in your ear.'

'Well, I suppose if I had incredibly large ears or if the cat was very, very tiny. People can change sizes, you know.'

Alice wasn't quite sure if Rita rolled her eyes or whether it was just the way a turtle's eyelids worked but she got a hint of exasperation from her.

'Let's assume that your ears are normal size and the cat is a normal size,' Rita exclaimed. 'Would you be able to put the cat in your ears?'

'Of course not,' said Alice defiantly. 'What's your point?'

'My point is that words are not the things they represent. The word "cat" can enter your ears easily but you can't put a cat in your ears. Words are labels. And when we use a word it's easy to assume that what you think it means is what the listener thinks it means.'

'When I use a word,' Alice said, 'it means just what I choose it to mean – neither more nor less.'

'Exactly!' Rita replied. 'The word that you use is the one that is meaningful for you. It's the one that is connected inside to the idea, thought or feeling that it represents. A different word might have a completely different meaning. What do you think of when you use hear the word "cat"?'

'I think of a Cheshire cat,' Alice replied, 'a grinning Cheshire cat sitting in a tree. What do you think of?'

'I think of a black cat that I know who is an excellent coach and really good at making sense of complicated situations. It's interesting, isn't it? When we hear the word "cat", we both think of cats, but our ideas are very different.'

'It's true,' Alice replied with a nod, 'and that's just with a very specific word like "cat". Imagine if we were using vaguer words like "slithy"' or "mimsy".'

'What does mimsy mean?' asked Rita. 'I've never heard of that word.'

'Mimsy means a combination of flimsy and miserable,' Alice explained. 'It's like a portmanteau — there are two meanings packed up into one word.'

'What's a portmanteau?' asked Rita, beginning to feel like the student now.

'Why a portmanteau is a dual-compartment suitcase. It has a compartment for hanging and another for folding,' said Alice gleefully. 'Humpty Dumpty taught me that word, you know.'

'Well, I never,' Rita said. 'It really is true that words are complex things and we need to be aware that their meanings can be very individual.

'Here is another example. Imagine that a person being coached uses the word "improve". This has some meaning for them, and it also has some meaning for each of us. We need to be aware that our version might be different. Let's say I change the word "improve" because it doesn't mean that much to me and I choose a different one, such as boost, develop, enhance, help, progress, raise, upgrade, augment, refine, sharpen, or touch up. My question might become "What's important to you about developing your presenting skills?" or "What's important to you about sharpening your presenting skills?", but developing and sharpening might not mean the same to the speaker.'

'That makes sense,' Alice nodded. 'I'm beginning to understand this now – different words might have different levels of meaning for each person and in a coaching conversation our questions will be most effective when we use the words that the person being coached uses.'

'Exactly,' said Rita. 'Of course, we probably won't do this all the time and to some extent we don't need to. What we're really listening for are important words for the individual. We might call these semantically dense words or semantically loaded words, these are words that have emotional connections or bring up particularly positive or negative reactions.'

Alice paused thoughtfully and reflected on her earlier statement about words and their meaning. 'So, in a coaching situation,' she began, 'it might make more sense to say the following: when you hear a word, it means just what the speaker chooses it to mean – neither more nor less.'

'Excellent summary,' said Rita, 'superb. Now we've established that there are open and closed questions and that there are certain things that make some open questions better than others. Do you remember what these are?'

'Yes!' said Alice, 'A good open question is one that is easy to understand, has a porpoise and influences the direction of a person's thinking without dictating it.'

'A porpoise?' queried Rita. 'Do you really mean an aquatic marine mammal?'

'No!' said Alice, laughing, 'I mean it has a purpose. Those two things always confuse me.'

They both laughed.

Rita continued: 'So, the next question is: how do you ask an open question? What are some of the ways you can create open questions easily?'

Alice was just thinking that what she needed was a list of good open questions. It would be helpful to have some examples which she could use to discover different ways of phrasing open questions but she was beginning to feel rather tired. She'd learned a lot this morning and her brain was full. Perhaps it was time to walk back home and take a rest.

'You look rather tired,' said Rita before Alice could say anything. 'Have I been talking too much?'

'Yes,' Alice muttered, 'I mean no. Yes, I'm tired but I've very much enjoyed talking to you. I hope we can do it again.'

'I hope so, too,' said Rita, smiling. 'It's been lovely to talk with you.'

Alice intended to trudge back to her house, but the sun was so warm and the soft grass so inviting that it seemed a shame not to make the most of it and have a nap. 'I'll just have a five-minute snooze,' she said to herself, 'and then I'll go home for it must be nearly lunchtime by now.'

&

'Alice, now that we've recounted the opening of the story, I think we ought to have a short summary of the main learning points.'

Where's she gone?

'ALICE!'

'Ben, I'm in the kitchen. Do you want some cake?'

'Did you bring cake?'

'No.'

'Then what cake is it?'

'It's a cake I found in your cupboard. It's absolutely delicious.'

'Does it say "Happy Birthday, Ben" on it?'

'Er ... it *did*.'

'Oh. That'll be the cake for my birthday tomorrow, then. I think I'll wait.'

'It's a lovely cake. What were you saying about a summary, Ben?'

'I think we should highlight the key takeaways so far.'

'Oh, I love takeaways. Pizza is my favourite.'

'You're thinking about pizza and you've just had cake. *My* birthday cake! Right, I'll do this summary while you finish your cake.'

And, for you reading this, please feel free to skip ahead to the next chapter if you want to get on with the story. Otherwise here are some reminders of what we've covered so far.

What is coaching?

My own definition is that coaching unlocks potential, increases flexibility, gives options and develops the individual. It's a way of working with someone that empowers them to take ownership of their own learning, problem solving and development.

Telling versus asking

Simplistically, in any conversation we are either telling or asking or some combination of the two. Coaching sits very much at the 'ask' end of the continuum; it's a process where we ask questions of someone else and they set the direction of the conversation. They also take ownership of the outcomes of the coaching.

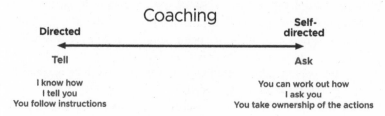

Figure 3.1 What is coaching?

The four levels of listening

There are a number of models for different levels of listening, though they follow similar themes. I first came across levels of listening in the work of Stephen Covey (2013; first published 1989), and my description here is based on some of that work.

Superficial listening is the appearance of listening without really taking in anything that is said. The amount of what the other person is saying that we register is very small.

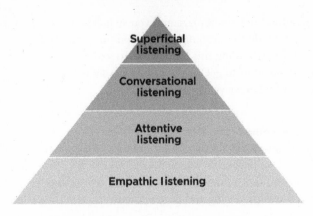

Figure 3.2 The four levels of listening

Conversational listening is often characterized by people sharing experiences or stories with each other. One person talks about a situation and this reminds the listener of their own experience or something similar that happened to them. There is a 'back and forth' conversation between the two and, although there is more listening and attention on the other person, the amount of listening is still relatively small.

Attentive listening is when the listener is paying attention not only to what is being said but how it's being said. The listener may observe their own thoughts, memories or feelings but will bring their attention back to the person talking and maintain focus on the other. Effective coaching requires listening at this level.

Empathic listening is about establishing a deep level of rapport with the speaker which can lead to an intuitive sense of the person and clear insights into what they are saying. This is the level where the greatest amount of information is attended to.

Open questions

An open question invites someone to participate and be involved in the conversation and typically stimulates thoughts, ideas and feelings. The criteria for good open questions are based on work by Starr (2016; first published 2008) who proposed that effective open questions are 'simple, have a purpose, and influence a person without being too controlling'.

In my own experience, when people are learning coaching, they sometimes don't know what open questions to ask and need examples to help them get started. The following table shows a few suggestions.

Questions	Purpose of question
What do you want? What don't you want? How specifically would you know that you've achieved it? What would that give you? / What would you gain? Would you lose anything by achieving this? When do you want it?	Identifying and exploring a goal
What/when/where/who specifically? Can you give me an example? How do you know that?	Eliciting specific information
What is important to you about that? What does that give you? For what purpose?	Discovering someone's motivation or values
Can you tell me more about that? What else is relevant? What else haven't you told me?	Eliciting general information
Imagine being him in this situation, what would you be thinking? If you were her in this, how would you be feeling?	Helping someone appreciate something from someone else's perspective

What are your thoughts about this now? What are your reflections now? How are you feeling now?	Checking on someone's current thinking or feelings
What specifically are you going to do? When do you want to start? What is the first step you can take?	Prompting someone to take action

Hopefully these questions are a useful starter to get you thinking. There are, of course, many, many open questions you might ask and will already know.

'Anything else you want to add, Alice?'

'No. I want to carry on with the story.'

CHAPTER 4

Ronald Makes a Breakthrough

AN EXAMPLE OF A COACHING CONVERSATION

● ● ●

Alice opened her eyes and had no idea how long she had been asleep. She was still lying on the grass, so she sat up. Her attention was drawn to a clicking noise that was becoming louder. As the noise increased, she saw a bicycle coming around the corner on the path. It was a shiny red bicycle ridden by someone wearing tight black Lycra, a cycle helmet and sunglasses. Something didn't look right about the rider's body. As the cyclist approached, Alice noticed something very strange – the rider's face was odd and he appeared to have fins as legs.

'Stop being ridiculous, Alice,' she told herself. 'Fish do not ride bicycles.'

Drawing alongside her, the rider removed his sunglasses to reveal some very goggle-like eyes that looked incredibly fish-like.

'Good afternoon,' intoned the Fish.

'Good afternoon,' replied Alice cautiously.

'Could you possibly help me?' said the Fish. 'I'm having some trouble.'

'What trouble are you having?' asked Alice.

'I'm exhausted,' said the Fish wearily. 'I have so many things to do and as soon as I finish one thing I have another 10 things to do on my list.'

'What's your name?' she said, extending her hand. 'I'm Alice.'

'Ronald,' the fish replied, offering her a slithy fin to shake.

'So, Ronald, what are all the things you have to do?' Alice enquired.

'I work as a manager for a large company that makes bicycles and have a team of people that work for me. My workload is unbearable. I'm in the office at 7am and I often don't leave until 7pm. When I get home I usually spend a couple of hours replying to emails in the evening.

I hardly ever get to spend time with my family, and I can't remember the last time I actually took some exercise and rode my bike for fun. I'm actually late for a meeting right now,' said the fish, glancing at his phone.

'What help is it that you want?' asked Alice, thinking back to her discussion with Rita.

'I want to be able to say no,' replied Ronald. 'I can't seem to say no to anything. When my boss asks me to do something additional, I always say yes, and when people in the team make requests I always seem to agree to them.'

'You want to be able to say no to your boss and people in your team,' Alice said. 'What exactly do you want to say no to?'

Ronald paused. 'I would like to be able to say no to additional work requests from my boss that are outside my responsibilities and I would like to say no when certain people in my team give me their problems to solve.'

Alice thought about her list of questions to do with exploring a goal. 'What would being able to say no give you?'

Ronald took a deep breath. 'It would give me more control, a greater ability to manage my workload, time to see my family and even some time for myself.'

'And what would you lose by saying no? What would be the consequences of saying no as you've described?'

Ronald thought for a moment. 'Well, my boss might not be happy; he's used to me sorting things out. But I'd be fulfilling my responsibilities; I just wouldn't be doing some of the extra stuff he piles on to me.'

'And what about the people in your team?' asked Alice.

'They won't like it at first,' said Ronald, 'but some of them need to step up and take more ownership of the work that they do.'

Ronald's goal seemed to be clear, and Alice wondered what she should ask next. He knows what he wants to achieve, she thought. I wonder why he hasn't been able to do this.

'What has stopped you from doing this up to now?'

'I hate letting people down,' said Ronald. 'I worry that they'll think badly of me.'

'What do you mean by "think badly"?' Alice probed.

'That they'll be disappointed in me or think I'm not a good person.'

'And how would you feel then?'

'Awful,' said Ronald. 'I'd feel guilty and uncomfortable.'

Alice felt a pang of doubt. What was she was entering into? She wasn't experienced in this and Ronald seemed to be talking about some powerful emotions. She thought back to what Rita had said about coaching being to do with raising self-awareness and letting the person being coached take responsibility for their own actions. It wasn't her job to solve this.

'So, you are telling me that you say yes to people to avoid feeling guilty and uncomfortable. Is that correct?' Oops, that was a closed question, she thought.

'I suppose that is correct,' said Ronald. 'I've never really thought about it like that.'

'How do you feel saying yes all the time?' asked Alice.

'Stressed, anxious and guilty,' said Ronald. 'I'm stressed about all that I have to get done, anxious that I won't complete it and I feel guilty that I don't see my family enough.'

'What will happen if you carry on like this?' pressed Alice.

'I'll burn out. It's not sustainable,' Ronald answered. 'I have to approach this differently but I'm not sure how. What do you think I should do?'

'Well, what ideas have you got?' Alice asked.

'I'm not sure really. For one thing, I don't know how to say no in the right way,' replied Ronald.

'Who do you know who *is* good at doing this?' asked Alice. 'I mean *really* good? Who do you know who can say no in the right way?'

Ronald pondered the question and his eyes moved around. Alice waited. Finally Ronald's eyes seemed to settle on something that appeared to be in the distance.

'What are you looking at?' asked Alice.

'I'm remembering my first boss when I was an apprentice,' said Ronald. 'He was a great boss and he often said no to people.'

'Tell me a bit more about him. How did he say no to people?'

'First, he would acknowledge what they've asked for and that it was important for them. Then he would say he was sorry, but he wouldn't be able to do it and he would explain why. He always gave clear reasons, and ones that were true. People didn't always agree, but he was honest about why he wouldn't do it. Sometimes he would suggest alternatives that the person might explore, though not always.'

'Interesting,' said Alice. 'What was it like to be on the receiving end of that approach?'

'I often was!' said Ronald. 'I was new in the team and would frequently go to him and ask for things. Sometimes he would use the approach I've talked about to say no. If I went to him with a problem, he would often ask me to think about how I could solve it myself and we would talk through a way forward.'

'And how was that for you?' Alice asked.

'When he said no I was sometimes disappointed or annoyed initially, but I respected him and understood his reasons. We maintained a good relationship even though he said no. When I went to him with a problem and he asked me what ideas I had I was uncomfortable at first; I just wanted him to tell me. But over time I started to learn a lot more and didn't need him as much. In fact, often I would go to him with a solution and just check he was happy with it.'

'How did you feel then?' asked Alice.

'I felt good,' said Ronald. 'I quite enjoyed having a bit more ownership over my work and working things out myself. It was more interesting.'

'So, when your boss said no in the way you've described, saying he was sorry he couldn't help and giving a reason why, you still respected him and your relationship was good. And when he helped you to work out solutions to problems yourself then you liked having more ownership and work was more interesting.'

'Exactly,' said Ronald.

'So, what do you think you could do in your own job?'

Ronald laughed. 'Yes, I see what you're getting at. I could try his approach, couldn't I?'

'I don't know,' said Alice. 'Could you?'

'Yes,' said Ronald. 'Yes, I could definitely use his approach to say no to requests from people.'

'Great,' said Alice, 'and what about when people come to you with problems?'

Ronald thought for a moment. 'I'm not sure,' he said. 'My boss was very good at asking questions to get people thinking, but I don't know how to do that.'

'How could you learn?' asked Alice.

'Maybe I could get someone to teach me,' said Ronald. 'I think it's a skill I want to develop. You know, you're very good at asking questions – could you teach me?'

'To be honest, I'm still learning myself,' said Alice, 'but I do know someone who is an excellent teacher. Maybe you'd like to meet her?'

'Definitely,' said Ronald, 'that would be really useful. Could you introduce me?'

'Of course,' said Alice, 'I'd be happy to. In fact, let's meet here tomorrow morning and I'll ask Rita if she can come, too.'

'Thank you,' said Ronald. 'Thank you very much, your advice has been really helpful.'

As Ronald mounted his bike and began pedalling away, Alice reflected on the conversation. I didn't give him any advice, she thought, but I asked quite a few questions. How interesting that he doesn't realize that he came up with his own solution. As the clicking sound grew quieter, Alice wondered what Rita would teach them the following day.

CHAPTER 5

Growing with Rita and Ronald

THE GROW COACHING FRAMEWORK

• • •

'Alice … Alice.' The voice grew louder. 'Alice, are you awake, do you want something?' Her father's voice slowly penetrated the sleepiness in Alice's brain as she realized it was morning again.

'I'm feeling better,' she replied, feeling excited about meeting Rita and Ronald. 'I'm going out for some fresh air.'

'OK, darling,' her father replied.

Alice decided to forgo breakfast so that she could go straight out to the river. It was another beautiful day, the sun was shining and she could hear insects buzzing. She saw a bee hovering above a beautiful flower and looked up at the birds as they sang. Turning the corner on the path she saw Ronald had already arrived. His red bike was leaning up against the seat.

'Hello,' she said.

'Hello to you, too,' replied Ronald. 'I'm really looking forward to meeting Rita.'

Just then the Turtle lumbered towards them, and Alice made some introductions.

Rita began with a question to Ronald. 'What is it you want to learn about, Ronald?'

'I'd like to change the way I have conversations with my team. When someone comes to me with a problem or difficulty, instead of just telling them what to do, I'd like to get them to think about it for themselves. I still want to support them, but I want to change the way I give that support and would like to encourage them to take more ownership and be more creative when it comes to solutions.'

'I see,' said Rita. 'What is it about this that you want to learn?'

'Well, I don't know how to have the conversation. I know I need to ask them questions but I'm not sure how to get to an end point where they have a way forward to work with.'

'So, when someone comes with a difficulty or problem you would like to coach them to think about it for themselves and support them in coming up with a solution they can take ownership of.'

'Exactly,' said Ronald, 'that's it.'

'In my opinion there is no single right way to do this, but I can share with you one simple structure for this kind of conversation that will get you started. It's called the GROW model. One of the reasons I like it is that there are only four steps, so it's easy to remember.'

'The GROW model,' said Ronald, pulling a pen and notebook out of his Lycra.

Alice wondered how well he would be able to hold a pen in his fin, but he seemed to manage just fine.

'To begin, let me explain with an analogy,' said Rita. 'Have you ever wanted to plan a journey and used an online route planner to help you work out which route to take?'

'Oh yes,' said Ronald, 'I use the *Rivers and Canals* website.'

'Ah yes, the RAC – I've used that,' said Rita. 'I also use the *Animal Atlas*, the AA website – that's good too.'

Alice hadn't ever used one of those herself but she didn't want to be left out. She'd heard her father talking about the AA and RAC and added, 'Oh yes, I know those two.'

'Good,' said Rita. 'Now, suppose you want the planner to help you with a route. In order for it to do so, you need to provide some information. What information is that?'

'You need to tell it where you want to get to,' said Alice.

'And you need to tell it where you're starting from,' added Ronald.

'Precisely,' said Rita. 'It can't give you a route without knowing your destination and where you're starting out from. A coaching conversation is exactly the same. The first thing we need to ask is where the person wants to get to, or what their *goal* is. Second, we need to discover where they currently are in the issue or problem – that is, *the reality of what they've done so far*.

'After you've given the route planner your destination and starting point, the next stage is to look at the *options* for the journey. There might be several: a fastest route, a shortest route, one avoiding toll canals or locks. Are you familiar with this?'

'Yes,' Ronald replied. 'I then usually examine the options and decide which one I will take.'

'Exactly,' said Rita, 'and the GROW model follows the same four stages – called Goal, Reality, Options and Way forward. The original model called the final stage "Will" but personally I prefer "Way forward". I'll say a bit more about that shortly.

'*Goal* is the starting point for the coaching conversation and we explore with the person where they want to get to – that is, what the outcome is. We might ask things like:

- What do you want to achieve?
- What is your goal?
- What do you want to solve?
- What outcome would you like from this session/discussion/interaction?
- When do you want to achieve it by?

'Only once we have clarified the goal can we move on to the second stage.'

'And,' said Alice remembering from the day before, 'you need to clarify what the person wants as a goal and not just what they don't want.'

'Well remembered,' said Rita as Ronald frantically scribbled in his notebook.

'The second phase of the conversation is *Reality*. This is about establishing where the person is currently at in the situation – what they have already tried, what is problematic or difficult. Here we might ask questions like:

- Where are you now in relation to your goal?
- What is happening now? (What, where, when, who, how much, how often? – be precise if possible.)
- What have you done about this so far?
- How do you feel about this?
- What is really going on?
- What is holding you back?

'The aim here is to explore fully the problem or challenge.'

'I notice that every question so far has been an open question,' observed Alice.

'Yes, indeed,' Rita replied. 'The Goal phase should result in a clearly defined goal or outcome but we still get there by asking open questions. The Reality phase is more exploratory and, if done correctly, should contain the seeds of the next phase – the Options phase.

'In the Options phase we help the person being coached to come up with options or ideas for how they might solve the problem or make progress. This can be the most challenging phase for someone new to the coaching approach as it can be tempting to suggest your own ideas for how they can solve it.'

'Isn't that a good thing?' asked Ronald. 'Surely, if I know the solution, it's better if I just tell them what to do.'

'Let's think about that for a minute,' said Rita. 'Remind me what your goal is for the people in your team and why you want to take a different approach with them.'

'I'd like to get them to think about the challenge for themselves and encourage them to take more ownership of the solution,' said Ronald.

'Good, that's what I thought you said. Tell me, Ronald, how do you feel when someone tells you what to do? Do you feel more or less empowered?'

'Well, less probably. If someone else has come up with the idea I feel as though they're better at it than me.'

'And when someone else has the idea, do you feel more or less ownership of and engagement with it?'

'Less again, to be honest,' Ronald replied. 'Is that bad?'

'I think it's very normal,' said Rita. 'We tend to feel more engaged with our own ideas and are more inclined to take ownership of them if we've been involved in their creation.'

'OK, good,' said Ronald, 'I'm normal then.'

Alice looked across at the fish in his Lycra clothing and cycle helmet, holding a notebook and pen with his fins, and began to wonder if she knew what normal was anymore. Her thinking was interrupted by Rita asking Ronald another question.

'So, let's come back to your question about telling someone the solution, what do you think about that now?'

'Oh!' said Ronald. 'I begin to see what you mean. If I tell the person being coached the solution, then it's *my* solution. They won't feel the same empowerment, engagement or ownership as when they come up with it themselves.'

'Yes,' said Rita. 'How important is it for you that your team are more empowered and take ownership?'

'That's what I want,' said Ronald. 'It's what I need. I need them to step up and take more ownership over tasks so that I have more time available to concentrate on other things.'

'I thought so,' Rita nodded. 'Since you're talking about time, though, we should consider the coaching approach from that perspective. It might be an obvious question, but which is quicker, telling someone what to do or having a coaching conversation with them?'

'It's definitely quicker to tell them,' said Ronald. 'That's why I do it. One of my team comes to me and I tell them what to do as quickly as possible because I'm so busy.'

'Exactly,' said Rita. 'And what do they do the next time they have a problem?'

'They come to me again,' said Ronald.

'And the next time?' asked Rita.

'They come to me again,' said Ronald despairingly, 'It's never-ending.'

'Precisely, in the long term your team learn to come to you to get their problems solved and you end up spending your time helping them. Now, let's consider what happens when you use a coaching approach. The first time one of your team asks for help, you will need to spend more time with them, helping them come up with a solution. Maybe also on the second and third time. If you successfully help them come up with a way forward each time, what do you think might happen when they come the fourth and fifth times?'

'Well, they might already have done some thinking for themselves and have a solution in mind,' said Ronald thoughtfully. 'And then, over time they might come to me only to check the solution. In fact, I think in many of the situations they could probably get on with it themselves and update me afterwards with what they've done. Now, that would be a good situation to be in.'

'So, a coaching approach is a long-term investment,' said Rita. 'In the short term it will take more of your time but, instead of being stuck in a situation where your team rely on you for ever, in the longer term they will need you less and be able to do more themselves.'

'You know, I'd never thought about it like that,' said Ronald.

'There are some exceptions, though, and we should talk about them,' continued Rita. 'Let's say something is very urgent. Do you think coaching would be the right approach then?'

'Perhaps not,' said Ronald. 'It might just be best to tell people exactly what to do.'

'I agree,' said Rita. 'If time is critical, then you might still choose to tell people. The thing to be aware of though is that if you consider everything to be time critical, then you'll never use a coaching approach.'

'Yes, I see that,' said Ronald. 'I also have another question. I have different people in my team – some of them have been with the business a long time and have a great deal of experience; others like my apprentice are newer. Would I coach them all in the same way?'

'No, I don't think so,' said Rita. 'Let me ask you, how would your apprentice respond to being asked for solutions?'

'I think she'd find it hard; she doesn't know much about the work we do yet,' Ronald answered.

'Exactly, so initially, a tell or teaching approach might be more appropriate so that she can gain experience and learn. Of course, you could still ask questions to stimulate thinking, too. Do you know how questioning affects the extent to which someone will remember an answer, even if they don't know and have to be told?'

'I'm not sure, to be honest,' said Ronald.

'I think they would be more likely to remember it,' said Alice.

'You're right, Alice,' said Rita. 'Studies show that if you ask someone to guess something and then have to tell them the answer, they are more likely to remember it than if you'd just told them straightaway.'

'Very interesting,' said Ronald, 'I'm going to remember that.'

'Great,' said Rita smiling. 'So, coming back to your team, how would coaching work with someone in your team who has plenty of experience?'

'I think they might find it strange at first,' said Ronald. 'They might wonder why I'm asking them all those questions.'

'Yes, I think they might,' agreed Rita. 'You may need to explain to them why you're taking a different approach.'

'Should I just say that I need them to step up and do more?' asked Ronald.

'Well, how important is it for you to be honest with them?' Rita enquired.

'It's important,' Ronald said. 'I aim to be honest and transparent with them wherever possible.'

'So, that's your answer. You might also want to consider how using a coaching approach might be good for them. Do you have people in your team who want to progress and develop their skills?'

'Definitely,' said Ronald. 'Not all of them, but most have some longer-term career aims.'

'And, how do you think coaching would support the aims that they have?'

'Oh, I see,' said Ronald. 'If they learn to think more themselves and develop their skills, then they further their own learning and future prospects.'

'Yes, I would think so,' said Rita. 'I'm not suggesting being disingenuous and saying you're coaching them wholly for their benefit because that's not true, but I think it's reasonable to consider that for those who want to develop themselves this is an approach that will offer that.'

'Yes, yes,' said Ronald excitedly. 'OK, I really get it now. So, tell me more about the GROW model. We start with the Goal, defining what the outcome is or what they want achieve. Next we explore the current Reality, what the situation is in detail and what they've tried or what the problem is. You said the third phase is Options.'

'Yes,' said Rita. 'The Options phase is where we help the person being coached to come up with options or ideas for how they might solve the problem or make progress.'

'This sounds more difficult,' said Ronald. 'Surely, if they've come for help, then they don't know?'

'You might think so,' said Rita, 'but often people have half-formed ideas or maybe they haven't even really stopped to think about it. In this phase we might ask:

- What are some options?
- What could you do differently?
- What haven't you tried?
- How have you tackled this / a similar situation before?
- Who might be able to help?

'And we help the person explore the ideas they come up with.'

'I like the question "How have you tackled this / a similar situation before?" – that's useful,' said Ronald.

'I remember once coaching someone about public speaking,' said Rita. 'His goal was to be able to stand up in front of 25 people and talk for 20 minutes confidently. I asked him if he had ever been in front of a large group of people before, and he said he used to be a drummer in a band. I asked what the largest group he'd performed to was. He said that his band had once supported a major artist and had played a concert to ten thousand people! Ten thousand people! Now, I'm not saying that playing the drums and speaking are the same thing, but it was a very useful experience to draw upon and there were many transferable things.'

'Yes, but what if the person really doesn't know what do?' asked Alice.

'Well, maybe that's the case,' said Rita, 'but as a coach it's important to recognize that people are often a lot more resourceful than we might think. I'm not saying that they will always come up with a workable way forward but part of the journey might be for them to try something for themselves even if it doesn't work (provided there wouldn't be serious consequences to that).

'In that situation one of my favourite questions is to ask the person who they know who would be able to make progress. And when I say "know", it might be someone famous, a character in a book or film or someone from history.'

'Good question,' said Alice. 'I like that one.'

Rita continued: 'The final phase of the GROW model is *Way forward*. This is about identifying which of the options will work best and identifying how to begin. In the original GROW model this phase was called "Will", as in the question "What *will* you do?" Many people still call it this. Personally, I prefer Way forward. Either way, some questions we might ask are:

- Which options work best for you?
- What will you do now?
- When are you going to start?
- What commitment on a 1–10 scale do you have to taking these agreed actions?
- What prevents this from being a 10?
- Is there anything else you want to talk about now or are we finished?
- What is the first step?

'The end of this phase usually concludes the coaching conversation,' finished Rita.

'OK,' said Ronald. 'So, it's Goal, Reality, Options, Way forward – that's the GROW model. How long does a coaching conversation usually take?'

'It depends,' Rita said. 'It could be really quick. Perhaps someone comes to you with a small challenge and you clarify their goal, establish the reality of what they've done, ask them what ideas they have, and then what the way forward is and the first step. It might be quite a short conversation. Other times, if you and they have time available, and if the challenge requires it then you may have a longer conversation to explore things in more detail. The amount of time it takes will depend on many factors including the complexity of the person's situation, the amount of thinking the person has already done and the amount of time available.

'I've been talking about the person being "coached" a few times but I prefer the word "client" in practice. It does sound a bit formal, but I like it because it reminds me that, as the coach, I am in the service of the other person. As the coach, I am there to help the person fulfil their own potential and learn for themselves.'

'That's interesting,' said Ronald. 'What about when I'm the person's manager, though? I do want them to fulfil their potential but I also want them to achieve certain things for my department and for the business. I couldn't honestly say I was just there to help them fulfil their potential, so using the word "Client" sounds a bit strange.'

'A great question,' said Rita, 'and a very important one. In the situation you've described I would agree that the person you're coaching isn't really your client as you aren't working entirely to their agenda when you have the objectives of your department and the business as a whole in mind. In that case, the person being coached is a team member or employee and so another word might be more accurate. I will probably continue to use the word "client" because it's straightforward, but from this point on let's be clear that in using this we are referring both to the situation where a coach is paid to work with the client and when a manager is coaching a team member or employee.

'In both situations, I think that what's important is that both the coach and client have a clear shared understanding of their responsibilities within the coaching and the role that each will take. Usually, it's helpful to have a short conversation at the beginning of the coaching to ensure this is understood.'

'I see ...' said Ronald. 'Well, sort of. What kind of things might I need to discuss?'

'Let me explain further,', said Rita. 'In coaching we use the term "contracting" to describe this part of the discussion. I don't like the word personally as it sounds rather formal and a better word might be "agreeing", but essentially it just means being clear about things before we get started. Some of the things you might discuss would be practical, like how long the coaching will be, whether there is the option to meet again and where you will meet, but I think it is also important to be clear about the roles and responsibilities of the coach and client and understand the expectations of each.'

'What are the roles and responsibilities of each – I'm not 100 per cent clear,' asked Ronald.

'The role of the coach is to guide the process, to pay attention to the client, to ask questions and to feed back observations where appropriate. The role of the client is to set the direction of the conversation and be the expert in the content of the discussion,' Rita explained.

'What about responsibilities?' Ronald asked.

'The client owns the outcome of the coaching: they decide which actions or ways forward to take and are responsible for following up on those. The coach is responsible for the process and for keeping confidentiality when this has been agreed.'

Alice groaned. 'This has suddenly become very boring,' she said. 'You sound like one of my teachers at school. I've got no idea what you just said. Can we go back to talking about space rockets?'

'Let's come back to that another time,' said Rita. 'I do think contracting is important, though, and your success in coaching will depend on navigating it successfully.'

'I've got a riddle for you,' said Alice excitedly. 'It's much more interesting. Let's see if you can work it out. What has fewer holes the more holes you make in it?'

'What has fewer holes the more holes you make in it?' repeated Rita. 'Mmm ... let me see.'

Both Ronald and Rita began muttering to themselves in a race to work it out.

CHAPTER 6

Christina

A COACHING EXAMPLE OF GROW AND THE DIFFERENCE BETWEEN COACHING AND OTHER APPROACHES

● ● ●

While Rita and Ronald pondered the riddle, Alice looked around at the grass where they were sitting. Her eyes settled on a beautiful ladybird crawling along a nearby leaf. She leaned over and carefully picked it up.

'Put me down. Excuse me, put me down please,' a high-pitched voice said.

Alice looked around. Rita and Ronald were both deep in thought, and there was no one else present.

'Excuse me. Who do you think you are, picking me up without asking?' said a voice that appeared to be coming from her finger.

'Are you talking to me?' said Alice, peering more closely at the ladybird.

'Of course, I am,' said the voice, 'and do you mind giving me some space? I get awfully claustrophobic when people put their faces close to me.'

'I'm terribly sorry,' said Alice apologetically. 'Let me put you back down.' There was a tree stump at Alice's eye level and she put the Ladybird gently on to the wood.'

'Thank you,' said the squeaky voice, 'that's better.'

'I really am very sorry,' said Alice. 'I didn't mean to upset you.'

'No harm done, I suppose,' said the Ladybird.

'I'm Alice.'

'I'm Christina,' replied the Ladybird.

'Nice to meet you,' said Alice. 'I really am very sorry for upsetting you. Can I make it up to you somehow?'

'Perhaps,' Christina said. 'There might be something you can help me with actually.'

'What is it?' enquired Alice.

'Well, I want to get a promotion at work and I'm not sure what I need to do,' answered Christina. 'Can you help with that?'

With the GROW model fresh in her mind, Alice felt sure she could help. She needed to start with the Goal phase. 'Tell me exactly what it is you want?'

'I want a promotion to be Director of Human Resources,' said Christina.

'You want to be Director of Human Resources,' repeated Alice. She wondered what human resources was, it sounded very grand and her mind boggled at the thought of this tiny ladybird being a director of such things. She decided to set her own thoughts aside. 'What is it you would like from us talking together?' she continued.

'I'm not sure what I need to do to get it,' said Christina. 'I want to know what I need to do to get the promotion. I'm hoping you can tell me.'

Alice thought about this. It seemed like a clear goal that was definitely about what Christina wanted and not what she didn't want.

She was about to continue when Rita – who had started listening in – interrupted: 'Can I ask you something, Christina – is getting the promotion entirely dependent on you?'

'What do you mean?' asked Christina. 'I definitely want it.'

'Of course,' Rita replied, 'but what I'm asking is whether getting the promotion is something you are 100 per cent responsible for or are there other factors involved?'

'Well, the current Director of HR is leaving and the business has yet to decide what to do with the role. There is some talk of a restructure. And I don't make the decision about who gets the role, if that's what you mean.'

'That's exactly what I mean,' Rita replied. 'You see, although you very much want this promotion, it's not entirely in your control. If Alice works with you on a goal that's not in your control, then it's not possible for you to be responsible for achieving it.'

'So, she can't help me get the promotion, then,' said Christina, somewhat irritated.

'Not at all,' said Rita, 'but we need to be clear about what it is she can help with and the goal needs to be something you can be responsible for. Getting the promotion isn't something that depends only on you. We need to look at the elements of this that you can take ownership of and focus on them.'

'Oh, I see,' said Christina more calmly, 'that makes sense, I suppose.'

'Good,' Rita replied. 'Now what are you responsible for with regard to the promotion and what can you affect?'

'Well, I'm responsible for what I say at the interview and I'm responsible for the application letter that I write.'

'Excellent,' said Rita. 'Either or both of those might be useful goals to work on.'

'Shall we pick one to start with,' suggested Alice, 'and see how we get on? Which one would be most useful for you?'

'I'd like some help with the interview. I haven't always done very well with interviews in the past.'

'What is your goal for the interview, then?' asked Alice, realizing that she now needed to reclarify the goal.

Christina thought for a moment. 'Well, I'd like the interview to get me the job, but as I realize that's not totally in my control I suppose my goal is to do the best interview I can and express myself as well as I can.'

'To do the best interview you can and to express yourself as well as you can,' said Alice, looking across at Rita for confirmation. Rita winked at Alice reassuringly.

'So, what do you think I need to do?' asked Christina.

'Tell me, what have you done so far?' Alice questioned, making a mental note that she was now moving on to the Reality phase of the GROW model.

'So far? ... Well, not much. I've finished the application letter and I'm waiting to go to the interview,' said Christina.

'And what are you intending to do before the interview?' Alice continued.

'Well, I'll reread my application letter so I remember what I've written,' answered Christina.

'Tell me about previous interviews you've had. You said you haven't always done very well in them.' Alice asked.

'Yes, I find them difficult. Some of the questions tend to catch me out and I'm not very good at thinking on my feet. Sometimes I just go blank and I can't remember things I've previously done. Afterwards I think of things I wished I'd said and examples I could have talked about.'

'How do you feel in an interview?' asked Alice.

'I feel confident,' said Christina. 'I'm not nervous or shaking, but I do feel the pressure of people looking at me and I'm not relaxed. So, what should I do?'

Alice was beginning to feel a bit uncomfortable with Christina asking her what to do. She didn't know what Christina should do, and, importantly, she remembered that Rita had said that coaching was about helping the client find their own Way forward or solution without there being any suggestions from the coach.

'I think perhaps I haven't been very clear,' said Alice. 'When I said I would try to help you, I didn't mean that I would give you advice or tell you what to do.'

'Oh,' said Christina despondently. 'Well, how else would you help me?'

'By helping you work out your own ideas and way forward,' said Alice.

'But I could do that on my own,' said Christina.

'Have you already?'

'No, I haven't.'

'Shall we continue and see if we can help you work out what you need to do?' Alice asked.

'If you think it will help, then I'm willing to give it a go,' Christina replied.

'You told me that your preparation for the interview is to reread your application letter. Is there anything else you do?'

'Not really,' said Christina. 'Sometimes I do some relaxation and breathing exercises beforehand.'

Alice decided she'd explored the Reality of Christina's current situation enough and it was time to move on to the Options phase.

'What else do you think you could do to prepare?' Alice began.

Christina paused. 'Well, I could make a list of situations I've dealt with successfully in my current role and note down specific examples to talk about.'

'Great, what else?' asked Alice.

'I don't know really. What else do people do to prepare for interviews?' Christina queried.

'Who do you know that is really good at interviews?' Alice asked.

'My friend Angela is amazing,' said Christina.

'How does she prepare?'

'I know this because I've helped her. She makes a list of all the questions she anticipates could be asked and then practises her answers to them. She asked me to do a mock interview with her so she could practise her responses. It was quite fun actually.'

'Is there anything stopping you doing the same thing?' asked Alice.

'No,' replied Christina thoughtfully, 'although I don't know what questions might be asked.'

'How could you find out?'

'I could ask my friend Angela for her list. There can't be that many different interview questions.'

'I don't know what Angela does. Would her questions apply to the role you're thinking of?' Alice asked.

'She works in marketing so it's a bit different,' replied Christina.

'How could you ensure the questions are relevant to your business?'

'I am good friends with the Director of Operations,' said Christina, 'and he wouldn't be involved in my interview process so I think it would be OK to ask him.'

'Great,' said Alice. 'It sounds like you have a plan. Talk me through what you're going to do.'

'First, I'm going to think about some of the challenging situations I've handled in my current role and some of my successes. I'll make a list with some specific examples. I'm going to talk to Angela about her list of questions and then ask the Director of Operations for anything that might be particularly relevant to our business. Then I'm going to ask Angela to return the favour and do a practice interview with me. In fact, I might ask the Director as well and do two.'

'How committed are you to doing this?'

'Really committed! I'm doing it,' said Christina formidably.

'It sounds like you know what to do now.'

'Yes, I do. Thank you, that's really useful, really useful.'

'When you think about the interview now, how are you feeling?' Alice asked.

'I feel better. I know what I have to do and I'll be more relaxed with this preparation behind me.'

'Will you let me know how you get on?' said Alice. 'I'm really interested to know.'

'Yes, I will. Thank you,' said Christina, glancing at her watch. 'Gosh, is that the time, I really have to fly. Thank you again.'

Alice glanced sideways at Rita, who had been watching and listening the whole time. Rita smiled and mouthed, 'Well done!' Alice smiled back.

'It's a net,' said another voice.

'Pardon?' said Alice.

'What has fewer holes the more holes you make in it? A net,' said Ronald, 'although can I just say that I have a strong dislike of nets.'

Perhaps that wasn't the most appropriate riddle to ask a fish, thought Alice to herself.

'Correct,' said Alice. 'Well done.'

'Took me a bit of time,' said Ronald, 'but I got there.'

'Alice, I want to bring something to your attention from that coaching conversation with Christina,' said Rita.

'What is it?' asked Alice.

'Do you remember the question Christina repeatedly asked you?'

'She kept asking me what she should do,' said Alice.

'Yes, exactly,' said Rita. 'She didn't completely understand your role and her role in the coaching conversation. You had to stop halfway through and explain to her that your role was to help her find a solution for herself.'

'Yes,' said Alice. 'I felt that I wasn't giving her what she wanted. It was awkward.'

'Indeed,' said Rita, 'and you handled it really well. This is an example of where a contracting conversation at the start would have cleared things up. It might have been as simple as asking Christina if she'd had coaching before and, if not, explaining that your role would be to ask questions and guide the conversation and she would be responsible for the ideas and following up on those.'

'I do see that now,' said Alice. 'I would have felt more comfortable if that had been clear at the beginning. Something else I'd like to ask about is when you stepped in to clarify the goal Christina had. Can you remind me about that?'

'Of course,' said Rita. 'When we identify goals with people there are several conditions which need to be met to ensure the goal is well formed. If these aren't met, it can lead to difficulties later on. The main conditions to consider are:

- Is the goal stated in terms of what the client wants (and not what they don't want)?
- Can the goal be initiated and maintained by the client? Is it in the client's control?
- Is it clear how the client would know that they've achieved it?
- Is it ecological? This last term refers to the wider consequences for the client in achieving this goal. Asking the client what they would gain by achieving it and what they would lose by achieving it can be a way to explore this.

'In Christina's case it was really the second condition that wasn't being met. If a client chooses a goal that is not in their control, then they are unable to be fully responsible for the result.'

'Yes, I see that now,' said Alice. 'I don't really understand number four, though. Surely if someone has a goal, it's something they want.'

'In theory perhaps, but sometimes people want something which may have unintended consequences. I remember coaching someone about dealing with his boss differently. When I asked him about his goal, he said he wanted to be powerful and tell his boss what he thought without fear. I checked the ecology of this and asked him what feeling this way would give him. He said he would feel great at finally being able to speak his mind. I asked him whether he might lose anything. His answer – his job! At which point he realized that his outcome wasn't to be powerful. I asked him what it would be more ecological for him to feel. His reflection was that he wanted to feel confident and be able to articulate his feelings and ideas appropriately. The ecology of this was much better.'

'So, as a coach I have a responsibility to ensure the client's goal is ecological?' asked Alice.

'No,' said Rita. 'I would say you have a responsibility to ask your client about the ecology of the goal and to help the client think through the consequences of achieving it. Then you let the client decide what is right for him or her. The client owns the decision about that.'

'What if I don't think it's right for the client?' asked Alice.

'Well, how would you know that?' asked Rita.

'Well ... I'm not sure. Maybe it's just my opinion; it's what I would do.'

'Ah!' said Rita. 'So, you're saying that you want to impose your ideas about what you would do on to your client?'

'I don't like the word "impose",' said Alice, 'it sounds very controlling.'

'Indeed, I would agree,' replied Rita, 'but that is what you're suggesting. You're saying you don't like the choice your client is making because it's not what you would do.'

'But, surely, as a coach I have a responsibility to make sure my client does the right thing?' asked Alice.

Rita raised her eyebrows. 'How do *you* know what the right thing is for your client?'

'Well ... um ...', Alice faltered. 'I guess maybe I don't.'

'Exactly,' said Rita. 'And who are you to tell your client what to do? Now, for sure, it depends on the situation. If you're a very experienced chief executive coaching a new director, then it might be appropriate to share the benefit of your experience. But that is really mentoring and not coaching. And, just to be clear, mentoring is a really helpful approach that can bring huge benefits but it's different from coaching. In the spirit of clarity I want to ensure we're clear about the differences.'

'So, would a mentor give advice?' asked Ronald.

'I would certainly expect that a mentor would share their experience. One of the main differences between a mentor and a coach is that a mentor will usually have experience in the subject area whereas a coach would not. Mentoring tends to have more of a focus on the content, whereas coaching has more of a focus on the individual. Each has its benefits depending on the situation.'

'What about counselling and therapy? How are they different from coaching?'

'Let's remind ourselves of what we talked about previously,' said Rita. 'One of the characteristics of coaching is an "ask" approach, questioning and exploring the issue or challenge with the client and listening carefully to their responses. This is something that is shared by both counselling and therapy and both counsellors and therapists typically have high skill levels in listening and asking effective questions.

'Mentoring, as we've discussed, tends to have more "tell" in it, often in the form of the mentor sharing their experiences and talking through how they might approach the situation. Good mentors will also ask questions and listen, so mentoring sits somewhere in the middle of the "tell–ask" continuum.

'Teaching (and training) typically involves instruction, demonstration and explanation from the teacher so is more towards the "tell" end of the spectrum. It's not right at that end as teachers ask questions of course, and, in reality, where teaching is situated on this continuum will vary with different teachers.

'I am generalizing here,' continued Rita. 'I would also put management consulting more towards the "tell" end, as typically in this situation the consultant is considered somewhat of an expert in their field and usually will give a diagnosis of the problem and suggest an approach to remedy this.'

'This makes sense,' said Ronald, 'and I get that we're making some generalizations here. There may be individuals who work differently within each.'

'Absolutely,' said Rita. 'I think it's useful to make some comparisons in order to understand the differences between each in general terms.'

'I get that consulting, teaching and mentoring involve more "Tell" than coaching,' Ronald said, 'but how is coaching different from counselling or therapy?'

'One of the differences between coaching and counselling or therapy is their orientation to problems and solutions. Typically, therapy and counselling will examine problems in great detail, often revisiting the past to look for the origins or causes of something. From the initial framing of a problem or challenge they may move quickly into looking at the client's childhood to understand the origins of the issue.

Coaching tends to be more solution oriented and future focused with an emphasis on what is happening now and what the client will do in the future. That's not to say that coaching never reviews past experiences, and there are times when a "block" from the past needs to be addressed in order for the client to move forward. But coaching doesn't set out to examine the past or the origins of a problem unless this is needed for the person to move forward. It's a different orientation.'

'Do you think coaching is better then?' asked Alice.

'Absolutely not,' said Rita. 'Sometimes people have deeply held patterns of thinking and feeling that need unpicking and tracing back to their origins. Counselling and therapy have helped a great many people, myself included.'

Alice looked slightly surprised. 'So, did you lie down on a couch and talk to a therapist?'

'Well, lying on a couch is a very outdated view of therapy. Most of the time it might look like a conversation between two people, but, yes, I worked with a therapist for several years.'

'But there doesn't seem to be anything wrong with you,' said Alice.

'Well, there doesn't need to be anything "wrong" to talk to a therapist or counsellor, or a coach for that matter,' said Rita. 'All of them are approaches that can help someone understand themselves better, live a happier life and be more fulfilled.'

'I see,' said Alice. 'So, why would someone choose coaching instead of therapy or counselling?'

'Some of this is about the context that these happen in. Coaching often happens in the workplace and the focus is on development, improvement and solutions to problems. It might not be appropriate to delve into the client's past in that relationship and the client might not give permission for that. Some people don't want to examine their childhood or maybe don't need to in order to make progress with something. So, that approach might be unnecessary. Coaching is an approach that helps people fulfil their potential and become more self-aware.'

'This makes sense,' said Ronald. 'I'm definitely clearer now on what coaching is and what it isn't.'

'Good,' said Rita. 'So, let's come back to Alice's question about wanting the client do "the right thing". For that we need to delve a little deeper into understanding people's maps of the world.'

'People's what?' said Alice, thinking about the map of the world she had at home. 'Do you mean the globe? I've got a lovely globe of the world with a light inside that looks really beautiful in the dark. Is that what you mean by map of the world?'

'Not exactly,' said Rita. 'I think we should explain this in the next chapter.'

❧

Before we move on to the next chapter, let's take a moment to reflect on what we've just covered.

'OK, Ben. Can I see your GROW model diagram? I really like it.'

'Of course, here it is. In the GROW model, the four stages are Goal, Reality, Options and Way forward. The original framework was created by Sir John Whitmore in the 1980s, and it is a proven structure for a coaching conversation.

'Alice, how about you remind us of each phase?'

'The *Goal* phase is the starting point for the coaching where we explore with the person where they want to get to – that, what they want the outcome to be and if they can be responsible for it and it is within their control.

'The *Reality* phase is about establishing where the person is currently at in the situation, what they have already tried, and what is problematic or difficult. The aim here is to explore fully the problem or challenge.

'The *Options* phase is where we help the person being coached to come up with options or ideas for how they might solve the problem or make progress. It's important to allow the person being coached to do this themselves and avoid making suggestions or planting ideas.

'The *Way forward* phase is about identifying which of the options will work best and identifying how to begin.'

'How was that?'

'Perfect, Alice. Great job. I should add that I prefer calling the final phase "Way forward" rather than "Will" as in the original model. I think this final phase isn't only about what the person will do but is more broadly about having an approach to move forward with the challenge or resolve the problem, so "Way forward" more clearly describes this.

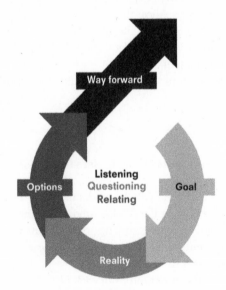

Figure 6.1 The GROW coaching framework

'In the last chapter we also introduced the idea of contracting in coaching, which means ensuring the coach and client have a clear shared understanding of their responsibilities and the role that each will take. It's also where we discuss confidentiality and the practical details of coaching.'

'My own experience of years of coaching has led me to realize that the contracting discussion is key to successful outcomes. I've learned the hard way by making mistakes and realizing too far into some coaching that I haven't set it up correctly. We'll return to contracting later in the book because I'd like to help other people avoid the pitfalls I found myself in.'

'And finally there was a discussion about the differences between coaching and other approaches. Where's your diagram, Ben?'

'This one, Alice?'

'Yes, that's it. I like seeing where each of the approaches fit and it helps me understand the differences better. I do have one question, actually.'

'What is it?'

'I understand why teaching, mentoring and management consulting are more towards the "tell" end of the continuum – they involve giving more direction whereas coaching, therapy and counselling and directed more by the client. I also now understand the difference

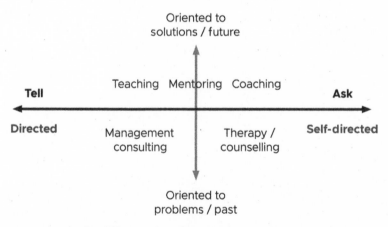

Figure 6.2 The difference between coaching and other approaches

between coaching and therapy and counselling, in that coaching has a primary orientation towards solutions and the future. What I don't understand is why you've put management consulting *below* the line?'

'Well, Alice, I might be criticized by some people for positioning it there. In my experience consultants are often called in to diagnose a problem and understand what has caused it. The consultant does some investigation and writes a report about what is happening with a way to remedy the situation. The focus is often on understanding the problem and its causes more than delivering a solution. There is a lot of variation between different consultants and consultancies, though, so it might actually be better positioned on the line halfway between problem and solution.'

'That makes sense. Do you know what else that diagram reminds me of?'

'I don't, Alice. Food probably. Most things seem to make you think of food.'

'Yes! You're right. It makes me think of ice cream.'

'What? How on earth does that diagram make you think of ice cream?'

'It doesn't. I'm just thinking about it anyway. I think it's because there's ice cream coming in the next chapter ... I can't wait!'

'In that case, shall we get back to the story?'

'Ice cream, ice cream, ice cream!'

'I'll take that as a yes, then, Alice.'

CHAPTER 7

A Trip to Naples

MAPS OF THE WORLD AND THE DIFFERENCE BETWEEN A CLIENT'S CONTENT AND PROCESS

● ● ●

Alice was contemplating the loveliness of her globe at home when Rita interrupted her thoughts.

'I want you to imagine that the three of us are going to visit a far-away city for the first time,' said Rita.

'Can we have ice cream? I want vanilla, strawberry and chocolate,' said Alice excitedly.

'And pizza?' said Ronald.

'It seems we're going to Italy then,' said Rita. 'Naples perhaps?'

'Will I be able to get a Neapolitan pizza there?' asked Alice. 'That's my favourite.'

'Yes, I'm pretty sure you will,' said Rita with a smile. 'Now let's suppose we arrive in Naples and we want to find the best pizza restaurant and ice-cream parlour. We've got a couple of different maps of the city to help us. It might be an obvious question, but why is a map useful?'

'It's a representation of the real world,' said Ronald. 'It will have the main features of the city and enough information so that we can find our destination.'

'Exactly,' said Rita. 'We know that there will be lots of information missing because if it contained everything it would be massive and unwieldy. As well as missing information, some information will a distorted version of reality, for example, buildings will be outlines on the map but we know in reality they will probably be several storeys high. Roads and streets will generally be represented without traffic on the map and with the street name written instead. We know that the street name won't be written on the tarmac but we accept this as a shortcut to convey the information.'

'When are we having the ice cream?' Alice asked.

'Not yet,' said Rita. 'We haven't arrived yet. Let's suppose there are two different maps – you have one and Ronald has the other. How would we know which map is best?'

'The one that has the most information on?' pondered Ronald.

'The one that gets us to the ice cream quickest!' said Alice.

'I'd agree with you, Alice. We could say that the most useful map is the one that navigates us most easily to our destination.'

Alice wasn't quite sure what happened but suddenly the three of them were sitting on a wooden bench in the middle of a busy street. People were walking past with cameras and Alice could hear strange voices. No one seemed to notice a fish and a tortoise sitting on a bench with a girl, though. How very odd, Alice thought to herself, but she had barely finished the thought when she noticed she was holding a bowl of ice cream with stripes of strawberry, vanilla and chocolate.

Rita took a spoonful of ice cream. 'Oh, that is delicious.'

'Itthertainlyis,' said Alice with her mouth full.

'I want to answer your question, Alice, so please bear with me while I explain the concept of a *map of the world*. I don't mean a paper map like the one we've been talking about but a conceptual map that exists in each of us. The fundamental idea is that we each live inside our perception of the world and that, while this perception is based on reality, it is not reality itself. Our perception is affected by a great many things, our beliefs, values, feelings, attitudes and personal history, to name a few. Since those things are different for each of us, our individual perceptions are often different, too, even of the same event. It explains how two people can see the same thing and infer completely different meanings.

'What makes our map of the world interesting is that most of the time we don't realize its existence. We're so used to living inside our own perceptual filters that we are no longer aware of them.'

'The three great mysteries: air to a bird, water to a fish, people to themselves,' said Ronald. 'Although I am well aware of water.'

'And many people are aware of themselves,' Rita resumed, 'but most of the time we are so accustomed to our own perception, thinking and feeling that we don't notice it. We call this combination of perception, thinking, beliefs, values, attitudes and so forth our map of the world.'

'Why do we have this?' asked Alice.

'Well, a bit like a paper map, our map of the world is a shortcut. It's a representation of reality that we use to navigate our way through life. And, like a paper map, there is lots of information that is left out. If we paid attention to everything we could see, hear, feel, smell, taste and think all the time, we'd be completely overwhelmed. Our conscious attention is limited so we attend selectively to things, completely deleting data that isn't relevant to us. Tell me, Alice, what car does your father drive?'

'A silver one,' said Alice.

'Do you remember when he first bought it?' asked Rita.

'Oh yes,' replied Alice. 'I went with him to collect it and I sat in the front on the way home.'

'Did you notice anything about the other cars on the road?' asked Rita.

'What do you mean?' Alice replied.

'About their colours?'

'I remember noticing that there were actually quite a few silver cars on the road. I'd never noticed them before.'

'Exactly,' said Rita. 'I think we can assume that they hadn't just appeared; it was just that you were suddenly noticing them at that point. We could say that your map of the world had changed and, because silver cars were now relevant and important, you were noticing them more. Prior to that you had been deleting silver cars from your experience and not paying attention to them.'

'So, what we notice in a situation is very dependent on what we know and are already aware of,' said Ronald slowly. 'And, although we might each notice different things in a situation, we tend to think that our own experience of the situation is the "truth".'

'Yes,' said Rita. 'Very often we don't realize that our experience or view of something is *our* experience or view of it and not what it *actually is*. We don't realize that someone else's different experience or view is just as true to them as ours is to us.

'As well as deleting information from our experience, we also distort the data and apply rules and generalizations. Turn over your map and tell me what it says on the back.'

Alice hadn't realized that there was something on the back of the Naples map. She turned it over and saw some text in a box:

I bgean rdeanig a setnnece adn fnoud taht alguoth nrealy all the wrods wree incerroct I cuold slitl uesdnatnrd tehm and it mdae ssnee. The pweor of the hmuan mnid is taht it deson't mttaer waht odrer the ltteers in a wrod are, the olny imnaorptt tnihg is taht the fsirt and lsat ltteers are in the rgiht pclae.

At first glance Alice thought it was gibberish but upon closer inspection she began to read the words.

'Am I correct in thinking that you can both read that?' asked Rita.

'Yes,' chimed Alice and Ronald in unison.

'Yet, most of the words are incorrectly spelled. They have the right letters but in the wrong order. Somehow, we are able to switch them round so as make them into a word.'

'Well, that's because we already know the words,' said Alice proudly.

'Precisely,' said Rita. 'We do a mental search and look for something that we already know as a match. When something is ambiguous or unclear we seek something that is close to it from our experience and use that to make sense of it.'

'So, are you saying that if we're confronted by a situation where we don't understand something, like, for example, a comment someone makes, then we use our previous experiences to make meaning of it?' Ronald asked.

'Yes, exactly that,' said Rita. 'Often there is a great deal of ambiguity in the things people say. For example, suppose someone in your team at work says, "There's no trust around here." It could mean a multitude of things. Maybe they don't feel trusted by someone or perhaps there's someone they don't trust. Or perhaps someone has behaved in a particular way which the speaker has interpreted as a lack of trust. As the listener it would be easy to fill in our own version of what we think the person has said and assume that's what they mean.'

'My first thought was that they meant management couldn't be trusted,' said Ronald.

'I thought you said "thrust",' said Alice. 'I was thinking about space rockets again.'

'Well, both are examples of distortion,' said Rita. 'Ronald on a meaning level and Alice at an auditory perception level, with both distortions relating to your own experience.'

'I'm starting to see how this might apply to coaching,' said Ronald.

'Hold on, we're getting there,' said Rita.

'We've talked about deletion and distortion. There is a third perceptual filter called generalization. This refers to the rules we have that we apply to our experiences. Now, look across the road at one of the shops.'

'I like the look of that clothes shop,' said Alice.

'I'm looking at the bookshop,' said Ronald.

'You haven't been in those shops before but I'm pretty sure you could walk across the road and open the door easily, right?'

'Of course,' said Alice.

'But you've never opened it before,' said Rita.

'Yes, but I know how to open a shop door,' Alice replied.

'Precisely,' said Rita. 'You have experienced lots of doors in your life and have generalized from your experiences how to open them. You know that you either push or pull or wait for the door to open automatically. There are some cues that will lead you to one of these actions in particular.'

'Like a handle,' said Alice.

'Exactly. When you reach a new door you automatically apply your generalization, or rule, about doors so that you can open one you've never used before. It's a shortcut in your map of the world. Generalizations are essential for us to make sense of the world quickly and are an example of applying learning from previous experiences to new situations. However, generalizations can also be very problematic. Perhaps as a young person, a client puts their hand up at school to answer a question, they get it wrong and the other students laugh. They decide, "I mustn't speak up again", to keep themselves safe. Years later in management meetings they struggle to express their views and fear being ridiculed.'

'Would that be an example of where we might revisit something from the past in a coaching situation?' asked Ronald.

'It could be,' said Rita, 'though you might not need to. It's perfectly possible to affect the person's feelings in their current life and enable them to update their map of the world for who they are now. Our mind tends to be efficient, so once something has been learned it appears again and again. The problem arises when someone's map of the world is outdated, inappropriate or too impoverished for the situation they are in. Imagine that we go to New York now and are trying to navigate with our maps for Naples because they're familiar and we are used to using them.'

'I don't think we'd find the ice-cream shop very easily. It would be very confusing,' said Alice.

'Exactly,' said Rita, 'but people have this experience frequently. Something is confusing or difficult or they feel stuck because their map of the world means they miss useful data, distort it or apply generalizations unhelpfully.'

'Can you give an example?' Alice asked.

'Well, I remember working with a client we'll call Hugo. He said to me, "I'm not confident", and listed a number of situations where he would feel uncomfortable and hardly speak. However, he was a professional gymnast, and when I asked him about his sport and the competitions he took part in, he said he felt confident talking to the coaches, judges and even the media. He was deleting or not recognizing the confidence he did have. In social situations, his experience was distorted as his attention was often on his own thoughts – wondering how people perceived him or what they thought of him instead of listening to what they were saying. It's pretty hard to have a good conversation with someone or a group of people if you're not really listening to what is being said.'

'How did you work with him in the coaching?' asked Ronald.

'Before I answer that we need to expand our ideas about what we're doing in coaching. So far we've discussed the GROW model as a way of having a coaching conversation.'

'Goal, Reality, Options, Way forward – or Will,' said Ronald.

'Well remembered,' said Rita. 'When we think about this approach we are typically working with the content of the problem and the intention is to help the client come up with some ideas to make progress.'

'What do you mean, the "content" of the problem?' asked Alice.

'I mean that we focus on the situation they are describing and what the client could do practically. So, if someone has a difficulty in social situations, we might ask what ideas they have for making conversation or how they might help themselves feel more comfortable and relaxed. All of which is very valid.'

'OK,' said Alice, 'I'm following. It sounds as though you're going to say there's something else we could be focusing on.'

Rita pointed across the road at a huge billboard which had a poster on it.

Content

Process

Client's problem / challenge

Client's thinking & feeling about
the problem / challenge
(their Map of the world)

Figure 7.1 Content and process

Alice was astonished. Surely that hadn't been there a moment ago. Sitting, as she was, on a bench in the middle of Naples with a now-empty ice-cream bowl in her hands, Alice began to wonder if Rita had superpowers. She was sure she would have noticed that billboard.

'Where did that billboard come from?' she said suspiciously. 'I didn't notice it before.'

'It's been there all along,' said Rita. 'It's just that it didn't have any meaning for you before, so your perception deleted it.'

'I noticed it,' said Ronald, 'but it made no sense so I didn't pay any attention to it.'

'The same thing happens when you are coaching,' said Rita. 'If you only listen for the content of what the client says, then all your questions will focus on the content of the situation. If you learn to pay attention to information that tells you about the client's map of the world – that is, how the client thinks and feels, what they believe – then you will ask questions about that. We might call this the *client process*.'

'So, if I'm coaching a client – how do I know whether to focus on the content or the process?' asked Ronald.

'You can pay attention to both,' said Rita.

'That sounds very difficult,' said Alice, 'and far too much to think about at once.'

'Do you remember when you learned to read, Alice?' asked Rita.

73

'Yes,' said Alice, thinking back to her days reading out loud to her mum and dad, concentrating on saying each word correctly.

'What was it like when you were learning to read?'

'It was hard,' said Alice. 'I remember reading out loud and looking at each word individually and thinking about how to say it.'

'When you were learning to read in that way, how much of the story did you pay attention to?'

'None at all,' said Alice. 'I was just focused on reading the letters and saying the words. I often had no idea what I'd just read.'

'And now when you read, do you remember the story?'

'Oh yes,' Alice replied. 'I love reading books, especially ones about space rockets.'

'So, you don't have to think about pronouncing each word and how to say it anymore?'

'No, I suppose I don't,' Alice pondered. 'it just sort of happens without me thinking about it.'

'Listening to a client's content and process is the same,' Rita said. 'When you begin, it can take all your attention to notice the process information and you might forget the content. Or, you listen to the content and don't notice the process information. As you become more skilled then you begin to be able to do it without thinking so that you can pay attention to the process information and still hear the content, too.'

'This relates to the learning ladder, doesn't it,' said Ronald.

'What's the learning ladder?' asked Alice.

Rita gave an encouraging nod to Ronald.

'Well, I'm not sure I can remember it all,' said Ronald, deferring to Rita.

'Give it a go,' Rita said encouragingly.

'OK, come with me then,' said Ronald, getting up from the bench.

CHAPTER 8

Irrationality on the Beach

THE LEARNING LADDER AND HOW THIS APPLIES TO BEING A COACH AND WORKING WITH CLIENTS

● ● ●

Alice and Rita followed Ronald across the street towards a brown wooden door set in the side of a stone-walled building. There was nothing written on the door or the building and the door had a single metal handle. As Ronald opened the door, Alice suddenly smelled the sea and had the salty taste of sea air on her lips. She looked behind her at the busy Naples street where people were still promenading with ice creams and cameras as she stepped through the door on to some soft sand.

'Alice, you need to eat less sugar,' she told herself. 'It's playing with your senses – you can't possibly go from the street straight on to a beach.'

'Ah, the sea,' said Ronald fondly. 'I'm looking forward to a swim.'

It was definitely the sea, and when Alice removed her shoes and socks she could feel the coarse sand between her toes.

'How is this possible?' she asked herself.

Ronald had picked up a stick and was drawing a picture of a ladder in the sand.

'Let me explain the learning ladder,' he said. The idea is that there are four different levels of learning, and as we become more skilled we progress from one to the next.

'Level 1 is called *unconsciously unskilled* or *unconsciously incompetent*. At this level we are unskilled but we're not even conscious that we are. We don't know what we don't know.'

'Surely, we would know that we don't know?' asked Alice.

'Did your mother or father read to you when you were young before you could read yourself?' asked Ronald.

'Oh yes,' said Alice, 'I loved stories being read to me.'

'What did you think about while they were reading?' asked Ronald.

'The story,' Alice replied. 'Spaceships and white rabbits and singing and pizza and adventures.'

'Did you ever wonder about the symbols on the page that your mother or father was reading?'

'No, I don't suppose I did,' said Alice. 'I didn't know what they were.'

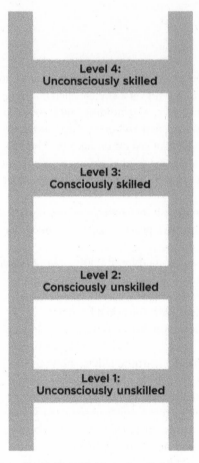

Figure 8.1 The learning ladder

'So, you didn't know about words or sentences?' asked Ronald.

'No,' said Alice, 'I couldn't read then.'

'Exactly,' said Ronald. 'You couldn't read and you weren't even aware that words existed and sentences existed. You didn't know what happened when someone looked at a page and read you a story, how they were able to look at the page and talk. That's Level 1 – *unconsciously unskilled*. You're not aware of what you don't know.'

'*Oh!*' said Alice. 'That makes sense now. My mother often says that "ignorance is bliss".'

'Well, that may or nor may not be true,' said Ronald, 'but what is often true is that moving from Level 1 to Level 2 doesn't always feel great. In Level 2 we become conscious that we are unskilled. This is where we become aware that we don't know or can't do something, and sometimes this lack of knowledge or experience can be overwhelming. Do you remember what it was like when you started to read, Alice?'

'It was difficult,' Alice replied. 'There were lots of long words that I couldn't say properly. I wondered if I would ever be able to say them, they seemed so hard. I remember when I couldn't say "fatigue". I kept saying "fatty-goo". It took me ages to learn that.'

'So, Level 2 is where we become conscious that we don't know something and are unskilled and is the phase where, if we choose, we can start to develop skills. If we practise and work hard, then, over time, we begin to perform better. Level 3 is *consciously skilled*, and at this stage we have learned to do the activity. We need to focus and concentrate, and, when we do so, we are able to perform well and have gained the skills. Do you remember what it was like when you could read for yourself, Alice?'

'Yes!' Alice replied. 'The first book I read on my own was *The Wonderful Wizard of Oz*.'

'Great story,' said Ronald, 'although it would have been even better if there were fish in it.'

'And some turtles,' said Rita.

'There is a lion,' said Alice.

'Well, anyway. What was it like when you read *The Wonderful Wizard of Oz*?' asked Ronald.

'It took me quite a long time,' said Alice. 'I sometimes had to read something more than once and it was quite tiring.'

'That's Level 3. We have gained the skills and, if we apply ourselves, we can perform well. We're not always able to do it quickly and it requires energy to use the skill.'

'So, what's Level 4?' asked Alice.

'Level 4 is *unconsciously skilled*,' said Ronald. 'This is where we have learned to do a skill "without thinking", or, at least, that's how we often describe it. What we mean is that we can do it without thinking consciously; it just happens automatically.'

'When I read now I don't have to think about the words, I just understand them,' Alice commented.

'Exactly, that's Level 4,' said Ronald. 'You're skilled and you've almost forgotten that you are. Anyone who demonstrates excellence can be considered to be unconsciously competent. Often, if you ask them how they do it, then they can't tell you. They'll say, "I don't know, I just do it." They are no longer conscious of what they're doing. This unconscious processing is much quicker than having to think about it consciously and feels effortless.'

'OK, so to get from Level 1 to Level 2 we have to discover what we don't know and learn how to do it. If we practise repeatedly, then we can move from Level 2 to Level 3 where we are consciously competent. How do we go from Level 3 to Level 4?'

'By practising more, usually over a period of time,' Ronald replied.

'Practice makes perfect,' said Alice.

'Actually, practice makes permanent,' said Rita. 'Repeated practice makes something permanent in our nervous system. Perfect practice makes perfect permanence.'

'Great explanation, Ronald,' said Rita.

'Thanks,' said Ronald. 'I can't remember how we got to talking about this, though.'

'And how did we come to be on a beach?' Alice asked herself.

'We were discussing paying attention to the content of what a client is saying as well as their map of the world, their thinking, feeling, beliefs and so on.'

'Oh yes,' said Ronald. 'I'd never really thought about that before. I guess I'm just moving into Level 2 then.'

'Quite possibly,' said Rita. 'Let's go back and look at the billboard poster again.'

The three of them turned around to where the door had been and saw a golden beach of sand stretching for miles.

'Oh,' said Alice.

'Oh,' said Rita.

'*Oh!*' said Ronald. 'And I haven't had any pizza, I'm not ready to leave Naples yet. I wonder why the hole has closed.'

'The hole?' quizzed Alice.

'It's a hole in the space–time continuum,' said Rita. 'We stepped through it to get here but it seems to have closed. I hate it when this happens.'

'A hole in the what?' said Alice.

'It's a mathematical model that joins space and time into a single idea called a continuum. The four-dimensional continuum is known as Minkowski space.'

Space was one of Alice's favourite subjects and she thought back to what she'd learned. 'Now come on, Alice,' she said to herself. 'There's Planet Earth then Mercury, Venus, Mars, Jupiter, Saturn, Uranus and Neptune. No Minkowski, though.'

'I don't think we've done four-dimensional continuums at school yet,' Alice said.

'Well, the hole has closed so let's think about this rationally,' said Ronald.

'No, let's not,' said Alice. 'It's an irrational problem so it needs an irrational solution. I have an idea. Come with me.'

Alice spotted an area of rocks further down the beach with rock pools and some large pieces of driftwood nearby.

'Come and stand so you can see your reflection in this rock pool,' Alice said.

'Why?' asked Ronald.

'First, I'm going to look at you both. Then I'm going to look in the rockpool to see what I just saw. Then we'll use the saw to cut one of those big pieces of wood in half.'

'How will that help?' asked Ronald.

'Well, two halves make a whole,' said Alice. 'Once we've made the hole we can put it where the door was and climb out.'

'An excellent idea!' said Rita. 'You know, Alice, your irrational solution has reminded me of something very important that I want to mention.

'Most of the time when someone comes for coaching they are considered to know more about the subject area than the coach. It's one of the differences between coaching and mentoring that we talked about. That's not always the case, of course; in the workplace a manager might have more experience and may still choose to use a coaching approach to develop someone in the team and give them opportunities to learn for themselves. Typically, though, the client is considered to be capable of finding ideas and solutions to achieve their challenges and goals. The coach's role is to help the client develop this thinking through questioning and exploration.

'One of the challenges for many new coaches is the tendency to want to "solve the client's problem". "Have you thought about doing *x*?" becomes a covert way of suggesting something by disguising it as a question. "What about *y*? Have you considered that?" is another thing I hear quite often when the coach wants to suggest an idea to the client.'

'I thought that in coaching the ideas should come from the client,' Ronald stated.

'Exactly,' said Rita. 'And, when they do, then things go well. Sometimes, though, the client seems unable to come up with any ideas and the temptation is for the coach to make suggestions or provide ideas. Typically, these are quite "rational" approaches to solving the problem. But here's the difficulty. If there was a "rational" solution to the problem, then the client would probably already have thought about it. People will usually try to solve something themselves if they can.'

'Except for when they don't,' said Ronald.

'Except for when they don't,' agreed Rita. 'In which case, *that* is part of the problem and is probably what they need help with. Again, though, a rational solution isn't what is needed.

'Let's consider the situation where a client presents a problem that they haven't been able to find a rational solution, too. It seems presumptuous of the coach to think that they are somehow more intelligent or creative than the client and will be able to come up with a solution that the client hasn't considered. Coaches sometimes talk about their set of "magical" questions they keep in order to solve the problem. But, in practice, if the way forward was so easily available, the client would have probably already found it.'

'So, what are you saying then?' asked Ronald.

'Well, if the problem isn't rational then neither should the solution be. Alice just reminded me of that. Instead of focusing on the content of a client's issue and looking for logical solutions, then the coach's job is often to explore the client's map of the world to discover where that is limited or incomplete in some way.'

'Are you saying that most of us are irrational?' asked Ronald.

'That is *exactly* what I'm saying,' replied Rita. 'In fact, personally I think that if we could understand and appreciate our irrationality more, then we would find things much easier.'

'I have to disagree with you,' said Ronald, slightly affronted. 'I consider myself a very rational person.'

'There are hundreds of well researched examples of our irrationality,' continued Rita unphased. 'Let me share some with you:

1. We are much more likely to buy when something else is offered for free (even if we don't want the freebie).

2. When it comes to helping people increase concentration and alertness, pink placebo (sugar) pills are more effective than blue ones and two pink placebo pills are more effective than one.

3. We think we are better drivers and funnier than we really are! Ninety per cent of us think we're in the top 50 per cent of drivers and 95 per cent think we're in the top 50 per cent of people who are funny.

4. Public speaking is often people's number one fear, yet no one ever died from it!

'We make decisions every day and have reactions that are non-rational yet we're usually not aware of this process. We justify ourselves using logic and reason afterwards so we can keep our sanity. In our own lives, we consistently overestimate our ability to make changes in our behaviour (how many people haven't kept a New Year's resolution?)

'We are significantly less rational than we think. Marketing experts know this, the advertising industry knows this, salespeople know this and technology designers know this, and they use this to their advantage all the time.'

Ronald looked as though there was a deep struggle going on inside him. 'I've heard of some of the things you mentioned. I know that the placebo effect is incredibly powerful: I read about research where people had pseudo operations and their symptoms improved afterwards even though nothing had been actually done. And I know what you mean about marketing and advertising – those two industries are founded on the idea that we aren't rational when it comes to our buying behaviour.'

'But ...?' said Rita. 'I can hear a "but" coming.'

'Yes, you're right,' said Ronald. 'I just consider myself a rational individual.'

'Well, that's part of the challenge. I would say that very often we aren't aware of our own irrationality and we become skilled at rationalizing our behaviour to justify it to ourselves. Let me be clear,' continued Rita, 'I'm not saying that we're all crazy. What I'm saying is that much of our behaviour and decision making is driven by thinking and feeling that we're not really conscious of.

'Have you ever met someone who has a phobia?'

'Why, yes,' said Ronald. 'My cousin Reggie has a phobia of clownfish. He gets completely freaked out when he sees one.'

'Well, you might not know this but it's surprisingly common. A phobia of clowns is one of the top 10 phobias in the population, with some studies estimating that up to 12 per cent of people are affected by it.'

'Oh, well if you're talking about people, then I'm sure they *are* irrational. But fish ...' – here Ronald drew himself up to his full height – '... fish are much more rational.'

'Well, there's nothing rational about a phobia of clownfish. Clownfish are small, harmless fish, aren't they?'

'Yes,' said Ronald. 'Beautiful colouring and very friendly. Tell lots of jokes.'

'Have you tried telling your cousin not to be afraid of them?' asked Rita.

'I have,' said Ronald. 'I've told him there's nothing to be afraid of and that clownfish are harmless. I said that the fear is just in his imagination and he needs to be sensible about it.'

'Did that help?' asked Rita.

'No,' sighed Ronald. 'He said he knows that. He said that logically he knows there's nothing to be scared of but that doesn't change how he feels.'

'So, how well did the rational approach to dealing with this work?' asked Rita.

'Oh!' said Ronald. 'I see what you mean now. Even though he knows rationally there's nothing to be afraid of, that doesn't change anything. Hmm.'

'Exactly,' said Rita. 'The feeling is irrational. You know that, and Reggie knows that. But it's still there. Trying to rationalize it doesn't change it.

'Now, I've picked a phobia as an example because it's more extreme and illustrates the point, but lots of other responses and reactions we have are the same.'

'So, if a rational approach doesn't work, then how do we affect what's happening?' asked Ronald.

'Actually, I'm not saying that a rational approach doesn't ever work,' said Rita. 'There are times when someone comes for coaching and they need help to think something through in a structured way and do some problem solving. What I am saying is that there are other times when this approach won't be effective, and the reason is that the problem isn't rational. This comes back to what I was talking about earlier with the client's content and process.'

'Done it!' shouted Alice, pointing at a hole where the door had been. 'Come on.'

Rita and Ronald decided not to waste any time following Alice through the hole in case it closed again. As they stepped through on to the busy Naples street again, Alice caught a smell of pizza and began to feel hungry.

'Perfect,' said Rita. 'We can see the poster again now. Let me continue what I was saying. Most of the time, when someone seeks coaching they are stuck or unable to make progress. They can't seem to find a solution to the problem.

'If we focus on the *content* and take a rational approach, then we look for solutions to the problem as the client describes it, in its current formulation.

Content

Client's problem / challenge

Process

Client's thinking and feeling about
the problem / challenge
(their map of the world)

Figure 8.2 Content and process

'If we focus on the *process* – on the client's map of the word – then instead we look at the way the client is describing the problem. We are interested in discovering if the client's map of the world is limited in some way, often in the form of implicit assumptions the client makes. Instead of focusing on the client's problem as the client defines it, we focus on *how* the client defines the problem. Or, if it's a goal, then instead of focusing on the goal as the client describes it, we focus on the client's way of describing the goal.'

'Surely, if clients are aware of their own thinking, though, they would know that themselves?' asked Ronald.

'Remember the learning ladder,' said Rita. 'Level 4 – unconscious competence. This is the stage where we can do something without thinking and we may not even consciously know how we're doing it. Well, people's problems can be at this level as well. Someone may have practised a particular way of thinking so much that it becomes automatic and unconscious – they don't even know they are doing it. If you ask them about it directly, they can't even describe it.'

'That does make sense,' said Ronald. 'I do know some people who seem to have the same problem again and again without really knowing why.'

'Exactly,' said Rita. 'So, in this situation we can consider the job of the coach to be to discover what the thinking or feeling is that the person is non-conscious of. If they don't know what it is or what's happening, then it's very hard to affect it.'

'So, instead of listening to the problem as it is defined, we are paying attention to the assumptions and ways of thinking and feeling that the client displays,' said Ronald. 'That sounds rather difficult,' he added.

'It requires a skillset,' said Rita. 'One that can be learned. The skills are to do with asking questions that explore the client's map of the world and paying careful attention to the responses of the client. One of the main roles of a coach is to ask questions enabling the client to separate their thoughts about a situation from the actual situation.'

'Can you say that last bit again?' asked Ronald. 'One of the main roles of the coach ...'.

'One of the main roles of a coach is to ask questions enabling the client to separate their thoughts about a situation from the actual situation.'

'To separate their thoughts about the situation from the actual situation,' repeated Ronald. 'I had never really contemplated the difference between those two things.'

'Well, we could discuss that for a long time but it's not a new idea. Many Eastern traditions have taught this concept for hundreds of years. Buddha said, "Pain is certain, suffering is optional", and he talked about how our thinking can add to or take away the suffering that we experience. In simple terms, and I am simplifying this, one of the goals of meditation and mindfulness is to begin to see our thoughts and feelings as they arise rather than being caught up in them. This is an example of separating our thoughts about something from the something itself.'

'OK, I understand this now,' said Ronald. 'I did some mindfulness once and it was very interesting. I never really got to grips with it but I understand the concept. So, are you saying that mindfulness helps people in a similar way to coaching?'

'In this particular aspect, yes. And the aspect I'm referring to is becoming more aware of your own thinking and feeling, and being able to observe it. In other ways, the two things are very different and have different purposes. But it's very hard to affect something if we aren't aware of it. Being able to "see" the thinking and feeling responses we have, which often happen very quickly, means we have increased opportunity to address them.

'Let me elaborate on why this is important in a coaching situation. If the coach focuses on the content of a client's specific problem, then the coach is likely to be trapped in the same thinking as the client, so not much progress will be made. If the coach focuses on the client's process – that is, the client's thinking and feeling about the situation – and looks at the client's map of the world, then it might be possible to discover a way forward.'

'Can you give us an example?' asked Ronald.

'Of course,' Rita replied. 'Let's come back to my client Hugo, who, you remember, said, "I'm not confident." We established fairly quickly that this was about social situations and that in his professional life he actually felt pretty confident. Let's consider some questions we might ask him.

'Some example *content* questions could be:

- Where and when do you have the problem?
- Who are who with?
- What have you already tried?
- What ideas have you got?

'Some example *process* questions could be:

- How is this a problem for you?
- What are you feeling/thinking?
- What are you paying attention to?
- Can you teach me how to have this problem?

'The questions have a different focus, but the main skill is listening to the answers.' Rita paused. 'This might be easier to explain with the actual example. Let's go back to the conversation with Hugo. Will you both come with me?'

Rita turned around and headed along the busy Naples street with Alice and Ronald in tow. She stopped at a manhole cover in the pavement and said, 'Give me a hand will you.'

Ronald and Alice helped her lift the cover and reveal the hole beneath.

'Oh no,' said Alice, 'is this one of Minkowski's holes again? Can we please make sure we get back this time?'

'Come on,' said Rita, jumping into the hole.

One by one, the three of them jumped into the hole and began to fall. Alice had a strange sense of déjà vu.

CHAPTER 9

A Hole Lot of Coaching

THE DIFFERENCE BETWEEN PRACTICAL SOLUTIONS AND WORKING IN A MORE TRANSFORMATIVE WAY

● ● ●

The three of them seemed to be falling for quite a long time, and Alice began to notice pictures on the inside of the hole. As she looked closer, she realized she was seeing pictures of herself when she was younger, each image being of a different situation she had experienced in life. She was reminded of when she changed schools and had her first day at her current school. She saw her eleventh birthday party when she'd bumped her head and had to go and lie down and miss the fun. As they fell further, Alice in the pictures was getting younger, until finally she landed on a huge bean bag next to Rita and Ronald.

'What just happened?' Alice asked.

'We've gone back in time,' said Rita. 'Did you both notice the pictures of yourself when you were younger?'

'Well, yes,' said Alice. 'I saw myself in lots of different situations.'

'I first worked with Hugo quite a few years ago so I wanted us to come back and revisit the first ever coaching session I did with him. I'm hoping it will provide a useful example of what we've been discussing.'

'I just saw my first day as manager in my current role,' said Ronald. 'I was so different then, desperate to please, saying yes to everyone. It's really interesting. I can see how much I've learned and how I approach things differently now. I wish I'd known back then what I know now.'

'What would you say to Ronald back then if you could give him some advice?' asked Rita.

'I'd say, "You're doing great. You need to get to know yourself more, get to know your strengths and recognize the areas you're not so skilled in. Instead of trying to push these away, welcome them and be more accepting of them. You don't have to be good at everything."'

'Interesting,' said Rita. 'How do you think that advice would have helped Ronald back then?'

'Well, he was trying really hard to be good at everything and please everyone. As a result, he was stressed and lost touch with what he was really good at. I think that, if he could have recognized the areas he felt less skilled in and acknowledge those, he would have felt more comfortable and learned more easily.'

'Hearing you say that makes me wonder what the future you would say when looking back on you right now,' said Rita.

Alice could tell it was one of those statements that was intended to make Ronald think and reflect and she decided not to say anything. Sometimes, she reflected, silence is one of the most powerful tools for insight.

As she looked around, Alice noticed that they were in a cave with a dimly lit tunnel leading off it. Rita began walking along the tunnel, and Alice followed behind her in silence, leaving Ronald to ponder. The tunnel seemed to curve round, although Alice felt disoriented and couldn't quite be sure.

Up ahead in the distance Alice noticed a light and, as they approached, she could see sunlight streaming in from above. Stepping out of the tunnel they entered a large clearing in a forest. She could smell the grass and foliage and there was a breeze gently rustling the leaves. 'How strange,' Alice said to herself. 'You imagined we were miles underground, didn't you?' On reflection, though, she decided that falling back in time needn't be downwards, it could be in any direction. 'Who says that time travel follows the laws of gravity?' she concluded.

Stepping into the clearing, Alice noticed two chairs in the middle and a number of chairs around the outside.

'Let's sit,' said Rita. 'They'll be arriving soon.'

Alice and Rita sat next to each other and were soon joined by Ronald who appeared from the tunnel. As Ronald sat down, Alice saw another turtle appear on the edge of the clearing. This turtle wore different spectacles from Rita and Alice thought it looked a little slimmer but otherwise they looked very similar.

'Is that ... you?' she stammered.

'It's a younger me,' said Rita.

Younger Rita appeared not to notice them and sat quietly in one of the chairs in the centre of the clearing. Shortly after there was a shuffling noise and a chimpanzee entered the clearing, wearing trainers, shorts, a T-shirt and a red baseball cap.

From her chair, younger Rita said, 'Hello, Hugo, have a seat. How are you?'

'I'm OK,' replied Hugo, looking down at the forest floor. 'A little nervous, I suppose.'

'What are you nervous about?' asked Rita.

'I've never really done something like this before,' Hugo replied.

'What do you mean "something like this"?' Rita queried.

'Well, talking to someone – professionally – about something that's bothering me.'

'Do you talk to other people about things that bother you?' asked Rita.

'Not really,' said Hugo. 'They probably think I do – my friends, I mean – but I tend only to talk about little things. I find it hard to talk about things that really bother me.'

'OK, well that's helpful to know. So, tell me what you want from our work together?'

'I'm not very confident,' said Hugo. 'I struggle talking to people I don't know. Actually, I often struggle talking to people I do know when I'm in groups.'

'What is it you want?' asked Rita again.

'She's establishing Hugo's goal,' whispered Alice to Ronald.

'I would like to feel more confident talking to other people,' Hugo responded.

'What does that mean?' asked Rita. 'How would you know if you were more confident?'

'I'd feel different. I'd feel relaxed and be able to speak without worrying what others think. I'd be able to enjoy myself more.'

'You'd feel relaxed and be able to speak without worrying what others think. If you weren't worrying what others were thinking, what would be happening instead?' asked Rita.

'She's heard what Hugo doesn't want and she's getting him to think about what he does want instead,' Ronald said to Alice.

'I don't know,' said Hugo. 'I suppose I'd be listening to what is being said.'

'What would this give you?' asked Rita.

'What do you mean?' Hugo replied.

'If you were more confident and you felt relaxed and able to speak and listen to others, what would this give you?'

'I'd be happier. I be able to enjoy social situations more. I might need to drink less to enjoy myself. Not that I drink loads but sometimes I feel I need a couple of drinks before I can feel comfortable. I'd make more friends.'

'Is there anything you'd lose by being more confident?' asked Rita.

'Lose? No.'

'OK, so tell me more about what happens when you're in a social situation. Can you give me an example?'

'This is exploring his reality,' whispered Alice and Ronald to each other in unison.

'I went to a friend's birthday last weekend,' Hugo began. 'When I arrived at the gathering I already felt nervous. I felt that everyone was looking at me when I walked in. My friend was talking to some people, so I hovered nearby until she was free. I know people were thinking that I didn't have any friends.'

'How do you know people were thinking that?' asked Rita.

'Well, I was standing on my own, so they must have been thinking that I didn't have any friends.'

'How does standing on your own mean that you have no friends? Have you ever known someone who had friends and stood on their own?'

'I suppose so,' said Hugo. 'I mean, maybe their friends haven't arrived yet or maybe they don't know anyone at that party but they still have friends.'

'What would happen if people thought you had no friends?' asked Rita.

'It would mean that I'm not likeable,' said Hugo, 'or I'm weird or boring.'

'So, in your mind, if you're not with friends, then people will think you're weird or boring?' asked Rita.

'Yes. I suppose I do think that. I never really verbalized it that way before.'

'Standing on your own means you have no friends, which means you're weird or boring,' said Rita.

'Yes, but that sounds a bit ridiculous,' said Hugo.

'What do you mean?'

'You see people standing on their own all the time, people go to bars on their own, to the cinema on their own, travel on their own ... they're not all boring or weird. In fact, sometimes quite the opposite.'

'Indeed,' said Rita. 'Standing on your own could mean any number of things. But in your mind it means you're boring or weird.'

'Yes, I see that,' said Hugo.

'How do you do it anyway?'

'What do you mean?' Hugo asked.

'How do you get into that mindset? Imagine you're going to teach me to have this problem. I'm going to go to a party and you're going to teach me how to feel unconfident.'

'OK ...' said Hugo, looking bemused. 'You want *me* to teach *you* how to be unconfident?'

'Yes, exactly. You seem to have practised it a lot – how do I do it?' said Rita, smiling.

'You have to start before you arrive. You have to make a picture of yourself at the party standing on your own. See yourself standing with a drink and no one else around you.'

'Ew ... that doesn't feel very nice,' said Rita.

'Right,' said Hugo. 'Now think to yourself that you don't know what to say to people and they won't want to talk to you.'

'OK,' said Rita. 'I feel quite anxious.'

'Now imagine that you're arriving at the party feeling this anxiety and see people looking at you as you arrive.'

'Oh yes, I can see some interesting-looking people,' said Rita.

'No, no. You have to think that they're wondering why you're on your own.'

'Oh right. OK. I'm imagining that they're thinking that. It's hard work this,' said Rita, smiling.

'It is, isn't it?' said Hugo, laughing. 'You have to do a lot of imagining what other people are thinking.'

'How do you know that they're really thinking these things?' asked Rita.

'Well ... I suppose ... I don't really,' said Hugo, 'but it's what's in my mind.'

'Exactly. It's what's in *your* mind. It's not necessarily what is happening, but it is what *you* imagine is happening.'

'Yes, it is.'

'If you are talking to a friend at a party and you saw someone arrive on their own, what would you think?' asked Rita.

'I might wonder who they were and maybe notice what they were wearing. To be honest, I probably wouldn't spend a lot of time thinking about it if I was talking to a friend. I'd be having a conversation.'

'Indeed. So, what makes you think that all these people are going to stop their conversations and make time to think things about you when you arrive?'

Hugo laughed. 'I don't know. It sounds kind of silly now.'

'I'm lost now,' said Ronald. 'I'm not quite sure what she's doing. Is this the options phase?'

'I don't think so. I think this is still the Reality phase but she's asking client process questions. She's separating Hugo's thinking about the situation from the situation itself and exploring his map of the world for that situation,' replied Alice.

'Oh yes, I get it,' said Ronald. 'She's showing him that this is how he thinks about the situation, not the situation itself.'

'So, in summary, this whole situation has begun before you arrive. You've started to picture yourself on your own in advance of arriving,' said Rita.

'Yes,' said Hugo, 'I can see that's how it begins.'

'And then you think to yourself you don't know what to say to people and they won't want to talk to you.'

'Yes, exactly.'

'So, what ideas have you got for what you could do differently?' asked Rita.

'Options,' said Alice, elbowing Ronald.

'Well, I could start by picturing the party differently,' said Hugo.

'What would you picture?' asked Rita.

'I could picture myself going up to someone and saying hello and introducing myself and having people to talk to.'

'What happens when you see Hugo going up to someone and saying hello?' asked Rita.

'I feel a bit nervous – I'm thinking to myself that I don't know what say,' said Hugo.

'Who do you know who would be good at this? Who would "know what to say"?'

Hugo considered this. 'My friend Mike is really good at talking to people. He'd know what to say.'

'Right, so imagine Mike in this situation. Picture him going up to someone and saying hello. What would he be thinking?'

'I don't know,' said Hugo. 'He wouldn't really be thinking anything. He'd probably be focused on the person he was talking to.'

'What would he be focusing on?' asked Rita.

'He'd be looking at them, maybe noticing what they're wearing, how they look, their expression and also aware of what is going on in the room.'

'What does he say?' asked Rita.

'He introduces himself and then says something he likes about the person's clothes or something about the party.'

'Like what?'

'Like ... "I like your jacket" or "I like your shoes, can I ask where you got them?" or "Great party! How do you know the birthday girl?" – something to just start the conversation.'

'What happens when you see Hugo doing the same thing in that situation?' asked Rita.

'Well, he sees someone to talk to. He takes a moment to observe the scene around him and the person and as he approaches them he considers what it is he's noticed about them. He says, "Hello, I'm Hugo", and offers his hand. They shake hands and he says, "I noticed your jacket. It's really great."'

'What happens then?' asked Rita.

'The person smiles and says, "Thanks." Actually, I'm noticing that the other person looks quite shy.'

'Really?'

'Yes, he looks slightly unsure of himself. I'm just going to talk about how I know the birthday girl before I ask him anything more to help him relax,' Hugo continued.

'How are you feeling?' asked Rita.

'Pretty good. I'm talking to someone new and probably helping him feel a bit better being on his own,' said Hugo.

'What are you thinking to yourself?'

'I'm not really. I'm just present in the situation,' Hugo replied.

'I don't really get this,' said Ronald. 'She seems to be rehearsing just this one situation with him. Other situations might be different. Is she going to rehearse all the possible scenarios he might experience?'

'I'm not sure,' Alice replied. 'She seems to have something in mind but I don't know what it is.'

'That's right', Rita replied. 'You're just present in the situation. Now let's go from the beginning again and, instead of seeing Hugo in the situation, I want to see it through your own eyes.

'Imagine arriving and seeing people having conversations. Maybe one or two look up but most are busy with the person or people they're talking to.'

'Yes, I see that.'

'What do you notice in the room?'

'There's music, the sound of people talking, it's loud actually. I can see the birthday girl talking to some people. I can see someone by the drinks area on his own.'

'Right,' said Rita. 'How are you feeling?'

'Pretty relaxed, I'm just looking around,' Hugo replied. 'I'm going to get a drink and say hello to the person I can see.'

'Tell me,' asked Rita. 'How are you being different now?'

'I'm more present and I'm paying attention to what's going on in the room and with the people there.'

'Exactly. How do you feel when you do that?'

'Much calmer. It's like everything slows down and I've got more time. I feel more relaxed.'

'OK, so let's imagine another situation. Something different where, if it had happened before now, you would have felt the old nervous feeling.'

'Interesting use of tenses there,' whispered Ronald. 'She's referring to the nervousness as something he used to feel.'

Suddenly Rita and Hugo stopped. In fact, the whole clearing stopped. The tops of the trees stopped their gentle swaying in the breeze. The occasional sound of the birds ceased. Alice and Ronald looked at Rita sitting next to them.

'I thought we should just stop and talk about what you've seen and heard,' she said. 'Do you have any questions?'

'This seems different from the previous coaching with Christina,' said Alice. 'It's not a practical problem to solve; the issue seems to be in Hugo's head.'

'Well, in his head and body. It's about how he feels physically as well as the thoughts he has. But, yes, you're right. This is an example of where the difficulty for Hugo lies primarily within his construction of the situation, in his map of the world.'

'Is that why she's – Rita's – been focusing on that?' asked Ronald.

'Yes,' said Rita. 'She explored in some detail his thinking and what he pictures in his mind beforehand. This is all part of his internal process.'

'So, the content doesn't matter that much?' queried Alice.

'Well, it's a problem which happens for Hugo in multiple situations. It's helpful to have a content example, but that's because it makes it easier to discover what Hugo is thinking and feeling.'

'But won't he feel and think different things in other situations?' asked Ronald.

'Not for social situations,' said Rita. 'This is a well-rehearsed pattern of thinking and feeling, and it probably just repeats in the same way each time.'

'What do you mean "well-rehearsed"?' asked Ronald.

'There's a saying which I like that explains how our brain's ability to learn and change: "Neurons that fire together wire together." It refers to the idea of neuroplasticity, the ability of the brain to form and reorganize synaptic connections, especially in response to learning or experience. Our brains literally change physical structure in response to learning and new experiences. Simplistically, we might say that the more a person thinks in a particular way, the stronger those connections or that pathway become. It's similar to physical training: if you train a particular set of muscles, they become stronger.'

'So, you're saying that Hugo has trained himself to feel nervous?' asked Ronald.

'No, I wouldn't put it like that,' said Rita. 'He didn't consciously choose to be this way, but our brains learn through conditioning – stimulus–response. Each time the stimulus is fired, the response strengthens, so in this situation it becomes a self-perpetuating pattern. Hugo anticipates feeling nervous, which in itself is anxiety provoking. Since he already feels nervous when he moves into a social situation, he finds it harder to talk to people and retreats into his own thinking. This increases his anxiety further and the whole thing spirals downwards. This then strengthens the belief about the problem for next time.'

'When you put it like that it sounds like such a big thing,' said Ronald. 'How can you help someone with something that is so pervasive across multiple situations?'

'Well, to some extent we use the same process that created the problem to help resolve it. That's a pattern of generalization. The problem has reinforced itself over time and spread across different situations.'

'Like a virus,' said Alice.

'Yes, I suppose so. That's an interesting metaphor,' said Rita. 'I guess the similarity lies in the fact that it replicates itself across different boundaries. Hugo might have started being nervous at a party where he doesn't know anyone, then it happens in a bar, at a dinner and in large groups with people he does know. If we use that metaphor, then what is needed is an antibody. Once the antibody is produced in the body, it can spread and begin to neutralize the virus. What I'm saying is that, once we have *one* example where Hugo is able to feel and think differently, this can begin to spread to all the other situations where it would apply. Sometimes this happens on its own; it's almost like the mind takes the new learning and says, "Well, if that applies in that situation then it also applies in this situation," and so on. Which is, of course, probably how the problem began. That's what I mean by using the same process to resolve the problem as the one that created it.'

'You said that sometimes it happens on its own. What if it doesn't?' asked Ronald.

'We can help the process as part of the coaching. Rita is going to get Hugo to think about other situations now and use the same new way of approaching them. This will help condition the response.'

'Will that be enough?' asked Ronald. 'Will he be cured?'

'I'm not sure "cured" is the best word to describe what's happening here. I know I used the virus metaphor but that was to describe the spread of learning. This is really about conditioning a new response in Hugo's nervous system and helping him learn a new way of approaching it. The honest answer is that the younger me sitting there can't be sure what will happen when her client leaves. The real test is when Hugo goes out into the world and finds himself in social situations. Only then will we know for sure. Hugo certainly appears to be feeling differently in the coaching session and looks more relaxed when he's imagining the social situations.'

'Yes, but that's only him imagining them,' said Ronald.

'If I may say,' said Rita, 'you seem a bit cynical.'

'Well, this isn't real,' said Ronald. 'Yes, he feels different but he's only imagining the social situations.'

'You are so right,' said Rita, smiling. 'None of this is real. And neither was the problem. It existed only in his thinking. Of course, the experience of the party was real for Hugo, but the problem began in his imagination before he even reached a social situation. The nervousness was when he imagined a social situation. That's how it began – he wasn't even physically there. Now when he imagines a social situation without being physically there he feels calmer and more relaxed. It's actually a very good comparison.

'The thing that tells me Hugo feels different is his physiology and body language. He's not just saying he feels different with the same body language he had at the start. He looks physically different. His head is up, his breathing is slower, he's fiddling less.'

'I understand,' said Ronald. 'That does make sense. To be honest, I hadn't particularly noticed how his body language had changed, I was really focusing on what he was saying.'

'Yes,' said Rita. 'Remember when we talked about the learning ladder on the beach. At the moment, you're consciously having to pay attention to what Hugo is saying so it's not easy to observe his body language, too. As you practise listening and become more skilled, you'll find it easier to notice the body language as well.

'Let's see what happens next. If I remember correctly, I ... er ... she ... er ... Rita has just asked Hugo to imagine another situation. Something different where, if it had happened before, he would have felt the old nervous feeling?'

Alice and Ronald returned their attention to Rita and Hugo sitting the centre of the clearing. The tops of the trees began swaying again and the birds came back to life.

Hugo replied to the question. 'I can think of a situation when I went to a kind of networking event with my sports club. There were various different sponsors there and I was asked to go as one of the athletes.'

'OK,' said Rita. 'Now I want you to imagine it now, just being present, noticing the people in the room, noticing the whole event and who is there.'

'Yes, it's like I'm less aware of myself and more aware of what is happening around me.'

'So, what's the first step here then?'

'The first step is to breathe and notice what's around me, notice who is in the room, who I might talk to,' said Hugo.

'What happens when you go to talk to someone?' Rita asked.

'I say hello, introduce myself. Perhaps I ask them what their involvement is at the event or what has brought them there. I can talk about myself as an athlete and why I'm there.'

'How are you feeling as you imagine that?'

'Calm. Calm and relaxed. I'll just see what happens, I don't need to overthink this. I'll talk to someone, see if we have a connection or a talking point, and, if not, say it was nice to meet them and see who else is there.'

'That's right,' said Rita. 'You don't need to overthink this. What's the first step in this situation?'

'Breathe and take in the situation – who's there and what's happening.'

The clearing stopped again and Alice and Ronald turned to Rita. 'What have you observed?' she said.

'I think you've ... she's ... just done what you talked about. Beginning to spread the antibody into different situations,' said Ronald.

'Indeed, and it's subtle. I want you to appreciate that this is quite a subtle piece of work in some ways.'

'What do you mean?' said Alice.

'Well, when Hugo says he doesn't feel confident and is nervous, it would be tempting to try to "fix" this by getting him pumped up, feeling great about himself, so he can talk to anyone. It might even work in the short term, but what helps Hugo here is switching his attention from his own thinking and internal pictures to paying attention to what's around him and being present. As he does so he begins to feel calmer and takes in more about the people and situation he's in. This is turn helps him enact the conversations he wants to have.'

'I'm curious as to why Rita over there didn't explore where this lack of confidence came from, what might have caused it?' said Ronald.

'This is coaching. We do sometimes revisit the origins of something but only when it's really necessary. Coaching is about helping someone in the now and future and raising their awareness of what's happening inside of them. Hugo now has something he can take responsibility for and is much more aware of the internal processes that have been taking place. With his awareness we hope that he has a choice to approach this differently,' said Rita.

'So, you didn't need to go into his past to unearth the roots of this?' asked Ronald.

'I didn't know back then,' said Rita. 'Honestly, I didn't. If Hugo had returned to the next session without making any progress, I would have been curious as to what was getting in the way. But, as a starting point, a coaching approach aims to work with what's happening now.

'By contrast, a psychotherapist might want to explore the roots of this and where it originates. That might be a useful line of enquiry depending how ingrained the pattern is. I would say neither is wrong and neither is better. It depends upon the individual and the situation.'

'This has really been enlightening,' said Ronald. 'I don't feel that I'm much nearer to being able to coach successfully myself yet, but I do understand much more.'

'Practice,' said Rita. 'When we discussed the learning ladder, we said that practice is what will move you on. I think it's time you each did some coaching yourselves.'

The clearing began to fade away and Alice felt herself falling again, but much more quickly this time. She felt herself pop out of the manhole and into the light of the Naples street. The smell of pizza was still there but more faint. No sooner had she registered this than the scene faded and she was back on the grass with Rita and Ronald looking at the tree stump where Christina had been.

✍

'That was quite an adventure, Alice.'

'The ice cream we ate in Naples was del-i-c-ious, Ben. I could eat it again right now.'

'Are you asking for some *more* of my birthday cake?'

'Oh yes please. I stopped last time because I thought it would be rude to eat more than half of it.'

'How restrained of you, Alice. Could you save me a piece, please?'

I can hear the cake tin being opened; she's not wasting any time. There's a lovely Victoria sponge with jam in the middle and a dusting of sugar on top – my favourite and, apparently, Alice's too.

While Alice is devouring my birthday cake, let's quickly recap the last chapters.

Maps of the world

Even though I say 'quickly', there were some fairly big ideas to understand, the first of which is that we each have our own map of the world and our reality is exactly that – our own. We live in a world that is created through our perception and, while this perception is based on reality, it is not reality itself. Our perception is influenced by a great many things – our beliefs, values, feelings, attitudes and personal history. Since those things are different for each of us, then our individual perceptions are often different, even of the same event.

The expression 'A map is not the territory' was first coined in 1933 by Alfred Korzybski who also said that 'the word is not the thing' (Korzybski 2010). Very often we do confuse the word with the thing or the map with the territory, and our map of the world is so intrinsic that we don't realize its existence. We're used to living inside our own perceptual filters and we're no longer aware of them – our map of the world has become unconscious. It's at Level 4 on the learning ladder – we've become so accustomed to our own ways of thinking that we're unconsciously skilled at using them.

The learning ladder

The learning ladder describes a typical progression when we learn and become more skilled. Its origins are uncertain, but a notable claimant for inventing it is Martin M. Broadwell (1969). I think the model can help you appreciate your own journey as you learn coaching, but it also applies to unhelpful bits of learning, the things we might call 'problems' in our lives, some of which have become so automatic and unconscious that we're no longer aware of how they happen.

As a reminder, Level 1 is called unconsciously unskilled or unconsciously incompetent. At this level we don't know what we don't know, we can't perform or complete a task, and we aren't even aware of what is involved. At Level 2 we become conscious that we are unskilled, aware that we don't know or can't do something. Level 3 is consciously skilled, and at this stage we are able to perform successfully provided we consciously focus and concentrate. Level 4 is unconsciously skilled, where we can do something 'without thinking' – it just happens automatically.

Content and process

One of the skills of a good coach is to help clients separate their thoughts and feelings about a situation from the situation itself – that is, to help clients realize what is their own map of the world. I call this the client's process and by focusing on the client's map of the word, we look at the way the client is describing the problem.

Focusing on the content means looking for solutions to the problem as the client describes it, in its current formulation. My own view is that focusing on the content is only occasionally useful, as most of the time a client will have tried to solve the problem rationally themselves before coming for coaching. The greatest leverage is usually found by discovering if a client's map of the world is limited in some way, often in the form of implicit assumptions, and instead of focusing on the client's problem as the client defines it, we focus on *how* the client defines the problem. One of the benefits of this is that exploring a client's map of the world will often apply to much more than the challenge the client has brought to the coaching, so there may be wider benefits to the coaching than just the resolution of the current scenario.

'That was a long summary, Ben.'

'I hope it's useful, Alice. I believe it's helpful to revisit ideas, and reiterating the main points makes them easier to remember.'

'That's true. I had to learn lines when I was in a play at school and the only way to really learn them was to go over them again and again.'

'You were in a play? What was it?'

'*The Wizard of Oz*. I played Dorothy. "We're off to see the Wizard, the wonderful Wizard of Oz ...".'

'It's not the time for a song, Alice. We're in the middle of something here.'

'Not even a quick song?'

'How about you tell us what happened when you returned to the tree stump?'

'I must have gone straight home to bed because the next thing I remember was waking up the following morning.'

'OK, well, I'm listening.'

CHAPTER 10

The Rules of the Game

COACHING AS A MANAGER AND CONTRACTING AS A COACH

● ● ●

'Alice ... Alice, how are you feeling?'

Goodness, is it morning already? Alice thought to herself. I don't even remember coming home or falling asleep. She tried to open her eyes but they felt heavy.

'How are you feeling?' asked her father again.

'Good,' she replied. 'Sleepy.'

'OK, darling. Well, just get up when you're ready,' Alice's father replied.

When Alice opened her eyes again she felt much more refreshed and was excited to go and see Rita and Ronald. She was enjoying what was becoming a daily meeting and learning something new each time. As she walked along the path to their grassy area by the river she saw Rita and Ronald already deep in conversation.

'Good morning,' she said.

'Come and join us,' said Rita. 'We've just started talking about a question Ronald raised yesterday.'

'What was that?' enquired Alice.

'Well, when Rita was talking about the client's "problem", she talked about the client's thinking about the problem and the problem or situation itself. She said that most of the time, if people could solve or make progress themselves with the issue, they would do so. There might be times when a problem-solving approach is useful, but very often the breakthroughs are made when we look at the client's map of the world to see where this is limited.'

'Yes, I remember,' said Alice. 'You talked about exploring the client's thinking and feeling to discover where there might be assumptions or distortions within their map of the world that mean the problem is formulated in a particular way.'

'Right,' said Ronald, 'and I'm much clearer on that now. Watching the example with Hugo gave me some insight into that. My question is about when Rita said, "Most of the time, if people could solve their problems, they would do." At the time I asked about what happens when they don't want to solve it. We've just begun discussing that.'

'But, surely, if they don't want to solve it, they wouldn't be engaging in coaching in the first place?' mused Alice.

'Well, that may not be true. There are a few different scenarios here that I think Ronald's question speaks to and I would like to consider each of them.

'First, in a business context, there's the scenario where the coach is brought in by an organization to work with one of the team. Typically, the coach is brought in by HR, or the person's manager, often to work with the individual in a particular area. That's the first situation we'll consider.

'Second, there are times when people may have a challenge or problem but they don't really want to solve or make progress with it. This might be for a number of reasons: maybe it's too much effort; maybe the gains aren't significant enough. I've coached people around the issue of weight, typically people wanting to be at a more healthy weight for them – and although they do want to lose weight, sometimes they're just not willing to put the effort in and the reward isn't that big. Sometimes there is a benefit to having the problem and the person doesn't want to lose that; on some level inside they would rather have it than not. Sometimes a person doesn't believe they can solve it or make progress; deep down inside they don't just believe it's possible for them. And then there's also the situation where people have learned to be helpless – I don't mean deliberately – but they have unconsciously learned that they can't help themselves so aren't willing to even try.'

'That's quite a lot of different scenarios,' said Ronald. 'More than I was thinking about.'

'Yes,' said Rita, 'but I've grouped them together because the strategies we might use will be similar.'

'I'm interested in the first scenario you've described,' said Ronald. 'Now that I know more about coaching and the benefits of it, I can envisage bringing a coach in to work with members of my team in the future, particularly for challenges which I don't feel skilled enough to work with or where my own interests might be difficult to keep separate.'

'Those are probably two of the main reasons an external coach might be asked to get involved. There is definitely a difference between someone who is a manager like yourself, Ronald, and who can apply some coaching skills and someone who is a full-time coach used to dealing with a wide range of issues and individuals. There is often a different level of expertise.'

'Yes, I see that,' said Ronald. 'It's something I'm really interested in for the future, but for now I can see that I don't have the experience and skills that might be required to deal with more complex situations.'

'The second part of what you said is also important,' said Rita. 'Sometimes a person's manager may not be able to separate sufficiently from their own interests or thoughts about the individual to make the coaching successful. There is also the situation where the closeness (or distance) of a working relationship means that the manager won't be able to establish a healthy climate for the coaching to work.'

'I suppose the same thing applies when potentially coaching friends or family members?' pondered Alice.

'Indeed,' said Rita. 'The complexity of the existing relationship can make it more challenging. That's not to say it can't be done, but some very clear contracting is needed at the outset and some clear boundaries are needed as well as permission from the person being coached. Trying to 'coach' your partner or friend when they don't want to be coached is only going to go badly. Trust me, I've been there!'

'So, how do you work successfully in the situation you've described. Let's say I decided to bring a coach in to work with a member of my team who needs to improve in a particular area. How would I begin with my team member?' asked Ronald.

'Well, therein lies one potential problem,' said Rita. 'If you only ever bring in a coach to remedy someone's performance or behaviour, then the person may resent it from the outset. It's like saying to them, "I'm getting a coach to fix you." That could immediately set up a dynamic where the person resists all attempts to coach them. The first step is the conversation between you and your team member to understand if the team member wants to improve their performance or behaviour.'

'What if they don't?' asked Ronald.

'Well, I would be very curious about why not and there could be some useful questioning and exploration to discover what's going on. I would certainly see that as the first step. Ultimately, though, we're talking about the workplace so it might mean more formal performance management. I do think that addressing a situation early with the right kind of conversation – usually asking and listening more than telling – can potentially avoid this.

In the situation where the person is willing to do something, then the next step would be to *offer* them some coaching and see if they would like it. Imposing it is unlikely to work. If the person would like to engage in coaching, then things are starting in the right way, as they have bought into the process.'

'Yes, I really see that,' said Ronald. 'It's really important to set that up in the right way.'

'The other thing to consider is that you might offer coaching to team members who are performing really well as a reward for their work or offer it to all team members. This changes the association of coaching with being a remedy.'

'Why might they want it?' asked Ronald.

'Well, remember that coaching is about helping someone fulfil their potential. Maybe an individual wants to develop themselves more or think about how they can improve further. Sometimes it's easy to ignore people who are working effectively because they aren't causing a problem. In the end it really comes down to contracting effectively, and that's what I think we should talk about,' said Rita.

'The squeaky wheel gets the grease,' said Alice.

'The what?' said Ronald.

'It's from a poem I heard somewhere,' said Alice. 'Something about the wheel that squeaks the loudest is the one that gets the grease. Let me see if I can remember it.'

'How do you feel about us talking about contracting, Alice?' interrupted Rita.

'It sounds boring,' said Alice. 'It sounds all formal and adult. Can't we talk about more interesting things?'

'What's your favourite game, Alice?' asked Rita.

'My favourite game?' said Alice thoughtfully. 'I like the one where you build hotels and collect rent.'

'OK, I want you to imagine that you're playing with a friend and you have each been given a different set of rules,' said Rita.

'What do you mean?' asked Alice.

'Well, for example, imagine that *you* are allowed to build hotels only when you own all the properties in a set but your friend can put them on any property individually. For your friend the hotels cost twice as much. The rents are different for each of you and the properties cost different amounts. Imagine also that some of these rules aren't made clear at the start and you discover them only as you play.'

'Oh, no, that would be horrible. It would be really confusing,' said Alice. 'The game would be weird; it would be uneven. It wouldn't be enjoyable if we didn't know the rules at the start.'

'Exactly,' said Rita. 'Without clear rules the game would be confusing. It wouldn't be as much fun. The same idea applies in coaching, we need some boundaries so that the coaching can work. Of course, we're not talking about rules in coaching but rather an agreement about how things should work and who is responsible for what.'

'Oh, I understand that now. You're saying that before we play a game we need to make sure we both understand the rules,' said Alice.

'Yes,' said Rita. 'Imagine you play with a new friend for the first time and instead of checking at the start you just begin playing. Except that your friend knows a different version of the game with different rules. How would that be?'

'Frustrating,' said Alice. 'We'd both be thinking the other was doing something wrong.'

'Exactly,' said Rita. 'It doesn't matter which set of rules you play to as long as you both agree at the beginning.'

'OK, I get it now,' said Alice. 'If we are clear at the start of the coaching what the expectations are and who is responsible for what, then it will make the coaching easier and more successful.'

'In the scenario Ronald is describing there are actually three people in the contract. There is the team member who is the client. There is the external coach who is being brought in to help and there is the manager who is paying for or authorizing the coaching, in this case Ronald.

'Let me ask you a question, who is the coach's client?'

'The client – I mean the person the coach is going to help,' said Alice.

'But who is paying for the coach's services?' asked Rita.

'The organization or the manager – from their budget at least,' said Ronald.

'So, who is the coach responsible to?' asked Rita.

'The client *and* the manager or organization?' queried Alice. 'Are they accountable to both?'

'Yes,' said Rita, 'but in different ways. And this is why it's so important to be clear about things. As the person engaging the coach's services the manager/organization may choose to define the scope of what the coach will work on with the client.'

'What do you mean "scope"?' asked Alice. 'If you mean telescope, I've got one in my bedroom and I use it to look at the stars at night. Sometimes I spot space rockets zooming through the sky. They go super-fast.'

'Not exactly,' said Rita, 'although it might be a way of explaining it. When you position the telescope it shows you one particular area of the sky which is magnified and you can see more of it, right?'

'Yes,' said Alice. 'I tend to adjust the telescope into one position and then just look through it to see what spaceships I can notice.'

'Well, the question of scope in coaching is a bit like that. It asks what is the area that we are going to focus on, or what is the range of topics that the work with the client can cover. The scope is the agreement on what the coach will aim to work on.'

'So, if I have a team member who wants to improve their communication skills, we might agree that broadly this will be the area to work on,' asked Ronald.

'Yes, as an example. And this means that the coach has a clear remit to work within. I remember one particular situation where I was asked to do exactly that. When I arrived to work with the client I began, as usual, by asking the client what their goal was. The client said he wanted to work on his interview technique to help him prepare for a new job.'

'What did you do?' asked Alice.

'I explained to the client that the scope of the coaching was to help him improve his communication skills, which he had already agreed to. I said I would happily work with him on that, but I wasn't being paid to help him find another job. It was totally fine if he didn't want to work on his communication skills, but then I wouldn't be able to work with him. His response was that, if that was the case, he didn't want the coaching.

'Did you go back and tell his manager that?' asked Ronald.

'Well,' said Rita. 'I had to tell the manager that the team member didn't want to engage in the coaching for the areas that had been set out. I had already agreed with the client that the coaching conversation would be confidential so it would have been wrong to say any more.'

'Didn't the manager ask more, though?' asked Ronald.

'Yes,' replied Rita, 'but I had already agreed with the manager that, although I would report back on the coaching in general terms, the specific content of the conversations would be confidential. Having agreed this in advance meant that there wasn't any difficulty going back to the manager.'

'I can see now why it's important to get this right,' said Ronald.

'And the thing is,' said Rita, 'it's actually pretty straightforward. Typically, I have an initial chat with the manager about what they are asking for. Then I ask the manager to have a conversation with the team member where they agree the outcomes that the coaching will work on. I send them a form and ask them to write these down and they both sign it. I also include on the form other information such as the confidentiality element – that the coaching conversations will be confidential between coach and client and I will report only on an overall measure of progress. I also include some terms about cancellations, so everyone is clear.'

'So, that's agreeing the rules at the start of the game?' said Alice.

'Exactly. It needn't be burdensome; it just means that everyone is clear at the beginning.'

'This is really useful,' said Ronald. 'I'm much clearer on what contracting means now.'

'Excellent,' said Rita.

'You've got me thinking about lots of different games now,' said Alice. 'It's the rules that actually *make* the game. Without them the game wouldn't exist.'

'It's not only about *having* the rules,' said Rita, 'but also about everyone taking part having a shared understanding of them and giving their agreement to play by them. If someone breaks the rules or cheats in a game, then it doesn't work.

'In coaching, if the coach or client doesn't maintain healthy boundaries around their own role and responsibilities, then things can become problematic. For example, if the coach becomes too involved in trying to help the client or solve the problem, this can disempower the client, which is, of course, very unhelpful.

'This conversation moves us on to the second set of situations I mentioned where someone might not want to be helped in coaching. I described some situations earlier when an individual might not accept the coaching help being offered. This might be because the client doesn't really want to make progress, maybe it's too much effort, or maybe the gains aren't significant enough.

'Sometimes there is a benefit to having the problem, something they gain by having it and the client doesn't want to lose that. Sometimes a person doesn't believe they can solve it or make progress; deep down inside they just don't believe it's possible for them. Let's talk about this set of scenarios.'

'Let's play a game,' said Alice. 'That would be much more fun than talking all the time. Do you both like board games?'

'Of course,' replied Ronald and Rita.

'My favourite is the game where you buy properties and then put houses and hotels on them.'

'We have our own game,' said Ronald. 'The animal game is set around rivers and woods.'

'I wish we had that game, I'd like to play that,' said Alice wistfully.

Suddenly there was a loud rumble of thunder and it began to rain. Big raindrops started to fall, becoming harder and harder. There was another rumble, louder this time, and a crack in the sky as a bolt of lightning forked its way down. Alice looked at Ronald and Rita.

'Let's find some shelter,' said Ronald.

The rumble got louder and closer. There was a flash right above them and an almighty crack. Alice looked up just in time to see a branch from the tree above falling right towards her. Suddenly everything went black.

CHAPTER 11

Foxed and Imprisoned in the Triangle

THE DYNAMICS OF A COACHING RELATIONSHIP AND THE DRAMA TRIANGLE

● ● ●

Alice opened her eyes and observed that she was sitting in a wooden boat in the middle of a river.

'How very strange,' she said to herself. 'How did you get yourself here, Alice?'

She stood up and nearly fell overboard as the boat rocked violently from side to side. Sitting down hurriedly and grabbing the sides, Alice looked at her vessel. On closer inspection it appeared that the boat was, in fact, half a giant coconut husk. The inside was smooth and, peering carefully over the side, she could see the coarse hairy outside of a coconut.

'Curiouser and curiouser,' she said. 'Why I do believe I'm on the river in a coracle.'

She tried again to lift herself up to climb out, but the coracle wobbled precariously, and she nearly fell out again.

'Oh dear, oh dear, Alice,' she chastised herself, 'you've got yourself into a bit of a pickle here.'

Looking around, she discovered that her craft was on a wide river with a grassy bank on the right-hand side. The river was hardly moving, and on the bank Alice could see that the land appeared to be divided into plots, each separated by some trees or a hedgerow.

She heard a splash and turned round to see Ronald swimming gracefully down the river. He was moving slowly, his fins gently fanning the water, and was focused on the riverbank. He seemed to be counting each plot as he passed and barely had time to shout, 'Hi,

Alice,' as he swam by. Watching with curiosity, Alice saw Ronald stop ahead at a brown earthy plot with a ramshackle stone ruin on it.

Where on earth was she? There was something familiar about the place but Alice couldn't quite put her finger on it. She heard another splash and turned to see Rita gliding down the river behind her.

'What's happening?' Alice shouted.

'Are you enjoying the game, dear? I told you we have a wonderful board,' Rita replied as she cruised by, her four legs propelling her gently forward through the water.

'Game?' questioned Alice, her voice slowing, 'You mean we're *in* the game?'

'I've rolled a three and a four,' Rita shouted as she passed, 'I'm off to try my luck on the merry-go-round.'

As Rita disappeared down the river, Alice noticed two large square men running along the bank. They looked like twins and stopped opposite Alice.

'Excuse me,' Alice shouted, 'But I don't suppose you know where we are?'

'Don't you know?' said the man on the left looking surprised. 'You're halfway round the board already.'

'And it's your turn, dear,' offered the man on the right.

'My turn?' said Alice, puzzled.

'Yes,' he nodded. 'Are you ready to roll?'

'Ready to roll?' said Alice.

'For your turn,' said the first man. 'Come on, dear, you've got a game to play.'

'Yes, I suppose so,' said Alice. 'I'm ready.' She watched as both men jumped up in the air and started doing somersaults. One landed and tucked his arms and legs in to do several roly-polies. The other did a couple of cartwheels sideways before finally coming to rest nearby.

'Four,' shouted the first man.

'Two,' shouted the second man.

Alice looked at them quizzically as they stood up and dusted themselves down. 'Come on, then,' said the man on the left, 'off you go. You're off to the merry-go-round, too, I think.'

'What do I do?' she asked.

'Two and four is six,' said the man on the right. 'You need to move along six plots.'

'But how?' countered Alice. 'How do I make this boat move?'

The two square men looked at each other. 'With the paddle, dear,' the left one replied winking at his twin.

Alice hadn't noticed a small sandy coloured wooden paddle on the floor of the coracle. 'They think you don't know how to paddle a coracle, Alice,' she said to herself. 'But you've been wanting to paddle a coracle for ages. Though that is mainly because you like the sound of the word.'

Alice thought back to the story she'd read about a coracle as she knelt in the boat and drew herself up to her full height. Slowly she began a figure of 8 motion at the front of the coracle. She glanced across at the square men who stared, mouths open in surprise, as her craft moved slowly down the river.

Looking to her right Alice noticed the next plot was very grassy with a big sign that said 'Lottery'. 'How odd,' she began to say to herself and then saw Ronald floating in front of the plot beyond.

'Hi, Ronald,' she said.

Ronald appeared to be studying a document carefully and looking at the land in front him. 'Sixty acorns,' he said. 'It's cheap, but I'm not sure if it's worth it.'

'I'll catch you up,' he shouted over his shoulder.

Alice continued down the river counting the plots as she passed them on her right. There was another ramshackle ruin followed by some slightly better-looking wooden houses on stilts.

'Where am I?' Alice asked herself. The two square-looking men had stopped back down the bank opposite Ronald, who was examining the plot in front of him and was deep in conversation with himself. Alice counted 6 plots and stopped her boat in front of what appeared to be a large merry-go-round.

'What fun,' Alice said to herself, 'you love a merry-go-round and you haven't been for ages.'

From her boat Alice could see some steps leading up to an entrance on to the ride. Around the edge were lots of words painted on the ground and Alice could read the ones nearest to her.

'Go to the Doghouse. Go straight to the Doghouse. You do not win 200 acorns,' she read. Oh, that doesn't sound very nice, she thought.

'Come to ride the merry-go-round, have you, dear?' said a voice.

Alice looked around and saw the fairground man standing in the control booth.

'I don't like the look of that,' she said, pointing at the 'Go to the Doghouse' words.

'Don't worry,' he said. 'That was the last player who had a go – you might be luckier.'

Alice climbed carefully out of her boat and stepped onto solid ground.

'On you get,' said the fairground man.

Alice went up the steps and sat on a horse as the ride began to turn. She could see the steps moving round next to her and different writing flashing past as the ride went faster and faster. No sooner had it become a blur than the ride began to slow and she was able to read the writing.

'Advance six plots. (Collect 250 acorns),' she read.

'Do some gardening on your land – For each hedgerow pay 50 acorns – For each treehouse, 150 acorns,' said another.

The ride stopped and Alice looked down the steps.

'Go to the Doghouse,' she read.

'Well, what are the odds of that, twice in a row,' said the fairground man. 'Sorry to be the bearer of bad news, young lady, but you're off to the Doghouse.'

Alice heard a siren approaching and saw a blue and white boat with flashing lights speeding down the river. Alice's eyes widened when she saw the occupants of the speedboat. At first glance she had seen two police officers but as they stepped ashore she realised they were actually Alsatian dogs wearing police uniforms.

'Come with us, young lady,' said the female Alsatian.

'What have I done?' asked Alice.

'You rode the merry-go-round and you landed on "Go to the Dog-house",' said the officer.

The officers escorted Alice back to her coconut boat and attached a tow rope from their speedboat to her craft. It seemed only a very short distance before they stopped and Alice saw a large wooden kennel with bars on the windows. There was a large grassy area outside for 'Visitor Mooring'. Maybe Rita will come and visit me and get me out, she thought to herself.

The police officers lifted the door to the kennel and ushered Alice inside along with her boat. She looked into the gloomy room and saw Rita was already there. Tucked away in a far corner she could just make out what appeared to be another boat with oars.

'You too!' exclaimed Rita. 'Oh dear, oh dear.'

'I'm not sure what is happening,' said Alice. 'I went on a merry-go-round and then the police arrived and brought me here.'

'Never mind, dear. I'm sure we'll get out soon,' said Rita.

'I don't think so,' said a voice.

Alice and Rita jumped.

'You're here for good now, trust me. I've been stuck here for ages,' said a voice that came from the darkness in the direction of the boat and oars.

Alice moved towards the voice, still unable to see who its owner was.

'Hello,' she said, peering into the darkness.

A pair of eyes looked up to meet her gaze and she saw some pointy ears above them.

'Hello,' she said, 'I'm Alice, and this is Rita.'

'Hello,' said the voice.

'May I ask who you are?' Alice enquired.

'Does it matter?' replied the voice.

'It matters to me,' Alice said softly.

'My name is Reynard.'

'Reynard. Nice to meet you. What are you doing here?'

There was a snort from the shadows. 'I've been stuck here for ages. No one has come to get me out and no one has been to visit.' There was a pause. 'Still, mustn't complain, I suppose.'

'Oh, poor you,' said Alice. 'I'm so sorry. Who has left you here?'

'Who?' Reynard replied. 'Everyone ... Everyone has left me here.'

'How awful,' said Alice. 'How can I help?'

'You can't.'

'Well, I'd like to try. Tell me what I can do.' persisted Alice.

'You can get me out of here and get me home.'

'Of course, I will. Don't worry,' said Alice. Good to establish the goal straightaway, she thought.

Alice looked around and began examining the kennel. The door she had arrived through was thoroughly locked. There was one small window and it had bars on it. She peered through the window and saw a splash in the river followed by the two square men in hot pursuit. That'll be Ronald, she thought, it's good that he's still OK.

The walls appeared to be solid, as did the floor and ceiling.

Alice looked at Rita, who shrugged her shell, as if to say, 'I don't know either.'

'See – I told you. Stuck.' The voice of Reynard was accompanied by movement, and Alice saw some orange fur appear in the light accompanied by first one paw and then another. As Reynard moved into the light, Alice saw a bedraggled-looking fox with dirty orange and white fur.

Poor thing, she thought.

'We won't get out of here,' said Reynard.

'We will,' said Alice. 'I know there's a way.'

'Oh you do, do you? Well, what is it, clever clogs?' said Reynard, his tone becoming harsher.

'Well, I don't know yet,' she said.

'You don't know. You don't know. I thought you said you were going to help, but actually you don't know what to do.'

'I'm sorry,' said Alice, 'I wish I had an idea. I'm not very good at escaping from the Doghouse. I've never done it before.'

'Never done it before,' said Reynard, 'but you still thought you'd come in here and promise to get me out and take me home.'

Oh dear, oh dear, thought Alice. 'I'm sorry,' she said, 'I've let you down.'

'Yes, you have,' said Reynard. 'But, don't worry, I'm always being let down. I'm used to it,' he said, retreating slowly back into the shadows.

'Oh, how awful,' said Alice, beginning to feel a bit helpless. Poor Reynard, what a life, being let down by others and stuck in here on his own. Here was a chance for something different to happen, for someone to help him, and she was useless.

'Don't be upset, Reynard,' she said. 'I'll get you out of here if it's the last thing I do.'

'Just leave me alone. It's better if you don't try to help me,' said Reynard's voice from the shadows. 'This is just how it is for me.'

How ungrateful, thought Alice to herself. I am trying to help him and he doesn't want it.

'You're right,' she retorted, 'it probably is best that I don't help you. You're obviously so self-absorbed that you don't want it. Selfish fox,' she spat at him.

There was a sniffle from the corner followed by a whimper. Then the sound of sobbing.

Poor, poor Reynard, thought Alice as she sat down on the floor. A tear rolled down one of her cheeks as she thought about the poor fox suffering in the corner. The tear became a second tear and a third.

'Stop your snivelling,' shouted Reynard from the corner. 'It's pathetic.'

Alice sobbed some more, and the tears began to flow down her cheeks on to the floor forming a puddle.

'What are you upset about, dear?' whispered Rita, sitting down beside her.

'I feel so useless,' Alice whispered back. 'Poor Reynard has been stuck here for ages, and it sounds as though he's been abandoned by everyone. I just wish I could help him.'

'Do you think you can help him?' asked Rita.

'What do you mean?' asked Alice.

'Do you think you can help him right now?'

'Yes, he wants me to get him out of here,' said Alice.

'And is it in your power to do so?' asked Rita. 'Can you give him that?'

'No,' said Alice. 'I don't think I can. There's no obvious way out.'

'In which case, if that is what Reynard wants, then you can't help him,' said Rita.

'But he seems so upset, poor thing,' said Alice. 'I thought maybe I could at least cheer him up.'

'Does he seem to want cheering up?' asked Rita.

'Of course,' said Alice, 'he's upset.'

'Yes, he is. But how do you know he wants you to cheer him up?'

'Well, my father said you should always try to help people, and my mother said you should always be positive, so I just assumed that's what I should do.'

'Ah!' said Rita. 'You just what?'

'Assumed,' said Alice. 'Oh, I see. You mean that being cheered up is what I think Reynard wants, not what he says he wants.'

'Exactly,' said Rita. 'I think it's time to share a model with you that might be helpful in understanding the interaction you just had with Reynard.'

Rita began drawing with her foot in the dust on the kennel floor.

'I want to talk about the drama triangle, also known as Karpman's triangle. It's a model which explains possible dynamics that can arise within a coaching relationship. That said, the model applies beyond coaching, and frankly, it could be relevant for any personal or professional relationship.'

'Sounds interesting,' said Alice. 'I'm guessing that the triangle isn't a spaceship, though?'

'You're right', said Rita, beginning to write at each corner of the triangle. At one corner she wrote 'Victim', at another 'Rescuer' and at the third 'Persecutor'.

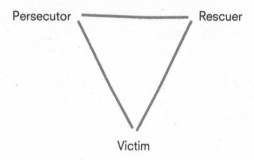

Figure 11.1 The drama triangle

'The drama triangle comes from a body of work called Transactional Analysis. This particular model was first developed in the 1960s by Dr Stephen Karpman to describe certain positions people can take in interactions. These positions are windows through which people view the world.'

'So, part of their map of the world?' asked Alice.

'Very much so, although these are very automatic patterns. The three positions are stances people take very unconsciously in their reactions and responses.

'Let me explain what they mean. In the Rescuer position a person seeks to 'rescue' someone they see as vulnerable. Typically, the Rescuer will contribute more and do more about the situation than the person they are rescuing. The Rescuer may offer their 'help' without being asked and may not find out if and how the other person wants to be helped. This means the Rescuer may help when help isn't wanted or may only offer help based on what the Rescuer thinks is wanted. Consequently, the Rescuer may not be appreciated or valued and can end up feeling resentful. People who rescue as a life position would usually be described as co-dependent. They need victims to help and in extreme cases sometimes can't allow the victim to succeed or get better.

'The person in the Victim position feels vulnerable, powerless, inadequate, and unable to take action. They don't recognize their own power to change their circumstances and instead try to find someone who can rescue them. If the Rescuer isn't able to create the outcome the Victim had hoped for, the Victim may feel disappointed and upset. Does this make sense so far?'

Alice nodded. 'I'm beginning to see why you're sharing this with me now,' she said, thinking back to her conversation with Reynard.

Rita continued: 'Very often, when the Victim feels the Rescuer hasn't helped, they will move to the Persecutor position and begin to Persecute their Rescuer.

'The position of Persecutor is "It's all your fault!" Persecutors criticize and blame their victim and can be overbearing, domineering and critical. Persecutors will be angry and lay blame, but they don't actually solve any problems or help anyone else solve the problem.

'Let me ask you, Alice, now that you understand the positions, can you identify the position you took with Reynard?'

'Yes, I can,' Alice replied. 'I jumped straight into rescuing. I felt sorry for him and saw him as vulnerable.'

'Indeed,' said Rita, 'that is very self-aware of you to be able to observe that. But we should recognize that you didn't take that stance all on your own, you had help.'

'What do you mean?' asked Alice.

'Think back to when Reynard first started speaking. What position would you say he was taking?'

'Oh, I see. He was definitely in a Victim position.'

'Yes, exactly. And when someone is in the Victim position, it invites the other person to step into the Rescuer position. The other person doesn't have to, of course, but for someone who has a tendency to rescue others, the appearance of a Victim will often trigger this.'

'I see that,' said Alice. 'I just wanted to fix everything for him. I would have done it all myself if I could.'

'Exactly,' said Rita.

'But surely it's good to help people, isn't it? Being a Rescuer isn't all bad.'

'We must make a distinction between helping people and being a Rescuer. Helping people can be a generous and kind thing to do *if* the person wants help and *if* the help being given *actually* helps them. The Rescuer position is an unhealthy stance. It is actually more about the Rescuer than the other person. The Rescuer takes this position to fulfil their own needs, perhaps to feel good about themselves or feel better than the other person.

'Suppose you rescue someone, get them out of a fix and do it all for them. You feel all powerful and you are the heroine. What message does this convey to the person you helped?'

'Perhaps that they're not as good as me, that they're not capable, that they're powerless?' said Alice.

'Yes, exactly. Some version of that. Is sending that message to them helping them?' asked Rita.

'No, not at all. It just makes them feel weaker and more dependent,' Alice replied. 'I never thought about this before.'

'Indeed, so your helping may actually be *unhelpful*. Your helping won't help. It will only continue the bigger problem of the person being in the Victim position.'

'I understand,' said Alice. 'It's why the coach and client roles need to be carefully understood.'

'Yes,' said Rita. 'Of course, very often this issue doesn't arise in relationships, whether that's doing coaching or not, but when it does it creates an entanglement that can be very problematic.

'Now, let's continue. Do you remember what Reynard said when you didn't know what to do?'

'He began to criticize me and said I was useless,' said Alice.

'Yes, he moved from the Victim position to being a Persecutor. This had an effect on your position, didn't it?'

'I felt powerless and useless,' said Alice.

'You felt like a Victim,' said Rita. 'This is a typical "dance" that we may observe happening. The initial Victim persecutes the Rescuer and makes them into a Victim, so instead of a Rescuer–Victim relationship there is now a Victim–Persecutor transaction. What we saw with Reynard is that he then switched back to being a Victim and you switched back to being a Rescuer again. The dance continued.'

'Yes, and then he remained in the Victim position and I became a Persecutor,' said Alice. 'I got angry with him for not wanting my help and began to criticize and blame him.'

'The cycle continues,' said Rita. 'Sometimes it can go on and on. People exist in relationships where they are both stuck in the cycle. The relative positions change but nothing really changes as they're still in it.'

'So, what's the answer,' said Alice. 'How do we avoid become entangled in this way?'

'Well, from a personal perspective it can be helpful to understand if there is a particular position that you have a tendency to slip into. For example, we saw that you quickly stepped into the Rescuer position. In other words, for you, personally, someone in a Victim position is likely to be a potential entry point into the cycle if you aren't careful. This may be different for different people, but since coaching is a helping type of activity it probably invites a Victim–Rescuer dynamic more easily. Self-awareness is the first step.

Of course, if your client adopts a victim position, then this might actually be the bigger issue.'

'What do you mean, the bigger issue?' asked Alice.

'Whatever challenge or problem the client might be bringing to the coaching, if they are in the Victim position they feel inadequate or powerless. They will be unlikely to make progress with this or anything else. So, until they can reconnect with their own power and agency, working on the issue is unlikely to be fruitful.'

'So, the first step is tell them to stop being a Victim?' asked Alice.

'I certainly wouldn't say that,' said Rita. 'Someone who is in the Victim position already feels powerless. Telling them to stop it almost sounds like being a Persecutor (though it depends how it's said). The way forward is to support them in recognizing their own involvement in the situation, that they can have some effect on what happens. Once they recognize that they have some ownership over what's happening, you can begin to work with them on that.'

'I see,' said Alice, 'but what happens if when you question them they don't think they can improve things or take ownership?'

'That's a possible outcome,' said Rita. 'Usually I begin by acknowledging that that's what they think. I accept that is their truth. Sometimes I even ask them how they could make things worse?'

'Make things worse? Why would you want them to do that?' asked Alice, astonished.

'Well, if they can make it worse – and usually they do know how to do that – then it means they can affect the situation, it means they have some power. Most of the time, if they recognize how to make it worse, then they recognize how to make it better. The "making it worse" ideas often contain the seeds for how to make it better.'

There was a noise in the corner of the kennel. 'What are you two whispering about over there?' came Reynard's voice from the darkness.

'We were just talking about how we can help you,' replied Rita.

'Well, I think we've already established that you can't,' Reynard retorted.

'I was just saying the same,' said Rita. 'You're absolutely clear that we can't help you, so we can't.'

'Well, at least we agree on something,' said Reynard.

'I don't agree with you,' said Rita. 'But I accept that your view is that you can't be helped and I respect that.'

'What do you mean, "you don't agree"?' asked Reynard.

'It's not important,' said Rita. 'This is about you and you can't be helped. Nothing can be done and no one can help.'

There was a pause.

'But that's not what you really think?' asked Reynard.

'No, it's not,' replied Rita, 'but it's what you really think and I can't change that. Let's just accept that you don't want anyone to help you.'

The kennel was silent.

'But ... I do,' said Reynard softly.

Alice smiled to herself. At last they were getting somewhere.

'No, you don't,' said Rita. 'You're just saying that because you think you should.'

Alice nearly choked. What was Rita saying. Reynard had just said he wanted help and now Rita was telling him he didn't.'

'No, I'm not,' said Reynard. 'I do want some help.'

'Well, I don't believe you. I don't see any proof of that,' said Rita.

'I do want some help. I'm unhappy,' said Reynard. 'Desperately unhappy. And all alone.'

'I see,' said Rita. 'That sounds horrible.'

'It is,' said Reynard.

'Even though we're in the same kennel, you still feel lonely,' said Rita.

'I do,' said Reynard. 'I do.'

'But I suppose you can't do anything about that?' Rita asked.

'Exactly,' said Reynard.

'That's a shame. It must be horrible being lonely.'

There was another pause.

'Can I come over there with you?' asked Reynard, his snout appearing into the light.

'It depends,' said Rita. 'If you're willing to talk to us as adults, then you're very welcome.'

The snout became a head, which was followed by orange and white fur as Reynard shuffled over to Rita and Alice.

CHAPTER 12

Reynard

AN EXAMPLE OF COACHING A 'DIFFICULT' CLIENT

• • •

Alice, Rita and Reynard sat silently perusing the kennel, each wondering why they were there and how they could get out.

'I haven't got a clue,' said Alice, echoing each of their thoughts.

'What shall we talk about then?' asked Rita.

'Can we talk about why I'm so lonely?' asked Reynard.

'It depends,' said Rita. 'What's your reason for wanting to talk about it?'

'I'd like to change it,' replied Reynard. 'I don't want to be lonely anymore. I was lonely even before I got in here. I wasn't really playing the game with friends; I was playing on my own.'

'How do you want to change?' asked Rita.

'I don't want to be lonely anymore,' said Reynard.

'Well, that's what you don't want. What do you want instead?' asked Alice.

'Oh, I see,' replied Reynard. 'I want to have friends.'

'Well, how is it that you don't?' Alice asked.

'No one likes me,' said Reynard, 'they don't want to spend time with me.'

'So, what can you do about it?' asked Rita.

'Nothing,' replied Reynard, 'nothing at all.'

'How do you do that anyway?' asked Rita. 'How do you get people not to like you?'

'What do you mean?' asked Reynard.

'Well, how do you stop people liking you?'

'I'm not sure.'

'What would you do if you wanted people to like you even less?' asked Rita.

'I'd be ruder, tell more lies, use them even more for my own ends and then blame them for it,' replied Reynard.

'That would make them like you less, so what would make them like you more?'

'I see what you mean,' said Reynard. 'Probably being less rude, telling the truth more and not using them.'

'What would you call the opposite of rude?' asked Rita.

'Hmm ... friendly?' said Reynard.

'And, if you weren't using people, then how would you be relating to them?'

'Well ... Um ... I don't know,' said Reynard. 'I'd just be honest ...'

'Exactly,' said Rita. 'You'd just be honest with them. You'd be friendlier, tell the truth and be honest.'

'Yes,' said Reynard.

'What's stopping you doing that?' asked Rita.

'They might not like me if I'm honest and tell the truth.'

'How come?' asked Rita.

'Well, I'm not a particularly brave fox or a very clever fox, so they might not like me.'

'So, instead it's safer to be rude, tell lies and use others. Then you know they won't like you and you're in charge.'

Reynard gulped. 'No one has ever said that to me before.'

'When you're rude to me and blame me for things, then I don't want to be around you. It's a very effective defence mechanism,' said Rita.

Reynard looked forlorn. 'I've never really thought about it this way.'

'I'm sure,' said Rita. 'It takes some courage to really look at yourself like this. What's interesting is that when you're honest with me I like you more.'

'You do?' said Reynard.

'I do too,' said Alice. 'It's much nicer when you're honest.'

'But don't you think I'm stupid for feeling like this?' said Reynard.

'No,' replied Rita. 'We all have our difficulties in life and it is sometimes our attempts to "solve" them that make things worse.'

'You mean me being rude to people and using them solves the problem of them not liking me for who I am,' said Reynard.

'Do you think that is what's been happening?' asked Rita.

'I think it might be,' said Reynard, 'but I don't remember deciding to do that.'

'No, it will be very unconscious I expect,' said Rita. 'You haven't recognized that this is a defence mechanism. It's just something you learned, probably when you were much younger. What is most important is that you're now aware of it.'

'Yes, I am. The question is what to do about it. I'm not sure I know how to be more honest and friendly anymore.'

'Well, I suggest that we get together another time to explore that,' said Rita. 'Once you're ready to get started on that journey, we'll sit down properly to talk about it.'

'Thank you,' said Reynard, 'thank you both. I really appreciate it.'

Alice and Rita nodded but before they could reply there was the sound of a key in the kennel door and it swung open. Bright light shone through the doorway and Ronald entered the Doghouse accompanied by the two Alsatians.

'Unbelievable,' he said, shaking his head. 'Double five put me outside a lovely looking treehouse and I snapped that up for a bargain of 140 acorns. Double two entered me into the Lottery and I won a prize of 200 acorns. I rolled again and got a double four. Suddenly the police turned up and brought me here. I don't know what I've done.'

Ronald looked over at Alice, Rita and Reynard sitting in the kennel.

'Oh, hello,' he said, 'I wondered where you'd got to.'

'Ronald,' he said, offering his slithy fin to the fox.

'Reynard.'

'So, we're all in this together,' said Ronald. 'Have you been here long?'

'I have,' groaned Reynard. 'I've been stuck here for ages ... But it's nice to meet you,' he added.

'Nice to meet you, too,' said Ronald. 'Hopefully we can find our way out of here.'

'We need to check the kennel from top to bottom and see if we can find a hole in the wall,' Alice said.

'There's no hole in the wall,' Reynard said.

'But we need to check. There might be a hole in the wall we haven't found,' Alice countered.

Reynard began humming a tune, which quickly became a song:

'There's no hole in the wall, dear Alice, dear Alice.
There's no hole in the wall, dear Alice, no hole.'

Alice began to sing:

'Then make one, dear Reynard, dear Reynard, dear Reynard.
Then make one, dear Reynard, dear Reynard, make one.'

'With what shall I make it, dear Alice, dear Alice?
With what shall I make it, dear Alice, with what?'

'With your claws, dear Reynard, dear Reynard, dear Reynard,
With your claws, dear Reynard, dear Reynard, your claws.'

'My claws are too blunt, dear Alice, dear Alice.
My claws are too blunt, dear Alice, dear Alice, too blunt.'

'Then file them, dear Reynard, dear Reynard, dear Reynard.
Then file them, dear Reynard, dear Reynard, file them.'

'With what shall I file them, dear Alice, dear Alice?
With what shall I file them, dear Alice, with what?'

'With a stone, dear Reynard, dear Reynard, dear Reynard.
With a stone, dear Reynard, dear Reynard, a stone.'

'But, where shall I find one, dear Alice, dear Alice?
But where shall I find one, dear Alice, but where?'

'On the floor, dear Reynard, dear Reynard, dear Reynard.
On the floor, dear Reynard, the floor.'

'But the floor is too dark, dear Alice, dear Alice.
But the floor is too dark, dear Alice, too dark.'

'Then shine some light, dear Reynard, dear Reynard.
Then shine some light, dear Reynard, some light.'

'But how shall I light it, dear Alice, dear Alice.
But how shall I light it, dear Alice, but how?'

'From a hole in the wall, dear Reynard, dear Reynard.
From a hole in the wall, dear Reynard, a hole.'

'There's no hole in the wall, dear Alice, dear Alice.
There's no hole in the wall, dear Alice, no hole.'

'Well, I think we've established there's no way out,' Ronald murmured.

'Quite,' said Rita with her head in her hands. 'If I ever hear that song again, it will be too soon.'

'I rather enjoyed it,' said Alice, winking at Reynard.

'Well, it's not going to get us out,' said Ronald. 'I haven't asked how you ended up in here. What happened?'

'We both landed on the merry-go-round,' said Alice. 'And both of us got given a "Go to the Doghouse".'

'What about you, Reynard?' asked Rita. 'We haven't asked how you got in here?'

'I landed on the "Go to the Doghouse" corner,' said Reynard.

'I see,' said Ronald. 'Can anyone remember how to get out of the Doghouse in this game?'

'I think I used to know,' said Alice, 'but I've either forgotten or I can't remember it.'

'Why are you here, Ronald?' asked Reynard. 'You said you didn't stop at the merry-go-round and you didn't stop at the "Go to the Doghouse" corner. What happened?'

'I don't know. I rolled a double five and stopped at a lovely-looking treehouse. I rolled another double and stopped at the Lottery and when I rolled again the police turned up.'

'You said you rolled a double the third time?' checked Reynard.

'Yes,' said Ronald, 'three doubles in a row.'

'Well, that's why you're here. It's in the rules, three doubles in a row and you go to the Doghouse,' Reynard said.

'That's it!' exclaimed Alice. 'That's it.'

'What's it?' asked Ronald.

'To get out of the Doghouse you have to roll a double. That's it,' Alice said. 'Where are they?'

'Where are who?' asked Reynard, 'the police?'

'The square men who do somersaults,' said Alice.

'I think I saw them just outside, waiting on the grass,' said Ronald.

Alice pushed her head up against the bars. 'Hello,' she shouted, 'Mr Dice Men, are you there?'

She heard a rumble and one of the square men appeared doing a roly-poly. 'Four,' he cried. The other appeared somersaulting, came to rest and shouted, 'Three.'

'Another round in the Doghouse for you, dear,' shouted the first man.

'Someone else have a go,' said Alice.

'I'll try,' said Ronald. 'My turn,' he shouted to the men.

They began jumping and doing their roly-polies. 'Six ... One ... Another round in the Doghouse for you, young man.'

'I'll go,' said Reynard. 'My turn,' he shouted.

'Five,' said the first man. 'Five,' said the second man. The kennel door swung open and the Alsatian appeared. 'You're free to go,' he barked, looking at Reynard.

Reynard looked round at the other three. 'See you outside,' he said, 'I'll be waiting.'

One by one Rita, Alice and Ronald continued with their turns. Rita was next to roll a double, followed by Alice. Ronald finally rolled his on the third go and arrived outside to join them.

'Hooray,' said Alice, 'we're out! Well done, everyone.'

'What do we do now?' asked Reynard.

'Good question,' said Ronald. 'I rather fear I need to get back to work.'

'What is your work if I may ask?' said Reynard.

'I'm a manager for a company that makes bicycles,' Ronald said. 'My team do some of the marketing for the brand.'

'Oh, how interesting,' said Reynard, 'I used to work in marketing and design myself.'

'Really?' said Ronald. 'In what capacity?'

'Well, mainly using social media, Foxbook and the like.'

'Mmm ... I could do with someone to help with that,' said Ronald. 'Are you looking for any work right now?'

'Well, I might be,' said Reynard, 'although maybe not full time. I've arranged to do some coaching with Rita in the coming weeks.'

'Why don't you come to the office later on and we'll talk properly about it,' said Ronald. 'Let's see if there's a fit.'

'Great, thank you,' said Reynard. 'I'll see you later.'

Ronald turned to Alice and Rita. 'See you both soon.'

Ronald dived into the river and swam off down a little tributary that Alice hadn't noticed before.

'Thank you, both,' Reynard said. 'I think this is the beginning of a different chapter for me.'

'You're welcome,' said Alice.

'I hope it is the beginning of a different chapter,' said Rita. 'I'll be honest though; I think you've got some work to do.'

'I know,' said Reynard, 'I really do. I can see that some of my patterns of behaviour are very automatic and that as soon as I'm in a stressful situation they'll probably come back. I really want to address this, though, so I'll be coming to see you. Thank you, both, again.'

'Goodbye, Reynard,' Alice said.

'Goodbye,' he replied and vanished right in front of Alice's eyes.

'How is that possible?' Alice asked to herself. 'He can't just vanish. He was stuck in the Doghouse for ages and now he just vanishes.'

'How do *we* get out of here?' Alice asked Rita.

'I'm not sure, dear,' Rita replied. 'How do you end a board game?'

'Well, at home, usually we just put the pieces away and fold the board up,' Alice replied.

'Come on then.'

Alice got back into her coracle and then followed Rita to the far edge of the river. When she had checked before it had looked like the edge of the world. As she approached and examined it more carefully, she saw there was a large drop on to what looked like carpet. In fact, it looked exactly like the carpet in her lounge at home.

'I think you should go down first, dear,' said Rita, 'and perhaps you can help me down. I'm not as agile as I used to be.'

Alice clambered out of her boat onto the edge of the river and lowered herself until she was hanging from the bank by her fingertips. Then she jumped down and landed on the carpet. Rita followed and Alice supported the turtle as she descended.

'Carpet,' said Rita, 'how unusual.'

'Well, we've left the board but how do we fold it up?' Alice asked.

'I'm not sure, dear. Let's sit for a moment and think about it,' Rita replied, settling herself into the comfortable carpet.

*

'Ben, I've been remembering *The Wizard of Oz* story. The Lion didn't have any courage and was frightened of everything. Do you think he demonstrated a Victim stance?'

'I suppose you could say that, Alice. The Lion certainly seemed to be a victim of life's circumstances. The person in the Victim position feels vulnerable, powerless, inadequate, and unable to take action. They don't recognize their own power to change their circumstances and instead try to find someone who can rescue them.'

'And the Wicked Witch of the West was in the Persecutor position. She wanted my ruby slippers.'

'You mean Dorothy's slippers?'

'Yes, but I was Dorothy in the play. I know it was only on stage but you could pretend it's true, Ben.'

'Right, yes, Alice. The position of Persecutor is "It's all your fault!" Persecutors criticize and blame their victim and can be overbearing, domineering and critical. Persecutors will be angry and lay blame but they don't actually solve any problems or help anyone else solve the problem. I think you could say the Wicked Witch of the West was a Persecutor.'

'Exactly!'

'What about the Wizard, Alice? What position would Dorothy – I mean you – say he was?'

'He started out as a Rescuer, supposedly the best Rescuer of all, and he was going to help me get back to Kansas. Once he was exposed as a fraud, he stepped into being a Persecutor.'

'It's a good example, Alice. In the Rescuer position a person seeks to rescue someone they see as vulnerable. The Rescuer position is unhealthy because it is more about the Rescuer than the other person. The Rescuer takes this position to fulfil their own needs, perhaps to feel good about themselves or feel better than the other person.'

'What about the Good Witch of the North? She wasn't a Persecutor, Rescuer or Victim.'

'I'd agree, Alice, she wasn't. Let's remember that all three of the positions are unhealthy. The Karpman triangle shows how power and responsibility shift with the different roles people play, all of which are dysfunctional. Karpman was a student of Eric Berne who created Transactional Analysis, a way of studying the transactions between people.

'The Good Witch is a great example of providing healthy, adult support to Dorothy without dysfunction. She gives Dorothy the ruby slippers that belonged to the Wicked Witch and tells her to return home by following the yellow brick road to the Emerald City and asking the Wizard of Oz to help her.'

'So, Ben, how do we maintain healthy boundaries like the Good Witch?'

'Contracting is the starting point to ensuring good boundaries. This means being clear at the start of the coaching what the expectations are and who is responsible for what. When working within an organization this is more complex because there are two clients, the person being coached and the person paying for or instigating the coaching, typically a manager.'

'I don't think I'll ever do any coaching in that situation, Ben, not until I'm older anyway.'

'True, Alice, this might not apply to you yet. My own approach when brought in to do some coaching is to ask the manager to have a conversation with their team member to agree the outcomes for the coaching. I often ask them to write these down and both sign it; that way we are all clear about the purpose and scope of the coaching. This means that when I begin to work with my client we have a clear starting point to work from.'

'I have another questions, Ben. I understand the drama triangle but I'm still not clear how to avoid getting caught in it when coaching. How do I know that I've agreed the right boundaries?'

'It's a good question, Alice. It might be that something feels "off" or you're not making progress, but this might not tell you what the problem is. Many coaches engage in supervision, which is where they work with another coach to help understand their own coaching with clients.'

'Ben, does that mean we're ready to introduce, Victor? He did some amazing supervision with Ronald.'

'We're not quite there yet, Alice. There are a few more things we need to explain. Why don't you tell us what happened when you were on the carpet with Rita?'

'OK, Ben. Here's what happened next ...'

CHAPTER 13

You Can't Eat the Word 'Cake'

RAPPORT, CLIENT RESISTANCE AND THE DIFFERENCE BETWEEN DEEP AND SURFACE STRUCTURE

● ● ●

Alice settled herself next to Rita on the carpet.

'I'd like to ask you something,' she said. 'It's about how you talked to Reynard when we were in The Doghouse.'

'What do you want to ask?'

'When Reynard said we couldn't help him, you said he was right and you agreed with him. And when he told us to stay in the corner and be quiet, you acquiesced and we waited until he talked to us. Why did you do that?'

'We need to talk about something called rapport,' said Rita. 'Are you familiar with it?'

'It's a French word, isn't it?' said Alice.

'It is,' replied Rita, 'although it's also used in English. The definition is "a close and harmonious relationship in which the people understand each other's feelings or ideas and communicate well".'

'Something we definitely want when coaching,' said Alice.

'Indeed,' continued Rita. 'The question is, though, how do you create rapport?'

'By listening?' wondered Alice.

'Listening definitely helps,' said Rita, 'but there is more. One of the main ways is by entering into our client's map of the world.'

'What do you mean?' asked Alice.

'Well, you remember we talked about how each of us has a map of the world?' said Rita.

'Yes,' replied Alice, 'it's our combination of beliefs, values, ideas, feelings and thoughts. Our own version of how the world is.'

'We build rapport with someone when we recognize and accept their model of the world,' said Rita.

'What do you mean by "accept" their model of the world?' asked Alice. 'I've met lots of people who I don't agree with. Mrs Parker at school says that science is the only real subject and art is a waste of time. I don't agree with her at all.'

'We need to understand that there is a difference between agreeing with someone and accepting that they have a viewpoint. Do you accept that Mrs Parker has that view of science and art?'

'Yes, but she's wrong,' said Alice.

'In *your* world she's wrong. In *her* world she's right. We have to acknowledge what is true for her even if we ourselves hold a different view. This isn't about right and wrong. There are plenty of things we might consider to be wrong. We're talking here about how to work with someone most effectively in coaching. If we want to build rapport with someone, then we do so by accepting that their version of the world is how it is *for them*.'

'So, if I was coaching Mrs Parker, I would accept that she thinks art is a waste of time.'

'Yes, if you wanted to build rapport with her. And, let's be clear. You are accepting that *she thinks* art is a waste of time; you are *not* saying that you think art is a waste of time. There is a big difference.'

'So, when you agreed with Reynard that we couldn't help him, you were really accepting *his* map of the world about that?'

'Yes, exactly. And here we get to the interesting part of this. Suppose I had disagreed with Reynard and said, "No, no, you're wrong, we can help you." What would he have said?' asked Rita.

'He'd have almost certainly said, "No you can't, no one can help me," or something like that,' said Alice.

'Exactly,' replied Rita. 'If I had pushed against what he said, then he'd have pushed back harder and resisted more. He would have become more entrenched in his position. Resistance often creates more resistance. Let me show you something.'

Rita held up her front leg and said, 'Push against my leg.'

Alice put her hand on Rita's foot and pushed gently.

'If I push back more, what will you do?' asked Rita.

'I'll push harder,' said Alice, increasing her effort.

'Indeed,' said Rita. 'And, if I increase my force, then you will increase yours. Note that neither of us is moving, we are stationary but exerting a great deal of effort to remain so.'

'Yes, it's hard work,' said Alice, beginning to puff. She wondered if she should have tried harder in gymnastics at school; Rita was very strong.

'So, both of us will put a great deal of effort and energy into getting nowhere. Eventually one or the other may give up or tire and one will "win". Except that it's not really a "win": the other person hasn't changed what they are doing; they've just been beaten into submission. As soon as they have recovered they will push back again.'

'I see that,' said Alice through gritted teeth.

'OK, let's start again.' Rita lowered her foot and then raised the other one for Alice to push against.

'Right,' said Alice, changing arms and getting ready to push hard.

She pushed on hard on Rita's foot and nearly fell forward as Rita didn't push back at all.

Alice stopped and took a step backward to recover her balance.

'You've stopped. Why aren't you pushing anymore?' asked Rita.

'There's nothing to push against,' said Alice.

'Exactly,' said Rita.

'So, if you don't resist, then there's nothing for me to push against,' said Alice. 'With Reynard you stopped resisting him and he didn't have anything to fight.'

'In the context of coaching, resistance is unhelpful. There may be lots of other times in life when it's unhelpful, too – and when I say unhelpful, I mean that it doesn't create the conditions for change, transformation and growth. Of course, there may be times when resistance is appropriate and necessary, but in a coaching environment I believe usually it is not.'

'So, is this really about creating the right conditions for change to happen?' asked Alice.

'That is certainly one way to think about it,' said Rita.

'So, rapport is really essential,' said Alice.

'If you don't have rapport, then you don't have much at all,' said Rita.

'So, when you agreed with Reynard as to how he sees things, you were building rapport with him?'

'Yes, I was entering into his view of the world, and this usually builds more of a relationship and rapport.'

'But you don't really want him to stay with that way of thinking,' said Alice. 'So, what do you do?'

'If I want him to be open to examining other ways of thinking, I first need to acknowledge his current thinking and not push against it. Metaphorically, I need to get alongside him. Once we've walked together, I might begin to change direction and see if he will come with me.'

'This reminds me of a cowboy film,' said Alice.

'I don't follow,' said Rita.

'Well, I've watched a few cowboy films with my dad on a rainy Sunday afternoon. They're all the same,' she laughed, 'but I quite like them. There's usually a runaway train and someone is chasing it down on horseback in order to stop it. If *you* wanted to board a runaway train, how would you do it, Rita?' Alice asked.

'If I was on a horse, I suppose I would get the horse alongside the train at exactly the same speed and then I'd jump from the horse on to the train. Good metaphor, Alice.'

'Exactly,' replied Alice 'No one ever rides head on into the train or crashes into the side of it. That wouldn't work. They have to go in the same direction as the train to get on board and only then can they alter the speed it is going.'

'Well, metaphorically, that's what we do when working with a client. We need to get alongside them, understand their world as it is and then lead them gently to explore other possibilities.'

'Presumably different people will require different amounts of this?' Alice asked.

'Indeed,' said Rita. 'We always want to build rapport. Trust and openness are essential to this work, and we always want to enter into the client's map of the world in order to understand what is happening. Of course, some people are more ready for change than others.'

'How would you know?' asked Alice.

'One phrase I like is: "Resistance is a sign of lack of rapport." There are no resistant clients, only inflexible coaches,' said Rita with a smile.

'Ha-ha, I like that,' said Alice.

'We need to remember that it's OK to challenge a client, to challenge their thinking and ways of viewing the world. Rapport is not about just going along with everything. In fact, the reality is that the more rapport you have, the greater the level of challenge the client will accept and respond to.'

'Because, if you have rapport, they won't resist the challenge, they'll actually consider it.'

'Yes,' replied Rita. 'Without rapport a person may well just push back on the challenge. When it's done with rapport the person may reconsider their thinking.'

'When you were talking to Reynard, there were some times when you didn't ask questions and you told him things directly. I thought the coach was meant to ask questions,' Alice asked.

'Well noticed,' said Rita. 'I would say that the primary role of the coach is to ask questions and listen, but there are also times when the coach might offer feedback to the client about what they have observed. A great deal of skill is needed with this to ensure it is feedback about the coach's observations and not telling the client what to do or the coach giving their opinion on something. Often when people are new to coaching I say that they should only be asking questions because there is often a tendency to enter "tell" mode otherwise.'

'Can you give me an example of the coach giving feedback to the client?' asked Alice.

'Yes,' said Rita, 'but let's just be clear about the definition. Feedback in this context literally means feeding back observations to the client and bringing things to the client's attention when it would be useful – for example, when a client says certain words, when a client changes their body language or tone in response to something, or when the coach notices a pattern of behaviour or thinking.'

'What words would you feed back?' asked Alice.

'Sometimes I feed back exactly what the client has said. I remember once coaching a client who said, "When that happens I just burn the relationship." I replied saying, "OK, you burn the relationship," and the client looked aghast. "Did I really say that?" she said. She was shocked at her own language, and when we explored it further it revealed a great deal more about her thinking. So, it may be that simply feeding back the client's words is useful. At other times there might be particular words to follow up on.'

'Like what?' asked Alice.

'Words like "should", "can't", "always", "never".'

'What's wrong with "should"?' queried Alice.

'There's nothing wrong with it. When someone says, "I should do X," it indicates a conflict. Typically, it means part of them wants to do it or believes they ought to and another part doesn't want to. They are conflicted internally. "Should" is an indication of a split, and therefore it can be helpful to discover what lies underneath it. Often, a person might not really be aware of what is in conflict and by bringing it to the surface we can help them understand what is happening.'

'What about "can't"?' Alice asked. 'Why can't you say "can't"?'

'You can say "can't",' Rita replied. 'But when someone says, "I can't do Y," the temptation is to ask, "Why not?" We discussed before that asking "why?" in this way often leads to them having to justify what they've said. In the case of saying "I can't do Y", this means the person has to come up with reasons why this is true. A much better question is to ask "What would happen if you did?"'

'So, if a random person who neither of us knows said, "I can't sing in public," then you would ask, "What would happen if you did?"'

'Exactly,' said Rita. 'What do you think this random person would answer, Alice?'

Alice blushed a little. 'They might say, "I'd be embarrassed and nervous and worried what people were thinking about me," but, of course, I don't know for sure.'

'Of course you don't,' smiled Rita. 'If we ask, "*Why* can't you sing in public?" you might say, I mean, *they* might say, "I'm not very good at singing," which may be true, but it doesn't really get us to what is actually happening in terms of the person's feelings and thoughts. The "What would happen if you did?" question often brings us much closer to what is actually holding the person back. In this example we know it's because you – I mean, the random person – would feel embarrassed and nervous and would be worried what others were thinking.

'The other effect of the "What would happen if you did?" question is that it changes the orientation of the person's thinking.'

'In what way?' asked Alice.

'Well, suppose it actually was *you* who said, "I can't sing in public." I know it's not, of course,' Rita said with a wink. 'And I ask you, "What would happen if you did sing in public?"' What do you have to imagine in order to answer the question?'

'I have to imagine doing it,' Alice replied.

'Exactly, so instead of thinking about why you can't do it, you're imagining doing it – that's a different orientation. There still might be reasons why you don't want to do it but we're more likely to get to the real problem.'

137

'Very interesting,' said Alice. 'There is so much in these words I never knew. I've heard people say that "A word is worth a thousand pictures", and now I know why.'

Rita laughed. 'Yes, it's something like that.'

'I'll never remember all this, though,' said Alice. 'Talking of which, what about "always" and "never"? What's important about them?'

'"Always" and "never" are examples of universal generalizations, along with "no one", "everyone", "nothing" and "everything". People might say things like: "No one ever listens to me"; "Everyone hates me"; "Nothing I do ever works"; "This always happens to me." These statements are usually not true. For example, it's probably not the case that no one ever listens to the person. There is something underneath the statement, though, some experience, thought or feeling that is driving it, and it would be helpful to understand what it actually is.'

'So, although the statement itself is untrue, we should accept it as being true?' Alice asked.

'Not exactly,' said Rita. 'We may want to challenge the generalization. People can form such generalized ideas in their mind and then these start to become ideas in and of their own right. We know that our map of the world affects our perception, so once someone has this idea they may then start to see the world through that lens.'

'If I think "no one ever listens to me", then I may notice more frequently when someone doesn't listen to what I say. Or, if someone doesn't acknowledge what I say, then I may interpret it that way,' said Alice.

'Precisely,' said Rita. 'Challenging the generalization is important but the main goal is to get us closer to the deep structure of the person's experience.'

'How would we challenge it?' asked Alice.

'We might just simply say, "No one?" with a questioning look or ask, "Has there ever been a time when someone did listen to you?"' Rita replied. 'We're getting into fairly advanced ideas now, and I want to talk about the difference between the deep structure and surface structure of experience. Tell me if this isn't interesting – I can talk for hours about this stuff.'

'What is the "deep structure of experience"?' Alice said in a monotone voice as she rolled her eyes out loud.

'I did ask you to tell me if it wasn't interesting!' said Rita. 'OK, I'll make this really quick. Remember when we talked about putting a cat in your ear?'

'Yes, we said it would have to be a very small cat or I would need very large ears,' said Alice.

'Indeed,' said Rita. 'We also talked about difference between the word and the thing itself. You can't eat the word "cake", can you?'

'No, although I rather wish I could,' Alice replied. 'I can say the word "cake" whenever I want. If I could eat the word, then whenever I was hungry I would just say the word and then sit down and eat it. Cake. Cake. Cake! CAKE!'

'It's a good example,' said Rita. 'The words we use are what is called the *surface structure of experience*. They are what surfaces from inside us, but we know that words are only labels for things. Somewhere inside is the *deep structure*, the actual experience itself and the real meaning. The word "cake" is the surface structure but the experience of eating a cake, of biting into it and tasting the strawberry jam and sponge, the sugar and the texture, that's the deep experience.'

'In that case, I think I prefer the deep structure of experience,' said Alice. 'The word doesn't taste nearly as good as the cake itself.'

'When we move from the deep structure of our experience and put it into words, then we subject it to a series of filters, deleting, distorting and generalizing. The richness and depth of the experience is usually too much to convey in our everyday conversation, so we shorten it. We say, 'This cake is nice," instead of "The texture of this cake is soft and spongey, the base is cooked slightly crisper and the jam in the middle tastes sweet on my tongue."'

'Remind me again why this is important,' said Alice.

'In coaching we need to remember that sometimes the words someone says aren't really the full experience they are describing. Words like "never", "always", "can't" and "should" are pointers to what is going on inside someone but may not be literal descriptions of it. We must take them seriously but not always take them at face value. As the coach we will work most effectively when we can uncover the deeper structure of the person's experience.

'A generalization like "always" is the surface structure that relates to a deeper experience. When someone says, "My boss always ignores my ideas" they might actually mean "This is the second time I've put an idea forward and my boss hasn't gone ahead with it. I feel undervalued and unappreciated."

'If we can get to this deeper structure and uncover it, then we can work with what is really going on. Sometimes the words we use hide what we really mean, and as the coach we have to seek out the deep structure.'

'So, is this like hide and seek?' said Alice. 'That's one of my favourite games.'

'Yes, I suppose it is,' said Rita. 'We could say that hidden in the client's words is the deeper meaning and structure of their experience and our job is to seek it out.'

'Why didn't you say this was hide and seek at the start?' Alice said. 'It sounds much more fun now.'

'There are lots of ways that people can "hide" their experience. Sometimes people use vague words and say something like "I felt hurt".'

'What's vague about "hurt"?' asked Alice.

'Well, someone could be hurt physically or emotionally; it could be a scratch or a wound or a feeling of loss or sadness or disappointment. The word is a loose description of something and it hides the deeper meaning.'

'Yes, I see that,' Alice said. 'Homework is another vague word.'

'How so?' asked Rita.

'Well, it can easily mean frustration, difficulty or boredom,' Alice replied.

Rita laughed. 'Yes, for you I guess it can.'

'So, how does the coach best play this game of hide and seek with the client?' asked Alice.

'Usually the client isn't deliberately trying to hide the deep structure of their experience; their choice of description, phrasing and words will be unconscious. The first thing as a coach is to realize that what the client says and what they mean may be different and to avoid making assumptions about what things mean.'

'To question then?' asked Alice.

'Specifically, to question the meaning of words where appropriate,' replied Rita.

'What do *you* mean by "where appropriate"?' asked Alice.

'Often it doesn't matter precisely what a person means by something. If someone says they had a great time on holiday, we may not need to know exactly what they mean by that. It's good enough to know they enjoyed it. But when someone describes something of significance like a feeling, value or important criteria, then we may wish to ensure they are precise about it.'

'Are you talking about those dense words again?' Alice asked.

'Semantically dense words,' Rita nodded. 'Words which contain a lot of meaning for the client. And we need to remember that some words are vaguer than others.'

Alice began to write on the ground: 'All words are vague but some words are vaguer than others.'

'Where did you get that from?' asked Rita.

'I read it in one of my father's books,' Alice replied. 'It was a book about pigs I think.'

'Talking of which, I have a client arriving shortly,' said Rita.

'A pig?' questioned Alice.

'Yes, a very successful one. She's in charge of a leading charity and wants some coaching.'

'Do you think I could watch and listen to you working with her?' Alice enquired.

'Well, I'm happy to ask her,' said Rita. 'If she agrees, then it's fine with me. Come on, we'd better go.'

'Go where?' Alice asked. 'We haven't put the board game away yet.'

'Well, just this once let's leave it out. I'm sure it won't hurt. We need to go,' Rita said.

'Where are we going?'

'To meet her for the coaching. Jump on board!' Rita motioned for Alice to sit on her large shell.

'Sit on your shell?' said Alice doubtfully.

'Yes, come on, we're going to be late ... Hold on.' Rita pulled a mobile phone out from her shell. 'I think we'll get a Ubird,' she said, pressing a button on the screen.

'A what?' said Alice.

'Ubird ... It's a taxi company, dear.'

CHAPTER 14

Eating Cake and Feeding Back

THE DIFFERENCE BETWEEN GIVING FEEDBACK AS A COACH AND GIVING FEEDBACK AS A MANAGER

● ● ●

Alice sat down on Rita's shell and tried to make herself as comfortable as possible on the hard seat. She glanced up to see a large shadow above them and a pair of huge talons descending rapidly in their direction. Alice screamed.

'It's OK, dear ... That's our taxi,' Rita said.

Alice hugged Rita's shell tightly as the talons came closer and landed in front of them. A giant bird with a huge beak and peaked cap stood in front of them. 'Where to, Ma'am?' the bird said.

'The conference centre,' Rita replied.

'Certainly,' replied the bird as he scooped Rita and Alice up carefully in his talons. The ground began to fall away and Alice looked down to see the grassy area a long way below her.

'Busy day?' said Rita casually.

'So so,' said the bird. 'I've just started my shift so you're only my second fare. It'll be busy later, I'm sure.'

'Business good, though?' questioned Rita.

'Can't complain,' said the bird.

The three of them settled into a comfortable silence that was broken only by the gentle flapping of the bird's wings. Alice found the rhythm relaxing, and the whooshing of the air made her feel drowsy. 'Is that a whooshing or a swooshing?' she asked herself. 'What is the difference? Is a whoosh longer than a swoosh, or is a swoosh longer than a whoosh? A whoosh or a swoosh, a swoosh or a whoosh, a swoosh or a swoosh, a whoosh or a whoosh.'

Alice began to feel sleepy, and she felt her eyes close. Her hands were still holding on to Rita's shell, and she began to dream about arriving at the conference centre. She knew it was a dream because she was arriving with her father instead of Rita. Her father spoke to the receptionist, and then Alice followed him into a large seminar room. There was a lovely-looking armchair at the back which Alice decided to settle herself into.

'There you go, dear,' her father said. 'Make yourself comfortable and have a nap.'

'I already am,' Alice replied, although she was unsure how to explain to her father that in reality she was flying through the air on Rita's shell.

'Good,' her father replied. 'Are you sure you're comfortable?'

'Not really,' Alice replied. 'I'm hundreds of feet in the air sitting on top of a turtle holding on for dear life.'

'You're what?' said her father with a puzzled expression.

'I'm sitting on Rita's shell,' she replied, 'but you can't see me because you're talking to me in a dream.' This is rather complicated, Alice thought to herself.

'OK, darling,' her father replied. 'Well, you carry on. As long as you're OK.'

'I love you, Dad,' Alice said as the dream faded and she opened her eyes.

The ground was getting closer and they were descending towards a large building with a glass front. The flapping of the bird's wings changed slightly, and their descent slowed until they were just above the ground. The talons relaxed, and Rita and Alice touched down on to a concrete pavement outside the conference centre.

'Thank you very much,' Rita said to the bird.

'You're welcome,' said the bird. 'Have a great rest of the day and hope to see you again.'

'Aren't you going to pay him?' asked Alice.

'The Ubird app does it automatically,' said Rita. 'It makes life very easy.'

'Who are we meeting here?' Alice asked.

'Camilla,' replied Rita. 'I've been working with her for a while now. Come on, let's go inside.'

The doors to the conference centre opened and Alice observed a light and airy atrium. She stopped for a moment. 'Alice, you don't know the word "atrium" – how on earth are you managing to say things like that?' she asked herself. 'I don't know,' she replied to herself, 'but I must know the word if I just used it. Perhaps I just didn't know that I knew it.'

An interesting idea, she thought. If you know something but don't know that you do, then do you really know it? Conversely, what happens if you think you know something but actually don't? Is it better to know something but not know that you do or not know something and think that you do?

Her musings were interrupted by Rita motioning her to follow her down the corridor. They passed an empty room, and Alice heard voices in the next room. Looking through the glass she saw Ronald standing in front of a table with a group sitting around it. He noticed Rita and Alice and raised a fin at them in greeting and smiled.

Alice and Rita continued to the next room on the corridor and went inside just as Rita's phone beeped.

'Oh, she's been held up,' said Rita. 'It looks like we have a bit more time than I thought.'

'I'm hungry,' Alice said. 'Do we have any snacks?'

'It'll be dinner time soon,' said Rita. 'You'll spoil your dinner.'

'Oh, I love a "spoil your dinner" snack,' said Alice, 'they're the best. The trick is to eat just enough to take the edge off your hunger without spoiling dinner. I never get it right, though, and I'm always full when dinner comes. You can't beat a "spoil your dinner" snack.'

'Well, I'm afraid I don't have any,' said Rita.

Just then Ronald appeared from next door.

'Good afternoon,' he said, 'guess what?'

'You've built a spaceship and we're going to the moon,' said Alice.

'No,' said Ronald.

'You've brought a picnic?' she said.

'Well, sort of,' he replied. 'It's my birthday today and I've brought cake.'

'Happy birthday!' shouted Alice and Rita together.

'I didn't know,' said Alice, 'or I would have brought you a card. Yippee, what sort of cake is it?'

'A Victoria sponge with strawberry jam,' Ronald replied. 'It's from the shop, though. I didn't bake it.'

'It doesn't matter,' Alice said. 'I'm sure it will taste good. I was just saying to Rita that I fancied a "spoil your dinner" snack.'

'A what?' Ronald quizzed.

'Let's cut the cake,' said Rita. 'We've got a bit of time before my client arrives.'

Alice loved a Victoria sponge. This one tasted delicious: there was a decent amount of jam in the middle and a generous dusting of sugar on top. 'Perfect,' she said to herself.

'Now that Ronald is here, let's talk a bit more about giving feedback in coaching,' said Rita.

'I'd like that,' said Ronald, 'and I need to catch up on what you two have been discussing.'

'Well, we talked about boarding runaway trains and the deep structure of experience and cake,' Alice replied. 'And I can tell you that actual cake is much tastier than the word "cake", so I'm very pleased that you've got some with you.'

'Right,' said Ronald, looking bewildered.

'I'll fill you in later,' said Rita, smiling.

'Tell us about feedback in coaching,' said Ronald.

'First of all I want to make a distinction between giving feedback as a coach and giving feedback in other areas of life,' began Rita.

'As a manager, for example?' asked Ronald.

'Yes,' continued Rita, 'there are some subtle differences. For example, in the context of management, feedback will typically be given to improve, remedy or enhance performance. When given effectively it will often begin with a factual description of a person's actions or behaviour, some interpretation of this and the impact or consequences of it followed by a suggestion for the future.'

'I'm not familiar with that,' said Ronald. 'I use the feedback sandwich.'

'I like the sound of a sandwich,' Alice said, 'although I rather think I've eaten too much cake and spoiled my dinner.'

'I think you'll find the feedback sandwich can be a bit empty. I'm not a fan,' said Rita.

'How come?' said Ronald. 'It seems like a good way to package some difficult feedback among some positives.'

'And that's really the problem. The pattern of beginning with positive feedback, giving improvement feedback and finishing with positive feedback, while great in theory, has, in my opinion, been marred by disingenuous use.'

'What do you mean?' asked Ronald.

'Well, how many times have you heard someone say something positive only as an introduction to giving a lengthy piece of critical feedback which is then followed by a cursory positive statement to conclude?'

'Sometimes,' said Ronald tentatively.

'And, when people hear some positive feedback now they are often waiting for the critical feedback to come next. Even if the positive feedback is genuine, it is often missed in anticipation of what is coming next.'

'So, what do you propose?' asked Ronald.

'I think positive and improvement feedback should be given separately and either at different times or with a clear distinction between them. For both, I think there should be an initial factual description of the action or behaviour followed by the feedback giver's opinion about this, the impact of the behaviour and finally a conclusion with a suggestion for the future.'

'Can you give an example?' asked Ronald.

'Of course,' said Rita. 'Let's suppose you have a team member who is consistently late.'

'I do!' said Ronald.

'So, you might say, "I notice that on Monday you arrived at 9.15, on Tuesday at 9.20, on Wednesday at 9.10 and on Thursday at 9.15. That is a total of 60 minutes late over four days. I'm unhappy about this because that is an hour of work lost during the week and we are particularly busy right now. In my opinion it is also unfair on other members of the team who arrive on time each day and who are contributing their full hours. From now on I want to ask you to arrive by 9am each day and I would like to monitor this over the coming days to see how you progress."'

'That seems very "Tell",' said Ronald.

'It is,' said Rita. 'We're not talking about coaching right now. This is you speaking as a manager and using the authority conferred upon you. Of course, you could also approach this in a coaching way and that might be a very effective approach.'

'How would I do that?' asked Ronald, 'I'm particularly interested in that approach with this team member who I don't think would react very well to being "told".'

'OK,' said Rita, 'let's do a simple example. Can you role-play the team member? You know this person, so just answer as you imagine they would to give us an idea.'

'Right, my name is Tom then.'

'OK, Tom, I'd like to talk to you about punctuality. Are you aware of what time you have arrived in the office each day this week?'

'I've been pretty much on time, give or take.'

'Give or take, what do you mean by that?' asked Rita.

'Well, I may have been late a couple of times but it's no big deal,' replied Ronald as Tom.

'Can you tell me how late you've been?'

'I'm not sure exactly, but not much.'

'I'm concerned that you're not sure how late you've been. Do you think it's important to arrive on time, Tom?'

'Well, yes, but a few minutes here and there isn't a big deal.'

'Well, let's say you arrive 15 minutes late each day, five days a week. How much time is that?'

'It's an hour and a quarter.'

'Right, so you would be doing an hour and a quarter less work each week. Do you think that matters?'

'Well, I guess so.'

'What would happen if everyone in the team did the same?'

'We'd lose a lot of time.'

'Exactly,' said Rita. 'What do you think the impact of that would be on the team's performance?'

'Well, it wouldn't be good. We might not achieve as much.'

'Indeed. Now, the other team members aren't arriving late, but let me ask you, suppose you always arrived on time and someone else was always late, how would you feel?' Rita asked.

'I'd feel annoyed probably. How come they get to arrive late and get away with it but I don't?'

'Exactly,' said Rita. 'How would you feel towards this person who's so often late?'

'I'd be annoyed with them. Do they think they're special or something?'

'I see. What do *you* think about being late now?'

'Well, I see that it might upset others in the team and it's not fair on them,' said Tom.

'Good,' said Rita. 'What can you do about it?'

'I need to arrive on time.'

'That's great to hear,' replied Rita. 'I'm wondering what you need to do differently to ensure you do?'

'I can see how this works now,' said Ronald. 'You could now continue with a coaching conversation to explore some options that would enable Tom to arrive on time.'

'Indeed,' said Rita, 'we could continue in that way and identify the first step towards that. Of course, I'm just using this as an example of how to have a conversation. The person may not always respond well, in which case you still have the option to put your manager hat back on and use a firmer "tell" approach.'

'That is really useful,' said Ronald.

'I thought we were going to talk about giving feedback as a coach,' said Alice.

'We are!' Rita replied. 'We got a bit side-tracked there. I was beginning to talk about the difference between giving feedback as a coach and as a manager.'

'Because the relationship is different,' said Ronald.

'It is. The coach–client relationship does not have any hierarchical element whereas the manager–client relationship does. In a coaching relationship I would expect there to be less of the coach's opinions than in a manager–client relationship. The role of the coach is to feed back observations in a factual way and to bring them to the attention of the client.'

'What sort of observations?' asked Ronald.

'There may be several things:

- It may be to do with the client's language or a way of phrasing something. The coach may draw the client's attention to how they describe the problem, for example to highlight something in the client's map of the world.

- It might also be some non-verbal information the client shows. Maybe the client nods while saying "no" or maybe they look away or their voice changes.

- It might also be an observation about a pattern of thinking or behaviour that the coach notices over time. Maybe the client repeatedly describes relationship difficulties with colleagues of the opposite gender. Maybe the client seems to avoid expressing anger, or maybe the client repeatedly asks the coach what they think.'

'Wouldn't the client asking the coach be a good thing, actually asking for feedback?' asked Ronald.

'It depends,' said Rita. 'If the client is requesting feedback as a way of avoiding taking responsibility for making a decision or owning something, then it would be unhelpful. Similarly, if the client appears to be reliant on feedback from the coach, then it might indicate a lack of trust in themselves or an inability to regulate their own emotional environment.'

'So, when would the coach give feedback?' asked Alice.

'When the coach notices something which may be relevant for the work the client is doing. There might be lots of things to observe about someone, but if they don't pertain to the client's goal and the purpose of the coaching, then they aren't relevant. Of course, many times the coach may notice something and be unsure whether it is relevant or not.'

'What happens then?' asked Alice.

'The coach might bring it to the client's attention and ask about it.'

'I've noticed that you often use words like "might" and "maybe",' said Ronald. 'Can you say something about this?'

Rita smiled. 'Well noticed. I do.'

'And?' prompted Ronald.

'I think there's several reasons. First, we are talking about example situations so it's less easy to be prescriptive about things. Second, because coaching involves working with others there are many factors at play and I'm uncomfortable being very black and white. There may be nuances that are important – most of the time we're talking about shades of grey.'

'Yes, I understand. That's two reasons. You said "several", which suggests to me more than two. Is there anything else?' Ronald pursued.

'Oh my,' said Rita smiling, 'you are becoming very observant – I can't get away with much anymore.'

'What are you wanting to get away with?' asked Alice.

'You may have noticed that I don't talk about myself very much,' said Rita, 'We have talked about both of you, but I haven't said much about myself during our time together.'

'You're right,' said Ronald. 'In some ways I don't feel that I really know you, despite us having spent the last few days working together. You are usually talking about coaching and explaining something or asking questions of someone else and working in their world. Can you say something about that?'

'I can,' said Rita, 'although I'm sure you both notice that I look a little less comfortable now.'

Rita took a deep breath. 'As a younger turtle I grew up in a large family. Things were very black and white. There was a clear definition of right and wrong, and my parents were very strict about this. If one of us transgressed and did something "wrong", then we would be in trouble. I did my best to meet the expectations of my parents but they were very high, so I always had a sense of not quite being good enough. The environment felt very rigid and contained, not in a physical way but in terms of how we could behave, think and feel. There wasn't much room for me to be *me*. I felt that I had to conform to a strict way of living and was very concerned with doing or saying something wrong.'

'That surprises me,' said Ronald. 'I wouldn't have guessed.'

'I am very different now,' continued Rita, 'but there are still some echoes of that in me and I sometimes shy away from expressing myself fully. It's one of the reasons I dislike my sister's parties so much. All her friends exalt their opinions to great heights and decree what they believe as if it is the truth. I prefer to soften what I say with "mights" and "maybes" in case someone thinks I'm wrong.'

'What would happen if someone thought you were wrong?' asked Alice.

'Well, I might be,' said Rita. 'There's lots I don't know.'

'That sounds like a very rational answer,' said Ronald. 'What would it really mean if you were wrong?'

Rita paused. 'You've learned a lot in these past few days, Ronald.'

'Thank you,' he replied.

Ronald and Alice looked at Rita expectantly.

'I see that I'm not going to be able to avoid this question,' said Rita. 'Well, I suppose if someone really thought I was wrong, then it would strike at the heart of my self-worth – and there are resonances from my childhood of not feeling good enough still there.'

'So, better to be less definite with your language than risk not being good enough?' said Ronald pointedly.

Rita nodded. 'That is pretty much it.'

'From acorns do oak trees grow,' said Alice.

'What are you saying?' asked Ronald.

'Well, this conversation came from you noticing that Rita says "maybe" and "might" a lot,' said Alice in amazement. 'It's fascinating how much we've discovered from that observation.'

'And that is one of my points about giving feedback as a coach,' said Rita. 'Sharing an observation with a client can be the starting point for discoveries and greater self-awareness.'

'We've talked about why a coach might give feedback and the different things that it might be helpful to bring to the client's attention. I'm curious about how to actually do it, though,' said Ronald.

Rita answered: 'I've said that feedback should be based on facts and observable behaviours, so let me give you an example. Consider a conversation where the coach observes the client take a deep breath and bite their lip. The coach could feed it back in one of the following ways:

- "I noticed that, when you said the words 'I want a promotion', you took a deep breath and bit your lip."
- "I noticed that you have some emotion about wanting a promotion."
- "You seem to be unsure about whether you want a promotion."
- "I don't think you really believe you deserve a promotion. That might be a real barrier for you."

'What do you make of these?'

'The first statement is very factual,' Alice said. 'It's an exact description of what the coach sees and hears.'

'The second statement involves some interpretation by the coach,' said Ronald. 'The coach is inferring that the deep breath and biting of the lip indicate some emotion, although there is no attempt to know what this is.'

'What about the third statement?' asked Rita.

'I don't know how the coach knows that,' said Ronald. 'It seems to me that the coach is making a leap from what they have seen to concluding that the client is unsure.'

'Indeed,' said Rita. 'There seems to some of the coach's own opinion leaking into that statement.'

'I don't like the last statement,' said Alice.

'Why not?' asked Rita.

'It seems very presumptive. How does the coach deduce the client's beliefs from this? I dislike the coach's suggestion that it might be a barrier.'

'I agree,' said Ronald. 'That last statement seems to tell more about the coach than the client.'

'Indeed,' said Rita. 'I really think the last two statements overstep the boundary of the coach–client relationship.'

'What about the second statement, would that be OK?' asked Ronald.

'I think that the first statement is the cleanest and most objective, so I would suggest that is preferable. However, I could imagine that, for a client with whom you have good rapport and have worked with previously, the second statement would not be a massive leap to make and could be just as helpful.

'What is important with either statement is that they are used to open up dialogue and I would follow each with a question.'

'Like what?' asked Ronald.

'"I noticed that, when you said the words 'I want a promotion', you took a deep breath and bit your lip. Are you aware of that?" would be a good start,' said Rita. 'I might then follow up with "What just happened when you said that?" to see if the client can articulate what they were feeling.

'The goal here is to bring to the client's conscious awareness something that might be a fleeting emotion or thought which may provide some additional information about what is going on.'

'I'm beginning to realize that this isn't about feedback in the traditional sense that I know from management training,' said Ronald. 'It's not about giving an opinion but about observations the coach makes that could increase the client's awareness.'

Rita's phoned pinged and she glanced at it.

'Camilla is here. I'll go out and meet her and ask if you can stay to observe.'

⌀⌀

And while Rita goes to find Camilla, let's take a moment to catch up on the key points from the previous chapters.

Rapport

Rapport is defined as a close and harmonious relationship in which the people understand each other's feelings or ideas and communicate well. As coaches we can build rapport with clients by entering into their map of the world. This doesn't mean agreeing with the client but accepting that their thoughts, feelings, values and beliefs are exactly that – their own – and metaphorically getting alongside them before exploring other possibilities.

'Resistance is a sign of lack of rapport.'

'Alice, you're here! You liked that idea, didn't you?'

'Yes, it makes sense to me. I can see that it's important to get to the deep structure of the client's experience to really understand what is happening.'

'Alice, you have only mentioned deep structure because it reminds you of cake. I know how you think.'

'I'm not talking to you anymore, Ben!'

Oops! Since Alice has reminded us of deep structure and surface structure, let's just recap what these mean. The words we use are what is called the *surface structure of experience*. They are what surfaces from inside us, but we know that words are only labels for things. Somewhere inside is the *deep structure of experience*, the actual experience itself and the real meaning. Our use of words can disguise what we really mean (deliberately or accidentally), and the coach must seek out the real meaning and experience.

Feedback

'Ben, I want to give you some feedback.'

'Ah! Do you Alice? OK ... Well, please go ahead.'

'The tin containing your birthday cake is now empty.'

'That isn't what I'd describe as feedback, Alice. In coaching, feedback means feeding back observations to the client and bringing things to the client's attention when it would be useful – for example, when a client says certain words, when a client changes their body language or tone in response something, or when the coach notices a pattern of behaviour or thinking. Your statement doesn't sound like feedback about an observation, Alice.'

'You're right, Ben. In that case, I want to give some feedback to the tin: "Dear Mr Tin, I notice that you're empty." Is that better?'

'It's definitely better in terms of the correctness of the feedback, Alice. I think we need to talk about where my birthday cake has gone, though!'

'I don't think we've got time for that, Ben. We need to find out what happened in Camilla's coaching session.'

'You're right, Alice, but we're coming back to this!'

CHAPTER 15

Camilla

AN EXAMPLE OF COACHING
RELATIONSHIP CONFLICT

● ● ●

Alice wasn't quite sure what she was expecting when Rita returned with Camilla but it certainly wasn't what greeted her. Rita had said Camilla was the founder of a leading charity and she hadn't anticipated an elegantly dressed pig wearing a blue-and-white pinstripe suit and high heels.

Camilla flounced into the room and held out a trotter as she introduced herself to Alice.

'Pull yourself together,' Alice said to herself. 'This is not the time to stare.' After all, Ronald looked nonplussed as he introduced himself, and Alice wondered if she was overreacting.

'Alice, my dear,' she said to herself, 'you've been learning coaching from a turtle and have spent the last few days working alongside a fish. Along the way you've helped a caterpillar and a ladybird and have observed a coaching session with a chimpanzee. And don't forget your time in jail with Reynard the fox,' she chastised herself. 'Really, you need to calm down. There is nothing unusual about a pig in a suit and high heels.'

Feeling suitably reprimanded, Alice regained her composure and smiled at Camilla. 'Thank you so much for allowing us to observe this coaching session,' she said.

'You're welcome,' said Camilla. 'Rita tells me you're her students so I'm happy to be able to help.'

'I've told Camilla that you will both keep the session in strictest confidence,' said Rita.

'Of course,' said Ronald and Alice, nodding.

'Let's begin,' said Rita, taking a seat. 'What do you want to work through today?'

Camilla settled herself in her chair and began talking. 'It's something of a long-term issue. As you know, I am the co-founder of our charity along with my colleague, Clarissa. We started the charity together six years ago and have been incredibly successful in our work. It hasn't been easy but we now have a thriving staff team who work incredibly hard. I've always known that Clarissa and I are different and we've certainly had our ups and downs, but recently things have become increasingly difficult. She maintains that we should continue operating at our current size and consolidate the success we have. I believe that we have to aim for growth and should be looking to expand our operation over the next 18 months.'

'So, what's the problem?' asked Rita.

'Things have come to a head, and I'm not sure I can work with her anymore. She is stubborn, pig-headed' – Alice muffled a giggle at this point – 'and refuses to listen to my point of view. I'm at my wits' end. I have tried to explain to her what we need to do, but she says that I'm being rash and my ideas are ill considered.'

'What do you want from our time together today?' asked Rita.

'Good question,' Camilla replied. 'I guess I want to work out a way forward. We're stuck at the moment. She refuses to listen and I'm beginning to resent her stubbornness. The problem is that I know I'm right. If I thought she had a point, I could understand but she doesn't think strategically at all.'

'You want to work out a way forward,' said Rita. 'You're stuck at the moment.'

'Yes,' said Camilla, sighing. 'Do you think it's an impossible situation?'

'I have no idea,' Rita replied. 'Tell me more about this way forward, What would that give you?'

'Well, it would make me feel better if we were doing the right thing, if we were taking the charity in the right direction.'

Rita paused. 'Let me check, when you say "way forward", what exactly do you mean by that?'

'I mean, a way to get her to see what we need to do, to listen to my proposal and to agree to go forward with it.'

'Ah!' said Rita. 'You want her to change her mind and go along with your proposal – that's what you mean by a way forward. It's less of "*a* way forward" and more "*your* way forward"?'

'When you put it like that then ... yes,' Camilla replied. 'I just need her to stop being so stubborn and be more open minded.'

Alice and Ronald exchanged glances. This was turning out to be rather tricky. Ronald scribbled on his notepad: 'I'm glad I'm not the coach right now.'

'Me too,' wrote Alice on her pad.

'I'd like to bring your attention to something,' Rita said. 'Do you remember what your goal was during the last coaching session?'

'Yes, of course. I wanted my staff team to be more strategic and pay more attention to our objectives when making decisions.'

'You were frustrated that they weren't listening,' said Rita.

'I was,' nodded Camilla.

'And the first coaching session you had, the one before, what was your goal then?'

'I wanted to increase our income from sponsorship,' said Camilla. 'We have some great sponsors but I wanted them to increase their commitment.'

'You were frustrated that they weren't responding to your request and felt they weren't open to hearing about your plans for the charity,' said Rita.

'Well, yes, that was a big part of it.'

'Do you notice a theme here?' asked Rita.

'What do you mean?' asked Camilla.

'Do you notice anything in common between these issues?'

'I'm surrounded by people who don't listen and who are closed to new ideas?' offered Camilla.

'That is one way to look at it,' said Rita. 'It's interesting how many people you are surrounded by who don't listen and are closed off – your sponsors, your staff, your business partner. Amazing really!'

'I know,' said Camilla, 'what have I done to deserve this?'

'What do you think they all have in common?' Rita asked.

'They don't listen?' Camilla said.

'Well, we could consider that. It seems like there's a lot of people who aren't listening to you. I was thinking about what else is common between them?'

'I'm not sure,' Camilla replied.

'Perhaps I should ask *who* else is common between them?' Rita asked.

'Oh,' said Camilla. 'Me. I'm in common with them all. I'm not sure what you're suggesting.'

'I'm not suggesting anything, but I want to bring something to your attention. You are the common link between them all and you're having the same problem with all of them. The common denominator is you.'

'So, I'm the problem?' Camilla said angrily. 'You're not listening to me. I come here to tell you the difficulties I'm facing with other people, and you turn it round and blame me.'

'I'm not blaming you at all and I promise you I am listening,' Rita replied. 'I don't for one moment think that you want any of this, and I really do believe that you're doing your best to make progress.'

'But?' said Camilla.

'And ...' said Rita, 'I'm curious to know what else might be going on, if perhaps you are inadvertently contributing to the situation.'

'I see,' said Camilla, calming down, 'so you don't think I'm an idiot?'

'Not at all,' Rita replied. 'I do not think you're an idiot. Although I'm curious about you asking that. What's prompting that question?'

'Well, when you suggested that the common denominator was me, I felt you thought I was an idiot.'

'Is that what made you angry?' Rita asked.

Camilla nodded. 'I hate the thought of people thinking I'm an idiot. It riles me.'

'You hate the thought of people thinking you're an idiot,' Rita repeated. 'What would happen if someone thought you were an idiot?'

'Well, they'd be thinking, "Who does she think she is, running this charity when she hasn't got a clue?" They'd probably think I shouldn't be in the job, that I'm not up to it.'

'I see. So, in your mind, if someone doesn't listen to you, then you imagine it's because they think you're an idiot and you're not up to the job,' Rita said. 'You then feel angry, very angry towards them.'

'I wouldn't say I get angry,' Camilla replied. 'I think it's bad to get angry.'

'How did you just feel with me when I suggested that you are the common denominator?' Rita asked.

Camilla pursed her lips.

Alice had never seen a pig purse her lips before. She had heard of pig lips but never seen them pushed together in such an expression. She looked at Ronald, who was scribbling on his pad. 'Is she doing GROW or something else?'

Alice scribbled a hasty reply: 'Doesn't seem like GROW. Only one Goal question. Lots of exploring the causes of the problem????'

'Ask later. Not the right time now,' Ronald wrote back.

'I notice that you are pushing your lips together and outwards,' said Rita. 'Are you aware of this?'

'Yes,' replied Camilla through gritted teeth.

'What are you feeling?' Rita asked.

'Angry,' replied Camilla, 'really angry.'

'Do you know why you're so angry?' Rita asked.

'Not really. I feel angry towards you for blaming me but, in reality, I know that you're on my side and you want to help.'

'Do you? Do you believe that I'm on your side and want to help?' Rita asked.

'Yes,' said Camilla, softening, 'I do, I really do.'

'Yet, you still feel angry towards me when I "blame you", as you describe it.'

'I do. It seems very irrational of me,' said Camilla. 'Rationally, I know that you're here to help but I still feel angry.'

'I think this is important for us to note,' said Rita. 'What is this angry feeling about?'

'It seems out of proportion,' said Camilla. 'I recognize it now. I hate it when I think people aren't listening to my ideas or taking me seriously and I get very angry inside. I don't usually let it out.'

'Which people?' asked Rita.

'My staff. Our sponsors. My business partner,' Camilla replied.

'So, if they don't listen to your ideas, then that means they aren't taking you seriously and you feel angry. Except that you don't let it out. You feel it, of course, so I imagine it shows itself somehow. What do you do when you're feeling this anger?' Rita asked.

'I try harder to get them to listen. I push my ideas more and more. I don't let it go until they back down,' Camilla said.

'What effect does that have? How well does it work?' Rita asked.

'Not very well. They seem to listen even less and start to distance themselves from me,' said Camilla.

'OK,' said Rita, pausing. 'I think we have a good idea of what's going on here. When you have an idea or point of view that you express, if you perceive the other person (or people) isn't listening then, you feel very angry. You tell yourself they think you're an idiot and not up to the job. You don't express your anger outright; instead you push harder with your ideas and don't let it go. This has the effect of them listening even less and distancing themselves from you.'

'Yes, that seems correct,' Camilla said.

'And when we talk about people, we're referring to your staff, your sponsors and your business partner, Clarissa. Is that right?' Rita continued.

Camilla took a deep breath. 'It sounds exactly right. I never really saw it like that before. It's like a set of dominoes: once the first one starts, then each falls down one after another.'

'You've said several times that this starts when you feel as though you're not being listened to. Let's start with Clarissa. How do you know that she isn't listening?'

'She doesn't accept my ideas and she dismisses them,' said Camilla.

'Do you accept every idea that someone gives you?'

'No, of course not, people tell me ideas all the time and lots of them are rubbish.'

'What do you do then?' asked Rita.

'Move on,' said Camilla. 'I haven't got time to deal with all that.'

'Does Clarissa ever suggest things?'

'Sometimes,' said Camilla, 'I always listen but she's the people person not the ideas person.'

'How do you respond to her?' asked Rita.

'I just move on. I don't want to waste time on something that doesn't have value.'

Rita looked over at Alice and Ronald and pointed at one of the vacant chairs. 'Would one of you be kind enough to bring that chair over here?'

Ronald picked up the chair and placed it opposite Camilla, as Rita instructed.

Rita pointed at the empty chair. 'I want you to imagine that Clarissa is in that chair and you're looking across at her. You're telling her something and you don't feel she is listening. Take your time and notice what you, Camilla, are feeling.'

Camilla looked across at the other chair, and Alice noticed her lips purse again.

'OK,' said Rita, 'now I'd like you to get up and leave Camilla with those feelings in the chair where you've been sitting. Just stand back and let those feelings stay in the chair.' Rita paused. 'When you're ready I want you to sit down in *that* chair' – Rita indicated the other, empty chair – 'and imagine that you are Clarissa. To be best of your ability just *be* Clarissa.'

Camilla sat down in the other chair and adjusted herself.

Rita continued: 'I want you to be Clarissa, and I'm going to talk to you as Clarissa. Take a moment to look across at Camilla over there' – Rita pointed at the chair where Camilla had been sitting previously – 'and notice how you, Clarissa, feel.'

'I feel annoyed.'

'About what?' asked Rita.

'Camilla thinks she's better than me. She won't listen to my ideas and just dismisses anything I suggest. I'm annoyed with her.'

'OK, good. Now, stand up and come with me over here,' Rita said, walking to the far side of the room.

Camilla joined her at the far wall. Rita continued: 'Imagine that you and I are looking at two people called Camilla and Clarissa from a long way away.

'We're looking at Camilla who feels she's not being listened to and is getting angry. The more she feels angry the more she pushes her point.

'Let's look at Clarissa who feels that Camilla won't listen to her ideas and dismisses them. Camilla thinks she's better than her, and Clarissa feels annoyed.

'As you're standing here, what do you notice?'

'Oh!' said Camilla. 'Well, they're the same. I mean, they're feeling pretty much the same towards each other.'

'Yes,' said Rita, 'they are. Who's to blame for this?'

'Both of them,' said Camilla, 'and neither. They're both trying hard. They're just stuck doing the same thing and don't know how else to communicate.'

'Standing here, what do you think would help?'

'If one of them would be willing to actually listen, not just to the other person's ideas but to their feelings, to show that they value the other person.'

'OK, good,' said Rita. 'Come and take a seat.'

The two of them sat down. 'I want to come back to your outcome. Take a moment to reflect on what you just observed over there. What do you want to do now?'

Camilla looked pensive. 'I can see that something has to change. One of us has to be willing to do something different, to listen in a different way and to value the other differently.'

'That's right, Camilla,' said Rita. 'One of you does. Can *you* change, Clarissa?'

'No,' said Camilla, 'I can't change her. She won't change. Why would she? It's me, isn't it?' Camilla said slowly, 'I have to go first.'

'You don't have to do anything,' said Rita, 'but I remember a teacher of mine saying that in relationships you can either be right or be happy.'

'Do you think if I make an effort to change then Clarissa will, too?' asked Camilla.

'How would you know?'

'By doing it,' said Camilla.

'Exactly,' said Rita, 'but I want to be clear, you don't have to. This is your choice; you are free to decide how to progress.'

'I want to make progress with this. It's making me very unhappy,' said Camilla. 'What do you think I should do?'

'What do you think would help?' asked Rita.

'I need to talk to Clarissa, listen to how she feels and acknowledge that I haven't been very fair to her.'

'So, what's your outcome?' asked Rita.

'To talk to Clarissa and have a different kind of conversation, one where I listen without judging her and without pushing my own viewpoint.'

'So, your goal is to listen to Clarissa. If you weren't judging her and weren't pushing your own viewpoint, how would you be instead?'

Alice and Ronald glanced at each other. 'We're on to the Goal phase at last!' scribbled Ronald.

'Making sure it's stated in terms of what she wants and not what she doesn't want,' Alice returned.

'I'd be patient and open. Accepting of her viewpoint even if I disagree with it.'

'Great. What's it like when you are patient, open and accepting?' asked Rita.

Camilla took a deep breath. 'I'm more relaxed, slower, more thoughtful,' she replied.

'I notice your breathing changed then,' said Rita. 'How do you breathe when you're relaxed?'

'More deeply,' replied Camilla, taking another deep breath, 'and more slowly.'

'Just notice now that you can take some deeper breaths,' said Rita, 'and notice that the more deeply you breathe the more you can begin to feel relaxed.'

Camilla nodded.

'Imagine now that you're looking across at Clarissa again, breathing deeply and feeling relaxed as she's talking. What do you notice?'

'I can see her better,' said Camilla. 'I mean, I can see *her* more clearly. I can hear what she's actually saying and what she's feeling.'

'That's right,' said Rita, 'you can see her more clearly, you can hear what she's actually saying and recognize what she's feeling.

'Just stand up for a moment, would you? Leave Camilla in the chair and, when you're ready, move to Clarissa's chair, sit down and be Clarissa. Be Clarissa looking across at Camilla who is seeing you more clearly, hearing what you're actually saying and noticing how you feel. What's it like for you as Clarissa?'

'It's so different. I feel important. I feel that she cares.'

'That's right,' said Rita, then, pointing at the now empty seat, she added, 'How do you feel towards her, Camilla?'

'Much more open, more willing to engage and listen to her.'

'Good,' said Rita, glancing at her watch. 'We're about out of time. Come back to being you in your own chair. Final question. What's the first step for you from here?'

'To breathe,' said Camilla. 'To breathe and stay present to Clarissa when we talk.'

There was a pause. Rita looked at Camilla.

'You might not be considering yet that what you've learned here is about more than your relationship with Clarissa. At some point you might begin to think about where else it applies.'

'Thank you,' said Camilla. 'Really, thank you.'

'You're welcome,' said Rita as Camilla rose from her chair.

'Lovely to meet you,' said Ronald. 'Thank you for allowing us to observe.'

'To be honest, I'd completely forgotten you were there. I hope it was useful,' said Camilla as she picked up her bag and shook Rita's flipper. 'Goodbye.'

'Goodbye,' replied Alice, Ronald and Rita.

CHAPTER 16

In the Position of Being Eaten

PERCEPTUAL POSITIONS EXPLAINED

● ● ●

Alice was unsure how much time had passed during Camilla's coaching session but she knew that her 'spoil your dinner' snack phase had passed. She was sure she could eat a whole dinner right now and it wouldn't be spoiled at all.

Rita turned to them both. 'An interesting session,' she said.

'I have a thousand questions,' said Ronald.

'I thought you might,' Rita replied.

'I'm starving,' said Alice.

'Me, too,' said Rita. 'There's a nice restaurant around the corner. How about we go there and talk some more. Bring your questions, Ronald.'

The three of them walked back to the atrium and left the conference centre. The sun was shining but it was lower in the sky now. Alice had completely lost track of time. In fact, the only clock she was aware of was the one in her stomach.

'Everyone OK with pizza?' Rita asked, pointing to an Italian restaurant in front of them.

'Sounds good to me,' said Ronald.

Alice nodded. 'Really, Alice, you've been eating an awful lot of pizza recently,' she said to herself. 'You're going to look like a pizza if you're not careful.'

The three of them sat down as the waiter approached. 'What can I get you?' he said.

'Asparagus, pumpkin and feta pizza with rocket,' said Rita.

'Me too,' said Ronald.

'Me three,' said Alice.

'Three pizzas coming up,' said the waiter.

'So, what questions do you have?' asked Rita. 'In fact, before that, tell me what you noticed during that coaching conversation.'

'I noticed you feeding back some observations you made,' said Ronald.

'I noticed that you focused more on Camilla's thinking about the situation than the situation itself,' said Alice.

'And she started out somewhat in a Victim position and then became a Persecutor,' said Ronald.

'I would probably say she started out in a Rescuer position, trying to do everything and save the day,' said Rita. 'She then became a Victim and a Persecutor, moving round the cycle.'

'I noticed that you really focused on her map of the world,' said Alice. 'The conversation was about her perceptions of the situations and her own feelings and thoughts.'

'I noticed you fed back some of her exact words and phrases,' said Ronald.

'Indeed,' said Rita. 'Really well observed, both of you.'

'Can you tell us about the thing with the chairs?' said Ronald. 'You know, when you asked Camilla to change seats – what was that?'

'Of course, but first I need to explain a little bit of theory to you,' said Rita, picking up three of the side plates that were on the table and arranging them. She pulled her lipstick out of her shell and began to write on each plate.

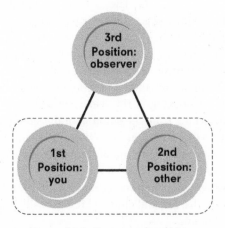

Figure 16.1 Perceptual positions

'In any situation there are three different positions from which we can perceive something.

'*1st Position* is YOU, feeling how you feel and knowing your own reality, your thoughts, beliefs, values, goals and needs. This position is essential for a strong sense of knowing yourself and your boundaries.

2nd Position is that of the OTHER person, experiencing the other's point of view, their feelings, thoughts, values and beliefs. This position is *not* being yourself and imagining what the other person thinks. That is you in 1st Position imposing your own map of the world on to them. 2nd Position is actually imagining being the other person with their map of the world.

'What do you think is useful about being able to take 2nd Position?' Rita asked.

'It helps us empathize,' said Alice.

'It helps us understand and appreciate someone else's point of view,' said Ronald.

'Exactly,' said Rita. 'Empathy comes from putting yourself in 2nd Position, feeling how the other feels.'

'Is that different from sympathy?' asked Alice.

'I would say that sympathy is a feeling of care and concern for someone but it does not involve sharing their perspective and feelings. Sympathy comes from being in 1st Position, being yourself and caring about the other, often with a desire for them to feel differently or be in a different situation,' said Rita. 'They are similar, but the subtlety is in the perceptual position and accompanying feelings.'

'What's 3rd Position then?' asked Ronald.

'*3rd Position* is that of a detached OBSERVER, someone who is outside the specific context or relationship. It is an objective perspective, standing back from the situation and seeing the bigger picture. It can be very helpful for looking at the wider consequences for everyone involved and detaching from the emotion of the situation.'

'We witnessed that with Camilla. When she stepped into 3rd Position, she saw both people more equally and the entanglement between them became more apparent,' said Ronald.

'Yes, that was very much the case,' said Rita. 'Both 1st and 2nd Positions were highly charged and emotive. It was really 3rd Position that unlocked the situation.'

'Is that usually the case?' asked Ronald.

'Not at all. In my experience there is typically one perceptual posi- tion that the client hasn't been attending to. For example, maybe they haven't really been appreciating something from the other person's perspective. I'm sure you've met people who can never see anything from someone else's point of view.'

'Yes!' said Ronald and Alice in unison.

'Right, so that's where they are missing 2nd Position, and so within the coaching context it may be helpful to provide this as a resource.'

'But surely everyone is already in 1st Position,' said Ronald. 'That's never missing.'

'Not so,' said Rita. 'There are some people who are very detached or dissociated and for whom connecting to their own feelings is difficult. They may have a tendency to take 3rd Position – the perspective of the observer – and may come across as somewhat cold. There are also those who default to 2nd Position and put themselves in other's shoes, always putting the other's needs and feelings first; these people also lack attention to 1st position.'

'Is that what is called co-dependent?' asked Ronald.

'It's certainly one way to think about it. If a person spends a lot of time in the feelings of the other, then their happiness is dependent on making the other person happy.

In either example the person isn't attending to 1st Position and may be missing crucial data there.'

'When would 1st position be the resource in coaching?' asked Ronald.

'Well, when would it be important for a person to be really in touch with how they feel?' asked Rita.

'When deciding what to eat,' said Alice, looking hopefully at the waiter. 'I'm starving.'

'That's actually a good example, Alice. Making decisions is often a time when it's important to feel our feelings. Would you buy a house or start a relationship based on an objective analysis of the building or other person?'

'I've never done either,' said Alice, 'but I wouldn't choose my friends simply based on a list of characteristics. I want to feel good being around them.'

'Exactly,' said Rita. 'It's not to say that 3rd Position doesn't contain useful data, but a person would probably need to pay attention to their own feelings, too, when making decisions.'

'I'm not sure I really understand 3rd Position,' Alice said. 'It seems rather hard to imagine.'

'Three pizzas,' interrupted the waiter. 'Asparagus, pumpkin and feta with rocket. *Buon appetito.*'

Alice was still thinking about what Rita had said as she looked down at her pizza. She noticed her mouth watering and began to feel rather excited about that first taste. She was about to pick up her first slice ('because', Alice said to herself, 'pizza is best eaten by hand rather than messing about with a knife and fork') when something strange began to happen. The pizza seemed to be sinking away from her – so that, by the time she reached out to pick up a slice, it was already quite a long way below, out of reach. 'Are you flying again, Alice?' she asked herself, but there was no Ubird carrying her this time.

She seemed to be on the ceiling of the restaurant looking down on people below her and was shocked to see that a young girl had sat down in *her* chair in front of *her* pizza. 'Why, who does she think she is, jumping into my chair the moment I'm gone?' Alice asked herself. The young girl seemed to know Rita and Ronald and the three of them were engaged in conversation. The girl was actually eating a slice of Alice's pizza.

'Stop, you thief,' Alice screamed, 'Leave my pizza alone.'

She looked down and could see the whole restaurant beneath her, but no one seemed to acknowledge her shouts.

Alice looked more closely at the girl eating her pizza and noticed that she was wearing the same clothes as her. In fact, she looked an awful lot like Alice remembered herself looking. She couldn't be sure, of course, because she'd been so busy recently that several days had passed since she'd looked in a mirror. 'I'm sure I remember looking very much like her,' she said to herself. 'In fact, she could be my twin.'

'That's it,' she realized. 'I have an identical twin who has only now chosen to reveal herself. How exciting, what fun we'll have.'

Alice looked down at her own body to make a more detailed comparison between herself and her twin sister and gasped. She had no body. There was nothing there. She turned around, looked up and looked down, but her body was nowhere to be seen.

'Alice,' she rebuked herself, 'you've been very careless this time – you've lost your body. Really, it's one thing to lose your homework or your Maths textbook but losing your body is intolerable. Now, young lady, think carefully, where did you see it last?'

168

Alice paused. I last saw it when I was sitting at the table, she thought. I distinctly remember my left arm reaching forward to pick up the pizza. 'Well, that must be where you've left it then,' she replied to herself.

'But, if I've left *my* body at the table, then that girl down there is *me*. And, if *she* is *me*, then who am *I*?' she asked herself.

'Think logically,' she commanded herself. 'If you're watching yourself right now then you're ...'

'In 3rd Position,' she heard a voice say. It sounded like her voice but she couldn't be sure. Nonetheless the voice was right. Now it made sense: she was no longer in 1st Position as herself and was somehow perceiving the situation in 3rd Position.

Now that she knew where she was, Alice calmed down and decided things weren't so bad after all. For a start, she was no longer hungry despite not having eaten the pizza. Looking round she began to observe the other people in the restaurant. On the table behind Alice, Rita and Ronald was a couple holding hands. At the neighbouring table was a family with a man, a woman and three children. Alice saw the waiter talking to them and nodding.

Looking back at Rita, Ronald and Alice below, she observed that they looked like good friends. There was still the slightly unusual fact that one was a turtle and the other a fish, but Alice didn't consider that for very long. They were talking animatedly, and Alice observed that Rita looked fondly at the other two while they discussed something.

'The question you must consider, Alice,' she said to herself, 'is how to get back from here. It's all very well being in 3rd Position and observing everything but you ought to begin making an effort to return to being yourself.' However, the problem, she considered, was that she didn't really know how she'd got here in the first place. She knew that she'd been saying that she wasn't quite sure what 3rd Position was when the strangeness had started to happen. In all honesty, she reflected, although she understood the concept, she wasn't entirely sure what 2nd Position felt like either.

No sooner had she thought that than things began to change. She dropped down from the ceiling like a stone and landed flat on the table. 'Ouch, that rather hurt,' she said to herself. She felt incredibly compressed from the fall. It was as if someone had rolled her out with a rolling pin and then smothered her.

Alice began to feel rather scared and this worsened when she opened her eyes and looked up to see a giant hand moving towards her. No ... No ... NO!' she screamed as the hand reached down to grab her. The hand picked her up and began moving her closer to a giant mouth with huge teeth. They looked like a row of white garage doors, all lined up next to one other.

Alice screamed again. 'Stop ... Stop ... STOP!' but the hand continued moving her towards a huge black void beneath the garage doors. Then, just as she was about to enter the dark hole of the giant mouth, the hand holding her stopped. She saw the mouth moving and making shapes in front of her like a vast cavern with edges that moved.

'What has happened?' she asked herself. 'Last thing I remember I was in 3rd Position on the ceiling but I don't know where I am now.' She thought back carefully over the previous moments. She had been wondering how to get back to being herself in 1st Position and had been wondering what 2nd Position would be like.

'Oh no,' she realized. 'I'm in 2nd Position – I've become the pizza.'

It was terrifying being the pizza. She was about to be eaten by a giant mouth. A giant mouth, which, by the look of it, needed to spend a bit more time brushing its teeth. 'Alice, you are never eating pizza again,' she told herself, 'you mustn't be so cruel.'

The mouth had stopped talking and was hanging open again. Alice felt the hand begin to move and suddenly everything went dark. She felt something slice her in half. 'Arghhh,' she screamed as she began to be tossed up and down in the darkness. Another slice and one of her arms disappeared. She tried to reach out with her remaining arm, but she couldn't see it in the darkness. Her head was next and she felt it being severed from the rest of her body. 'Oh really, this is most inconvenient,' she said to herself. 'I really have lost my head now.'

Suddenly the cavern changed and she felt herself falling. She was falling inside a large cave but this time there weren't any pictures on the sides. She reached out and touched the slippery sides as she fell. 'Well, this is what it's like to be eaten,' she said to herself. 'I suppose it is interesting to discover. Perhaps I shall write about it at school. *If* I ever find my arms again.'

'Alice?' Ronald's voice slowly infiltrated Alice's thoughts, 'Alice, are you still with us?'

Alice gave a shudder. 'Yes, but I've lost my arms.'

'You've what?' asked Rita.

'I've just been eaten,' Alice continued. 'It was truly horrible at first.'

'What are you talking about?' asked Ronald.

'I've just been eaten. I was the pizza and that giant mouth ate me. It was very unpleasant.'

'When you were the pizza?' said Ronald, his eyes squinting in disbelief.

'Just now, I was in 2nd Position and felt what it was like to be the pizza. I was screaming but no one could hear me,' Alice replied.

'I think you've been daydreaming, dear,' Rita said. 'Besides, pizzas don't have feelings and pizzas can't talk or scream.'

'Well, this one did,' Alice replied.

'It's called anthropomorphism, dear,' Rita said.

'Ant-rope-what?' Alice asked. 'What have ants and rope got to do with this?'

'Anthropomorphism,' Rita repeated. 'The attribution of human traits, emotions or intentions to non-human entities. Pizzas can't talk or feel or think. I think you've been getting carried away, dear.'

'Of course,' Alice replied. It was some time in the future, when the word came up again, that Alice giggled to herself about how she had learned it. 'To think that anthropomorphism was explained to me by a talking turtle,' she chuckled.

'We were just talking about some coaching Ronald did earlier today,' Rita said.

'I did some coaching with one of my team before I joined you,' said Ronald, 'and I had a few difficulties.'

'I've suggested that we go to see a friend of mine who is somewhat of an expert in working with other coaches,' Rita continued. 'Would you like to come along?'

'What about pudding?' Alice said.

'A worthy question,' Ronald added.

'Well, if we're going to see *him*, then we probably ought to take something sweet anyway. How about we stop on the way and pick up something?'

'In that case I'm coming,' said Alice.

⚓

'Ben, if I was Rita, I wouldn't have felt very confident working with Camilla in that coaching session.'

'Thank you, Alice. You've just given an excellent illustration of how people get confused about 2nd Position.'

'What do you mean, Ben?'

'Well, if you *were* actually Rita working with Camilla, you would have felt confident because Rita knows what to do. What you're saying is that, if *you* were coaching Camilla, then *you* wouldn't have felt very confident.'

'Oh, yes, I see what you mean.'

'It's a really good example of how people get confused. When you say, "If I were so-and-so, I would do ..." you're not using 2nd Position.'

'Then, what is it, Ben? It *sounds* like 2nd Position?'

'It's 1st Position superimposed on the other person. It's 1st Position because you have your own thoughts, feelings and beliefs and you're imagining the situation as if you were in it. True 2nd Position is being the other person, seeing the situation through their eyes with their map of the world. Of course, none of us can really do that because we're not actually the other person, but we can do our best to take their world view. That gives a really different perspective from being ourselves and imagining being in the situation.'

'Oh, I like that, Ben. Mrs Parker in Science sometimes says, "If I were you, Alice, I'd stop daydreaming and concentrate on your work." Next time I'm going to reply, "Actually, if you were *really* me, you'd carry on daydreaming because it's much more interesting."'

'Hmm ... that might not be best way to educate Mrs Parker about perceptual positions, Alice, and let's remember that we are talking about the use of perceptual positions in coaching.'

'Can you remind me about that, Ben?'

'The idea of taking different perceptual positions can be useful with a number of coaching challenges. Conflict and disagreement are a starting point, but a client with any coaching issue involving interactions with others will often benefit from exploring the three perceptual positions. People who have challenges presenting or speaking are often unconsciously in 2nd Position – that is, they are seeing themselves from an audience perspective (and often not very kindly) and there can be some strength in connecting to their own 1st Position. The concept of perceptual positions come from the field of Neuro-Linguistic Programming (NLP) and is very useful in the coach's toolkit.

'Alice, let's try something. How about you put yourself in my position for a moment. Imagine someone named Alice has just eaten all your birthday cake. How would you feel?'

'Ah! I might be a bit annoyed with her and disappointed that I didn't get a piece.'

'Yes, you might.'

'Ben, we've done enough about perceptual positions. Let's move on. Time for the next chapter.'

'I thought you might say that, Alice. OK, time for the next chapter. I just hope it doesn't remind me of cake!'

CHAPTER 17

Victor's Super Vision

AN INTRODUCTION TO COACHING SUPERVISION

● ● ●

The trio left the restaurant and crossed the road to a small patisserie with a brown wooden frontage and beautiful cakes in the window.

'We'll take a selection of fancies,' Rita said, looking at the selection of cakes. 'He'll complain and say he's on a diet but he'll still eat them.'

'Who are we going to see?' asked Ronald.

'We're going to see the Cat,' said Rita. 'He's the wisest and most experienced coach I know.'

'And he'll tell me what I should have done yesterday with my client?' asked Ronald.

'He works as a coach supervisor, so yes, he'll help you' said Rita.

'What's a coach super visor?' asked Alice, pronouncing 'supervisor' as two words. 'Is it some sort of magical glasses that let you understand coaching better? Some kind of x-ray spectacles for coaching?'

'Supervisor, it's one word. A supervisor offers supervision,' said Rita.

'He has super vision?' questioned Alice. 'My eyesight is quite good I believe, but I'd be interested in having super vision. Why, imagine being able to see for miles, that would be incredible ...'

'Let me explain,' interjected Rita. 'Supervision – it's one word. Supervision is where a coach gains insight into both the client and themselves as part of the coach–client relationship. They do this with the help of a supervisor, usually someone more experienced and who is not working directly with the client.'

'So, it's an actual recognized thing?' asked Ronald.

'Yes, you could think about supervision as coaching the coach. I go to see the Cat once a month for supervision to help with my own client work.'

'But, you've been coaching for ever. Surely you know how to deal with everything a client might present,' said Ronald. 'Why do you need supervision?'

'I'm not *that* old,' said Rita. 'I'm only 117.'

'117! That's ancient,' said Alice. 'I'm 12 and I'm already quite old.'

'My uncle lived to be 149 years old,' said Rita. 'I consider myself middle aged. Back to your question, though, Ronald. I engage in supervision for several reasons. Coaching is a process which is about much more than knowledge and skill. There is an interface between the skills and the person using them. The skills can't be observed on their own because they exist in and through the coach.

'What I'm saying is that the coach can't *not* bring themselves to the coaching. It's one of the reasons why no two coaches are the same.'

'Surely, that's the same with most professions?' asked Ronald.

'Coaching is not unique, that's for sure,' continued Rita, 'and there are many other skills where a person's own opinions will have an impact. Medicine, for example, has very well-documented procedures and approaches for diagnoses and treatment, but two hospital consultants may have different opinions on something. It's not black and white.

'Coaching, however, is not just about the coach's opinions: the entire map of the world of the coach can have an impact on what is happening. Of course, as a coach we aim to suspend our own judgements and views and work with the client's world but there are times when our own life experience, emotions and histories may impact on what is happening and this may be problematic.

'I do have a lot of coaching experience but that doesn't stop me being tripped up by own biases and assumptions. Many of these are, of course, unconscious – I'm not aware I'm making them.'

'How do you know they're there, then?' Ronald asked.

'Well, usually in supervision I discuss a client with whom I'm feeling challenged or wonder if I'm missing something, or perhaps the client isn't progressing. Often, when we explore the situation, I discover that I have been making some assumptions that I was unaware of and these have been getting in the way.'

'So, supervision is about the coach understanding themselves better?' asked Ronald.

'That's one aspect. It might also be about exploring different approaches to use within coaching, developing skills and considering strategies that would help that particular client. It is also about development as a coach.'

'It sounds fascinating,' said Ronald.

'I'd still prefer to have a pair of glasses that give me super *vision*,' said Alice.

'You know, Alice, in some ways that's exactly what supervision does. It gives you some different lenses to view the coaching through and this helps you see more clearly. But I've said enough – I'll let the Cat explain.'

The trio had arrived at an old-looking telephone box. Alice had only seen one once before when she'd been on holiday in the Lake District. They had been driving along a remote road in her father's new silver car, and she had noticed a strange small glass building and wondered what it was. Her father explained that in the past people hadn't had phones in their pockets and if you needed to use a phone you had to go to one of the glass buildings.

Rita opened the door to the phone box and the three of them stepped inside. Alice was expecting to see a phone in front of her but, instead, a wooden ladder led upwards into the darkness.

'Up you go,' said Rita, and Alice began climbing the ladder. She climbed cautiously, expecting to bump her head on the roof of the phone box but no roof appeared. They continued climbing for what seemed like an age until they arrived at a wooden platform with a door. It reminded Alice of the treehouse that she had played in with her sister and, although the treehouse had had a wooden ladder, it definitely didn't begin inside a phone box.

Rita knocked loudly on the door and a deep voice came from inside.

'Come in and leave your shoes at the door.'

Rita took off her red hat, and for the first time Alice saw the top of her head. It was wrinkly and the skin looked leathery and Alice thought for once that Rita did look her 117 years of age.

The three of them stepped into a small and cosy room with an open fire. Alice saw a large black cat reclining on a chaise longue and wearing a pince-nez. 'My, my, Alice, your French is improving,' she said to herself. 'Fancy using such words as "chaise longue" and "pince-nez"; Madame Dubois at school will be very pleased.'

Alice realized that she wasn't in the least surprised by the appearance of the Cat. After all, she thought to herself, what is one more talking animal among all the rest she had encountered.

The cat looked ancient. His whiskers were long and grey, and there were wrinkles around his eyes. His coat was a shiny black colour, and his paws were white like he was wearing snow boots.

Rita held out the box of cakes. 'A little something for you.'

'I've told you not to do this,' the Cat said angrily. 'You know I'll eat them. They do smell good, though,' he continued with a wink. 'You can't beat the sugary scent of a fresh cake.'

Rita introduced Ronald and Alice.

'Victor,' said the cat, holding out a paw. 'Pleased to meet you.'

'Here's a question for you both. In the word "scent", which letter is silent, the *s* or the *c*?'

'The *s*,' said Alice.

'The *c*,' said Ronald.

'Well, scent without the *s* is cent and scent without the *c* is sent, so I think it's rather hard to say. We can't say for certain which one is silent and which one is pronounced, but to take one away would change the word completely and give it a different meaning.'

'It cost one cent for the scent to be sent,' said Alice.

'Clever girl,' said Victor.

'The scent of a cent can't be sent,' Alice continued.

'Different meanings but they sound exactly the same,' said Victor. 'Here's another question for you. When you hear the words "scent", "cent" or "sent", how do you know which one it is?'

'It's the words around it,' said Ronald. 'They provide clues as to which one it is. If someone says, "The parcel has been sent," we understand it differently from "The parcel has a strange scent" or "That parcel isn't worth a cent".'

'Exactly,' said Victor. 'It's the words around it that provide the context and give meaning. A word on its own doesn't mean very much. Meaning comes from the context something occurs in. Enough of my ambiguous metaphors, though. You didn't come here to listen to me blather on.'

There was a pause.

'Well, maybe one more metaphor then,' Victor said.

'He's like this,' Rita said, rolling her eyes. 'I should have warned you.'

'Here's a puzzle for you,' Victor continued. 'Imagine you're walking down a street at night and you see a light in an upstairs room. Two figures are struggling and the smaller figure is halfway out of the window. What's happening?'

'Two people have had an argument, they're fighting and one is trying to throw the other out of the window,' said Ronald.

'A burglar has been disturbed by the houseowner and he's trying to escape out of the window,' said Alice.

'Interesting suggestions,' said Victor. 'What if I tell you there's a net beneath the window with people holding it.'

'I'm not a fan of nets,' said Ronald.

'And the light in the room is actually flames. One figure is a man and the other is his daughter.'

'He's trying to save her,' said Alice. 'The house is burning down and the only way out is to jump into the net.'

'Exactly,' said Victor. 'Two people struggling is two people struggling. We don't know what it means until we put the context around it. All meaning is dependent on context.'

'Not all meaning,' said Ronald. 'Gutting someone with a knife is always a terrible thing.'

'Unless you have appendicitis and the person holding the knife is a surgeon,' said Victor. 'In that case it might be a life saver.'

'Would you like a cake?' Rita injected hurriedly.

'Yes, thank you,' said Victor, taking three cakes out of the box and giving Alice a cheeky wink. 'Why don't you tell me why you're here?'

Rita nodded to Ronald.

'I'd like some help, please,' Ronald began. 'I was coaching one of my team yesterday and I had some difficulties. I'm hoping you can tell me what to do.'

'I see,' said Victor through a mouthful of cake. 'I'll do my best to help. Tell me about your client.'

'He's a member of my team,' said Ronald. 'He came to me because he is struggling with a project he's working on. He's having some difficulties with a website we're building; there are some technical aspects to it that he's new to and he was unsure how to go about it.'

'I asked about your client, not the problem,' said Victor.

He doesn't pull any punches, thought Alice, shrinking back in her chair slightly. He's straight to the point!

'Yes, sorry, I didn't mean to ...' said Ronald, beginning to get in a fluster.

'No need to apologize,' said Victor. 'Take your time. Let us just note for now that your answer to my request was to describe the problem and not your client.'

'He's called Simon and in his late twenties. He's been with the company for about two years and in my team for six months,' said Ronald.

'How would you describe Simon?' Victor asked.

'Disorganized, excitable, lacking focus and thinks he's better than he actually is.'

'How do you know that? asked Victor.

'That he thinks he's better than he actually is?' asked Ronald.

Victor nodded.

'He can be quite blasé about things,' continued Ronald. 'He will often volunteer for tasks or projects without considering the difficulties, he disregards and discounts problems and will be very positive about what he can achieve. The trouble is that he often doesn't actually deliver the goods.'

'How do you feel towards him?' Victor asked.

Ronald glanced at Rita and back at Victor. 'Perhaps I haven't been clear with what I'm asking for,' Ronald said. 'I'd like some help to understand what I could have done differently in the coaching session – for example, are there some better questions I could have asked or perhaps a different process to follow that would have helped us reach a better outcome.'

'Do you go to the doctor and tell him or her what treatment you need?' asked Victor.

Ronald looked slightly puzzled and shook his head.

'Do you take your car to the garage and tell the mechanic how to fix it?' he continued.

Ronald shook his head again. 'No, no I don't.'

'Then why are you telling me how to help you with your client?' asked Victor.

'I'm not,' said Ronald.

'Yes, you are,' said Victor. 'You want me to give you some better questions to ask or a different process to follow.'

Ronald looked at Rita again, with an expression that Alice interpreted as a silent plea for help. Nothing came back. He looks like a fish out of water, she thought to herself.

'Would you like some help with your client?' asked Victor.

'Yes ... Yes I would,' stammered Ronald.

'Good,' said Victor. 'You seem to be a motivated young man and I will help you to the best of my ability, I promise you. Now, you were describing your client. "Disorganized, excitable, lacking focus and thinks he's better than he actually is" was your description, I believe. So, can you tell me now, how do you feel towards Simon?'

'I don't feel particularly generous towards him,' said Ronald. 'He creates problems for me when he doesn't deliver what he has committed to.'

'Not particularly generous ... Are you always so mild mannered?' asked Victor.

'Well, I don't want to be unkind to him,' said Ronald. 'He means well.'

'You said he creates problems for you,' said Victor.

'Well, yes,' Ronald agreed.

'So, how do you really feel towards someone who creates problems for you?'

'Irritated,' said Ronald. 'Annoyed. Angry even.'

'You feel angry towards Simon. How do you express this?' asked Victor.

'I don't,' said Ronald. 'I don't like being angry with people; it's not who I am.'

'I see,' said Victor, his eyes narrowing. 'You're better than that?'

'I like to think so,' said Ronald.

'I'm sure you do,' said Victor. 'Tell me about the conversation with Simon. How did it begin? And, by that, I mean, how did he come to be having a coaching session with you?'

'I've fairly recently discovered coaching and Rita has been teaching me some skills to assist me in working with my team differently. I had a team meeting yesterday and explained to them that I would be taking a different approach with them and asking them to think more rather than me just giving them the answers,' said Ronald.

'How did they respond to that?' asked Victor.

'Pretty well, a bit mixed perhaps, but I explained why I'm doing it and some of the benefits to them and the business.'

'OK, so how did Simon approach you?'

'He said he was having a difficulty with some of the website work and would like me to do a piece of it for him.'

'What did you say to him?' asked Victor.

'I explained that I would like him to do the work himself but I would support him and talk it through with him, so we agreed to sit down and I would coach him.'

Victor nodded. 'It sounds like you've set it up in the right way, that's good. How did you begin the session?'

'Well, I asked Simon what the goal was, what he wanted to achieve,' said Ronald. 'He was fairly clear on that. He knows what the outcome needs to be as it's specified in the project plan.'

'Would you say he has bought into the outcome?' asked Victor.

'Yes, I would. He's not unmotivated; he wants it to work,' said Ronald.

'What happened next?'

'I began exploring the current Reality – what he'd done so far and what he understood. This was quite short – he hasn't done much and he doesn't get it.'

'And then?' asked Victor.

'We moved into the Options phase and I asked him what ideas he'd got. He suggested something which I knew wouldn't work. I didn't say that, though, but instead questioned him so he could explore it until he himself could see that it would fail. I asked him what other ideas he had, and his second suggestion was also poor. Again, I didn't want to be in "tell" mode, so I questioned him until he began to see the flaws in it. This was when things got difficult.'

'Things got difficult at *this* point!' exclaimed Victor with raised eyebrows.

Alice was beginning to see the problem herself. It was interesting to watch the interaction between Ronald and Victor.

'Yes,' said Ronald. 'I asked him what other ideas he had but he didn't have any more. I then asked him who would be able to solve it and he said he couldn't think of anyone. He started to become a bit sulky.'

'Sulky?' quizzed Victor, tilting his head to one side.

'Sullen, quiet, uncooperative, he wouldn't say much,' said Ronald.

'Mmm ...' murmured the Cat.

'I may not have helped things,' said Ronald.

'How so?' asked Victor.

'Well, at this point I said he needed to sort his attitude out, I was feeling exasperated with him,' said Ronald.

'When you began the coaching with Simon did you think he could solve this?'

'Probably not,' Ronald replied.

'But you went ahead anyway?' asked Victor.

'Well, I wanted to give him a chance,' said Ronald.

'Perhaps,' said Victor, 'or perhaps not. What would you say if I postulated that you wanted to show Simon what he doesn't know and illustrate that he's not as good as he thinks?'

Ronald's mouth opened. And closed. And opened again.

'You're angry with him because he thinks he's better than he really is and he causes you problems and you thought you'd "coach" him so that he could see just how little he knows,' Victor continued.

Ronald looked aghast. 'I don't know what to say.'

'Do you think there's any truth in what I'm saying?' Victor asked.

Ronald looked at floor. 'I feel terribly ashamed,' he said.

Alice saw Victor's expression change and his whole demeanour soften. 'I don't think you've any need to feel ashamed, Ronald.'

'But I think what you're saying is true,' Ronald said. 'I am angry with Simon and part of me wanted to put him in his place. That's a terrible thing to do as a coach.'

'Did you set out to put him in his place?' asked Victor.

'No,' said Ronald, 'I intended to help him, but I can see that my feelings got in the way and led me to pursue a particular line of questioning that wasn't supportive.'

'Let's pause a moment and talk to Alice and Rita,' said Victor, dipping his hand into the box of cakes. His hand fished around from one corner to another trying to find something. Eventually, he looked in the box.

'Where are the cakes?' he cried.

Alice looked at the floor. She could feel her cheeks going bright red. She also noticed a large collection of cake crumbs had gathered in the folds of her dress and she hoped Victor couldn't see them.

'Alice!' said Victor. 'Have you got something to say?'

'Yes, yes I have,' said Alice, wondering what on earth she should do.

'Go on,' said Victor slowly.

'I would like to perform a poem for you,' she said.

'A what?' said Victor. 'I want to know why you've eaten all my cakes!'

Alice stood up, cleared her throat and pulled herself up to her full height.

> *'What is this life if, full of cakes,*
> *We cannot make a few mistakes.*
> *No time for us to get it wrong*
> *And learn by doing as we go along.*
> *No time to hear, when questions we pose,*
> *The answers from our client who knows.*
> *No time to see, within the story*
> *Expressions and body language in all their glory.*
> *No time to separate process and content,*
> *And explore them both as time well spent.*
> *No time to backtrack and explore*
> *Something we missed that came before.*
> *A poor life this if, full of cakes,*
> *We cannot make a few mistakes.'*

'Bravo,' said Victor, clapping his paws in appreciation. 'A wonderful poem and a version that I've not heard before,' he said with a wink.

Alice took a small bow. 'I'm ever so sorry about eating all the cakes,' she said. 'I didn't realize that I'd eaten so many.'

'Never mind, my dear,' said Victor. 'I probably shouldn't eat that many, so you've done me a favour.'

'Let's return to you, Ronald. What are your reflections now?'

'I can see very clearly now that my own feelings have had an impact on my coaching and were the reason things didn't go so well. I realize now that I should turn my feelings off when I'm coaching if I'm to be successful.'

'Hold on,' said Victor. 'Let's not get too far ahead. Yes, I would agree that your own feelings had an impact on the coaching work that you did with Simon and are the primary reason the session wasn't fruitful. But let's remember that it wasn't your intention to respond in this way and that you were hijacked by your unexpressed feelings.'

'Which is why I need to turn my feelings off when I'm coaching,' said Ronald.

'*Plus ça change, plus c'est la même chose,*' sighed Victor.

'Pardon?' questioned Ronald.

'"The more things change, the more they stay the same,"' said Alice, somewhat confused. Where had she learned how to speak French so well? Perhaps she had been paying more attention to Madame Dubois than she remembered.

'The solution to the problem perpetuates the problem or becomes a new problem itself,' said Victor. 'What appears to be making a change and making progress just continues or creates the problem at a different level.'

'I'm afraid I don't follow,' said Ronald.

'Let's consider how this began. How have you been feeling towards Simon?' asked Ronald.

'Angry – I admit I've been feeling angry and irritated with him,' Ronald replied.

'And how did you deal with that?' asked Victor.

'I kept my feelings to myself,' said Ronald. 'I tried to ignore them and suppress them.'

'That's right,' said Victor, 'and how well did that work?'

'Not very well it seems,' said Ronald, 'since they have had an impact on my coaching.'

'Exactly,' said Victor. 'And your solution to this is to ignore your feelings and suppress them some more. You want to solve the problem by doing more of the thing that caused it.'

'Ah!' said Ronald. 'I do see your point.'

'What do you see?' asked Victor.

'I can see that this problem began before the coaching started. It's really about my way of dealing with Simon.'

'It's really about your way of dealing with your feelings,' said Victor.

'Is this still coaching?' asked Ronald.

'I think we've gone a bit beyond standard coaching here,' Victor said. 'I call it coaching plus.'

'There's a reason I come to see Victor,' said Rita. 'I've been sitting in your seat plenty of times.'

Ronald nodded. 'I'm learning a lot here,' he said, 'even if I can't quite explain what it is yet.'

'Well, let's return to a more traditional approach, Ronald. What is your goal from here?'

'To no longer suppress my feelings and bottle them up,' said Ronald.

'Well, you know as well as I do that that's what you *don't* want to do anymore,' said Victor.

'Indeed,' nodded Ronald. 'I guess I need to find a way to express what I feel,' he sighed.

'What's with the sigh?' asked Victor.

'I just hate upsetting other people. It's why I keep things to myself.'

'And yet, look what happened when you did that,' said Victor.

'I upset Simon,' nodded Ronald. 'I see that now. I do want to work on expressing myself more. I can see how important it is.'

'Indeed, when you learn how to express your feelings appropriately and effectively instead of bottling them up, then I think you'll find that your relationships improve significantly,' said Victor.

'I'm nervous about it. It doesn't feel very natural to me,' said Ronald.

'Of course you are,' said Victor. 'It's something new and it won't feel natural if you're not used to it. Natural is another word for something we can do without thinking. Anything that is new to us won't feel natural. Would you say riding a bike feels natural?'

'I would,' said Ronald. 'It's the most natural thing in the world to me.'

'And yet there was a time when you were a child and you couldn't do it when it felt very unnatural.'

'Yes,' nodded Ronald, 'there was. I remember having stabilizers on my bike to help me balance. It felt very unnatural.'

'Exactly,' Victor continued. 'Natural is another word for something we can do without thinking.'

'Level 4 – unconsciously competent,' said Alice.

'Yes, on the learning ladder, something we do naturally is something we do without being conscious of how we do it,' said Victor.

'So, I'm at Level 2 with my expressing my feelings,' said Ronald. 'I'm consciously unskilled.'

'Yes, that's probably true,' said Victor. 'You haven't learned yet how to do it skilfully and effectively.'

'I feel a bit better now,' said Ronald. 'If this is something I can learn how to do, then I'm less worried.'

'It is something you can learn how to do,' said Victor. 'Tell me how far did you ride the first time you sat on a bike?'

'Not very far,' said Ronald.

'Well, remember that when it comes to dealing with and expressing your feelings. You might even find it helpful to have some stabilizers at the start to keep you balanced.'

'What kind of stabilizers?' asked Ronald.

'There are some simple ideas that can help you express how you feel to someone in a way that will allow them to receive it more easily,' said Victor.

'What are they?' asked Ronald.

'Let me give you an example. If I say to you, "You've been really lazy and you make me really angry and annoyed," what might be your response?'

'I might say, "No, I haven't,"' said Ronald.

'Exactly, you might defend yourself against my accusation. My way of phrasing it invites you to push back and we're in a disagreement.'

'So, how should I say it?' asked Ronald.

'You could say, "When you arrive without the project work complete I feel angry and annoyed." What do you notice about how that is different?' asked Victor.

'It doesn't accuse the other person – my feelings are my own,' said Ronald.

'Can the other person disagree with what you've said?' asked Victor.

'No,' said Ronald, 'I suppose they can't. They can't say, "You don't feel angry," that would be ridiculous. I'm saying how I feel and it's true for me.'

'Exactly, there's nothing for them to argue about. They might not like it, they might have a different viewpoint, but they can't say it's not true. By owning your feelings – by saying, "When X happens I feel Y," instead of saying, "You're Z and you make me Y" – there is less opportunity for discord.'

'Which makes it easier to do! The thing that stops me is worrying that the other person will argue or disagree,' said Ronald, pulling out his notepad and pen. 'When X happens I feel Y,' he wrote.

'One of the important elements here is "I". When you make the feelings your own, the other person can't dispute them. There is definitely a bit more to this and some finessing which will make it even more effective, but I think you get the idea. I'll let you take things from here, Rita.

This is now a piece of coaching work with Ronald. From a supervision perspective I think we're done.'

Rita nodded. 'We can follow up on this when you're ready, Ronald.'

'Thank you,' said Ronald. 'This wasn't what I was expecting but you've opened my eyes today.'

'You're welcome. It's been a pleasure to meet you both, even if you did eat my cakes,' Victor said, giving Alice a wry smile.

'I'm sorry again,' Alice said. 'I promise I'll bring some more next time.'

'Thank you, Victor,' said Rita. 'That was very interesting to watch, I've learned a lot.'

'Be careful descending the ladder,' said Victor. 'I'll turn the light on for you.'

'Thank you,' said Alice. 'We climbed up here in the dark.'

He opened the door and shook hands with each of them as they got up to leave.

'Thanks again,' said Ronald.

The three of them began slowly and carefully descending the ladder, and Alice could see the light of the phone box far below them. She still didn't quite understand how the phone box could contain such a long ladder that was invisible from outside; some other quirk of physics, she supposed. 'A bit more attention in science is needed, Alice,' she told herself, 'then you might understand how all this is happening.'

CHAPTER 18

The Solution Becomes the Problem

COMPARING FIRST-ORDER AND
SECOND-ORDER CHANGE

● ● ●

The sun was beating down as they exited the telephone box, and the trio decided to cool themselves down with a visit to the lake for a swim. As they approached the lake, Alice saw a commotion in the water and the three of them rushed to the lake shore.

Something bright green was thrashing around in the water, occasionally coming to the surface with a splash, and then diving down. Alice couldn't see anything in the lake as it was all churned up and full of mud rising from the silty bed.

The three watched as the lake got cloudier and cloudier until, eventually, the bright-green thing came to rest. Alice recognized the frog who had played the mandolin a few days ago.

'Hello, Mr Frog,' she cried. 'Is everything OK?'

The Frog looked up and came leaping towards them. 'I need your help,' he said in a rush. 'My precious mandolin is lost in the lake and I can't find it anywhere. Will you help me look for it?'

'Of course,' said Alice. 'What can we do?'

'Well, you'll need to get wet,' replied the Frog, 'but I see at least two of you can swim.'

'*Three* of us can swim,' said Alice firmly.

'Well, what are you waiting for?' said the Frog. 'Let's start looking!'

'If I may say,' said Rita, 'it strikes me that the more you swim in the lake, the muddier it gets.'

'Yes,' said the Frog, 'which is all the more reason why I need help. The muddier it gets, the harder it is to see and the more pairs of eyes will be needed.'

'And the muddier it will get,' said Rita.

'And the more eyes will be needed,' said the Frog.

'But the more you look, the muddier it gets.'

'And the muddier it gets, the more we must look,' said the Frog. 'Don't you see? It's simple logic.'

'But there's a chance you'll stir up all the mud and the mandolin will be buried,' said Rita.

'All the more reason to get in there before that happens,' said the Frog.

'I tell you what,' said Alice. 'We'll all help you find your mandolin if you can solve my puzzle.'

'You'll all help?' asked the Frog doubtfully.

Alice looked at the other two who reluctantly nodded in agreement.

'It's a deal,' said the Frog. 'What's your puzzle?'

Alice began to hunt for some stones on the lakeshore, and when she had collected nine in total, she laid them out in a square formation.

Figure 18.1 Alice's puzzle

'The puzzle is to join all nine dots by drawing four continuous straight lines,' she said.

The Frog looked at her. 'That's simple,' he said and began to draw.

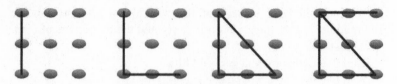

Figure 18.2 The Frog attempts a solution

'That's four lines,' said Alice, 'and you haven't joined all the dots.'

'Oh no,' he said and frantically started again.

The trio watched the Frog begin to work on the puzzle until Ronald spoke. 'I've been thinking about something from our meeting with Victor, about the idea that the solution continues or becomes the problem. It seems that this is something to be aware of in coaching.'

'Indeed,' said Rita, 'it's a more advanced concept that merits some discussion.'

'What does it mean, "the solution becomes the problem"?' asked Alice. 'I don't really understand.'

'Sometimes when a person faces a difficulty or challenge they attempt a solution which itself creates a problem and perpetuates the initial difficulty. Look at our friend here searching for his mandolin. The more he searches, the muddier the lake becomes and the more difficult it is to see. His solution has created a new problem, the existence of which impedes progress with the initial difficulty.'

'What would be an example in coaching?' asked Ronald.

'One example would be attempting to solve something by denying it is a problem.'

'Burying your head in the sand,' said Alice.

'Exactly,' said Rita, 'that's how people talk about it, although pretending something isn't happening is only one form of denial.'

'How is denial a solution *and* a problem?' asked Ronald.

'Well, one way to deal with something is to ignore it and hope it will go away or simply just pretend it's not there. Sometimes people choose this approach to dealing with a problem. In the short term it might even seem like it works. The problem, of course, is that by denying the existence of the issue there can be no real chance of resolution. Another way of denying a problem is to find an element of it that is amenable to progress and focusing on that, even if it's not really the heart of the issue. Again, that approach isn't going to bring a helpful resolution.'

'How else do people deny their problems?' asked Alice.

'Well, one fashion of our time is positive thinking. Being positive can often perpetuate a difficult situation.'

'But surely being positive is a good thing?' asked Ronald. 'There's so much negativity in the world that we need to be more positive.'

'And therein lies the problem,' said Rita. 'Your response to negativity is to be more positive. The solution creates the problem.'

'I don't follow,' said Ronald.

'In my experience, a lot of so-called positive thinking is about the reframing of a situation to find something good in it; it's the "Every cloud has a silver lining" approach. Often it involves a statement that begins "At least you're not X, or at least Y isn't happening to you ...". Some people would call it "looking on the bright side", and at times this may be a good thing. I'm not suggesting that being positive isn't ever helpful, but I am saying that it can become a defence against acknowledging difficulties and problems as they really are. The outlawing of negativity breeds a climate where issues can't be raised or addressed. Blanket positive thinking can be a covert denial of a situation and an often unspoken rejection of things as they are.'

'I had never thought about it like that before,' said Ronald. 'Can you expand on how this "solution" becomes the problem?'

'If there is a refusal to accept our feelings and thoughts or the feelings and thoughts of others, then there is an inability to acknowledge things as they are. As we know from coaching, acknowledgement of what is actually happening is required in order to begin a process of change. It's very difficult to successfully change things if we don't begin from the current reality. The journey doesn't have a solid platform to start and ideas are not grounded in the actuality of what is happening. In this way, positive thinking functioning as a denial may lead us further from a solution.'

Alice began humming a tune and started to sing:

> *Some things can make you frown,*
> *They can really bring you down,*
> *Other things just make you feel so stressed.*
> *When things are getting sticky,*
> *Acknowledge that they're tricky,*
> *And this'll mean that they can be addressed.*

'So ...
Always look at your own sort of strife,
[Whistling from Alice, Rita and Ronald together.]
Always caution when pos-i-tive is rife ...
[Whistling.]

'If there's a problem you have gotten,
There's something you've forgotten,
Change needs the cur-rent re-al-it-y,
Recognize your thought and feeling,
It will let you start the healing,
Denial will only make the problem cling.

'I don't know where you get these ideas from,' Rita said, looking at Alice.

'You were talking about being positive and the song "Always Look on the Bright Side of Life"* just popped into my head, although I don't think I got all the words right,' Alice replied.

'I have a question,' said Ronald, 'are we talking about optimism and pessimism?'

'Yes and no,' Rita replied. 'People often use those words to describe traits or patterns of thinking. There has been a lot of research into this, and optimistic thinking is about how we explain things to ourselves and attribute causes; it has little to do with being positive. What I'm talking about here is how positive thinking can be a way that people deny the existence or extent of a problem.'

'Is denial an example of a solution becoming the problem?' asked Ronald.

'Yes, it's one example,' said Rita, 'but not the only one.'

'What are the others?' asked Ronald, 'I'm curious now.'

'Broadly speaking, there are two other ways in which people can exacerbate a "problem" through the "solution" and both are relevant for coaching. The next one is when someone defines their problem in a way that doesn't allow for a solution. I remember a client saying he wanted to feel permanently happy and peaceful and was struggling

---

* Always Look on the Bright Side of Life © 1989, 2006 Virgin Records Ltd.

because he couldn't seem to attain it. He'd travelled the world looking for ways to achieve it – he'd visited gurus, he'd meditated for days, he'd fasted, learned yoga, run long distances, started a family and nothing had worked. He came to see me because he believed he had some block and wanted coaching to remove it.'

'How did you discover what the block was?' asked Ronald.

'I didn't,' said Rita. 'The real "problem" as I saw it was him trying to attain something that couldn't be attained through *trying*. The problem was the trying.'

'You don't think that people should aspire to be happy and peaceful?' asked Ronald.

'Aspire? Yes. Try too hard to attain it? No. And that's because the trying to attain it gets in the way of attaining it. What happens when you try really hard to relax? You can't. Relaxing is the absence of trying.'

'This reminds me of trying to get to sleep,' said Ronald.

'What do you mean?' asked Alice.

'Have you ever woken up in the night and be unable to get back to sleep?' asked Ronald. 'You're lying in bed and your mind is whirling.'

'Yes!' cried Rita.

'The more you will yourself to sleep, the more awake you become, and the more awake you become, the more will power it takes. And the more willpower it takes, the more awake you become, and now you're worried and anxious, too. And the more worried and anxious you are, the more alert you feel.'

'I never try to go to sleep,' said Alice. 'Instead I remember all the nice things that have happened in the day and make a note of them. I always fall asleep before I count them all.'

'A good example, Alice,' said Rita. 'The only way to solve the problem is not to try.'

'I'm beginning to understand,' said Ronald. 'It's the way of defining the problem that is difficult. By defining happiness and peace as something to strive for, your client looked for the solution in a way that would never lead to it.'

'Exactly. The difficulty is in the understanding of the problem and the subsequent attempt to find a solution,' said Rita. 'It's like lying awake at night and thinking that you just need to do one more thing to get back to sleep and you'll be successful.'

'This is why we listen so carefully to the assumptions inherent in the client's world, then,' said Alice. 'We're talking about surface structure and deep structure again.'

'Well remembered, Alice. Understanding the assumptions made by the client is certainly part of this,' said Rita.

'DONE IT!' shouted the Frog, pointing at four lines on the ground. 'I've solved it.'

The three of them looked over to see four lines drawn on the ground.

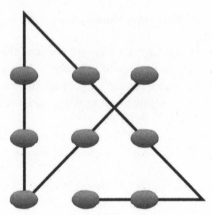

Figure 18.3 The solution

'Well done,' said Alice. 'Not many people work that out.'

'The difficulty is not with the solution but with the problem,' said the Frog. 'For a long while I imagined that all the lines needed to be inside the square and that the problem was how to arrange them in this way. But then I realized that it was me who had made that definition of the problem, not you. Once I realized that the lines could go outside the square, the solution was easy.'

'Very impressive,' said Ronald.

'Can we go and search for my mandolin now?' begged the Frog.

'Of course,' said Alice, 'a deal is a deal.'

The four of them turned around to face the lake and now saw a mere of crystal-clear water in front of them.

'Let's go,' said the Frog, 'while it's clear.'

'How about we take a walk round the edge to decide where the best place is to enter the lake?' prompted Rita. 'You two', she said, indicating Alice and the Frog, 'go one way and we'll go the other. While we're walking we may as well see if we can spot the mandolin.'

Alice and the Frog set off around the small lake and began to look. The sun was dropping lower in the sky and cast a beautiful orange light across the still water. The pair could see the bottom of the lake right the way to the middle, but there was no mandolin in sight. As they reached the farthest point they met Rita and Ronald.

'Nothing?' asked Alice.

'Nothing!' said Rita. 'I suggest that each pair continue circling the lake in case the other pair has missed it.'

Alice and the Frog continued round the lake looking carefully at the water and the lakebed, but there was still no sign of the mandolin.

When the four regrouped the Frog began to cry. 'You said you'd find it,' he wailed.

'Are you absolutely sure it's in the lake?' asked Alice. 'How did it get there?'

'Am I sure?' said the Frog. 'Not at all. In fact, I would say with some certainty that I lost it in the forest over there.'

'What?' screamed Alice. 'You lost it in the forest! Please tell me *why* we are looking in the lake then?'

'The forest is dark and it's awfully hard to move around. I'm an excellent swimmer and I like the water so it's easier to search in the lake,' said the Frog.

'Incredible!' said Alice, astounded. 'Right, we're going to the forest. Keep your eyes open.' She grabbed the Frog by the hand and pulled him along as Rita and Ronald trailed behind.

'What's your name?' she asked. 'I'm sick of calling you Mr Frog.'

'Tad,' replied the Frog.

'Tad?' quizzed Alice.

'Tad Pole,' said the Frog with a laugh.

Alice groaned. 'Do you ever tell the truth?' she asked.

'Of course,' replied the Frog, 'but I can tell you with complete certainty that all frogs are liars.'

'That makes no sense,' declared Alice. 'If it's true, then that means it's false.'

'It's called a paradox,' said Rita.

'What's one of those?' Alice asked.

'A paradox is something that combines logically unacceptable features or qualities, a statement which has apparently sound reasoning but is self-contradictory.'

'Like "I'm going to put lots of effort into going to sleep,"' said Ronald.

'Exactly,' said Rita.

'So, a paradox can't be solved then?' mused Alice.

'Well, it depends. It certainly can't be solved at the level of thinking on which it exists.'

'What does the "level of thinking" mean?' Ronald asked.

'I'll explain,' she said, 'though, in order for me to do so, we need to talk about change more generally. You both ride a bike, don't you?'

Ronald and Alice both nodded.

'What do you do if you want to go faster?' asked Rita.

'Pedal quicker,' said Alice.

'Change gear,' said Ronald.

'Or change gear,' added Alice.

'Exactly! There are two ways. You can pedal quicker in the gear you're in or you can change gear and pedal at the same rate.'

'How does this link to coaching?' asked Ronald.

'I remember a client who presented with the problem "I want to be more motivated". I find that a curious statement. *If* someone isn't motivated for something, it suggests they don't want it and yet their goal is to be more motivated. It seems that what they want is to "want it" – that is, they want how they feel to be different from how it actually is.

'As the coach we must ask ourselves what is happening. Is there something getting in the way, and is it a case of helping the client to connect more easily with the source of their drive (pedalling quicker) or of exploring why the client wants their feelings to be what they are not (changing gear)?'

'So, changing gear is looking at the problem at a different level?' asked Ronald.

'Indeed,' said Rita. 'People often call this first-order and second-order change. First-order change is change within the problem as it is defined. Second-order change is changing the definition of the problem.

'I remember another client who came to me for some help with his team. He told me that his team weren't working hard enough. He not only wanted them to work harder but he wanted them to *want* to work harder. He wanted to change gears and create a second-order change, not just a change in behaviour but a change in attitude. The problem here was that a change in behaviour would have been sufficient. He actually only needed the team to work harder, but he had told himself that they must also want to do that. Again, the solution became the problem.

'Often people will go to great lengths to "solve" something at the wrong level. One of my recent clients – a very successful entrepreneur – was pushing himself so hard he was on the verge of a breakdown. His business had grown significantly in its first year, and he set himself a target of increasing it again in the second year, again in the third, and again in the fourth. He had achieved each of these targets but at a great cost to his own well-being. His target in Year 2 had been difficult so in Year 3 he had increased his hours, spent less time at home, driven efficiencies and made considerable personal investment. In Year 4 he had done more of the same, pushing harder and harder, and his goal in the coaching was to explore how he could work more efficiently and harder again.'

'He wanted to pedal faster but it sounds like his legs were already spinning too fast. Essentially, he wanted you to help him get closer to having a breakdown,' said Ronald.

'Exactly,' said Rita. 'So, what should I do as a coach? I could agree to work with him on the outcome as it is – after all, he is paying me and he owns the outcome. But then I would be enabling him to have more of the same problem.'

'So, what did you do?' asked Ronald.

'I explored with him what would happen if he achieved the goal. What would he want then? He said that he would still want to increase profits the next year. I asked him when he would finally be satisfied. He said, "Never!" I pointed out that it wouldn't matter what he did; in his mind, it would never be enough. He was stuck in first-order change.'

'Could he recognize that?' Ronald asked.

'Yes, but he didn't know what else to do. We had to look at the situation from a different level, from the level of purpose. I asked him what was so important about continually increasing profits. What did that give him? His reply was that it made him feel important and significant; he felt good about himself.'

'Except, of course, that he didn't,' said Alice. 'He was about to have a breakdown.'

'Exactly,' said Rita. 'The purpose had got lost in the doing and he began to see that his endless goal was taking him farther away from the original intention.'

'He couldn't see the wood for the trees,' said Ronald. 'So, what did you do?'

'Once he could see that his current approach wasn't achieving his purpose, we could start work. The coaching had a different focus: instead of it being about him working harder and harder, it became about his desire for significance and importance.'

'A second-order change,' said Ronald.

'The beginning of it,' said Rita. 'It still took some exploration and work to get to the bottom of it, but once we had dealt with his issues around significance, he was able to take a step back from the business and get other people involved. He'd never been able to do that before because his own need for importance meant he had to do it himself.'

'That's really interesting,' said Ronald, 'because, thinking practically, it's the obvious solution. If a person running their own business is overworked, the first thing they would think of would probably be to employ others and delegate some of the responsibility.'

'Exactly,' said Rita, 'but if you'd suggested that to him at the outset, he'd never have done it. He might have been able to appreciate rationally that it was the right way forward but his unresolved thinking would have either prevented it happening, or, if he'd done it, I imagine things wouldn't have really worked because of his need for significance.'

'So, it was his lack of understanding about the problem that was preventing the solution.'

'FOUND IT!' shouted the Frog, 'I've found it. My precious mandolin.' He began to strum a ditty:

'I know an old lady who swallowed a fly ...'

Alice cleared her throat. 'I'll take it from here,' she said. 'You just play the mandolin.'

'*I know an old lady who got scared of the sun.*
I don't know why she was scared of the sun –
She had no fun.

I know an old lady who stayed indoors;
Her days were bores doing endless chores.
She stayed indoors to avoid the sun.
I don't know why she was scared of the sun –
She had no fun.

I know an old lady who had lots to drink;
It made her depressed and unable to think.
She drank to cure her bores indoors;
She stayed indoors to avoid the sun.
I don't know why she was scared of the sun –
She had no fun.

I know an old lady who ran out of food;
It ruined her mood when she ran out of food.
She ate all the food to soak up the drink;
She had lots to drink when she stayed indoors;
She stayed indoors to avoid the sun.
I don't know why she was scared of the sun –
She had no fun.

I know an old lady who ate her dress;
What a mess to have eaten her dress!
She ate her dress because she ran out of food;
She ate all the food to soak up the drink;
She had lots to drink when she stayed indoors;
She stayed indoors to avoid the sun.
I don't know why she was scared of the sun –
She had no fun.

I know an old lady who went naked to the shop.
The sun was out but she didn't drop –
She laughed non-stop!'

'And that, Alice, makes an excellent point. Sometimes the solution comes in the most unlikely form,' said Rita.

'It's like we said earlier: irrational problems require irrational solutions,' said Ronald.

'Except they're not really irrational,' said Rita. 'Often they're at a different level of thinking to the problem and aren't the "logical" solution that might be expected.'

'I'm really beginning to understand this now,' said Ronald. 'When a client comes for coaching, say to be more motivated about something, the logical thing is to look for reasons why they should do it. Like, for example, if someone says I need to be motivated to finish my dissertation, a rational approach would be to explore the benefits of doing so, make a list of the positives and why they should do it.'

'And that may be worthwhile', Rita commented, 'if it changes how the person feels. If it's only a rational thinking process where they're trying to convince themselves of the value of doing it, then it's unlikely to have any lasting impact.'

'The so-called "irrational" approach is to explore why they want to be motivated about something they don't want to do and what is the purpose of being motivated,' continued Ronald.

'And this may or may not unveil a deeper problem which has been keeping their thinking in place,' Rita said.

'What are some other common irrational approaches in coaching?' asked Ronald.

'If I think about common coaching issues, then one category is people who want to change a behaviour. Typically, they either want to start doing something (or do more of it) or they want to stop doing something (or do less of it).'

'Like someone who wants to start going to the gym or start exercising?' asked Ronald.

'Or someone who wants to stop eating cake or cut down?' Alice added.

'Exactly, a behaviour that the person wants to change. They want to speak up in meetings or finish their projects on time. A rational approach to this might be to look at how they might do it, what gyms are nearby, when they're open, what time of day would be best to exercise. Or what they might eat instead of cake that would be healthier, how they can buy less cake in the first place, how they might distract themselves and what they could do instead. The rational approach looks at substituting behaviours or controlling the behaviour.'

'That's a change at the same level then?' said Ronald.

'Exactly,' nodded Rita. 'Sometimes this approach works. *Sometimes*. In my experience, though, more successful is when we examine what drives the behaviour, uncovering what it is the person is feeling that leads them to do the behaviour (or not do it) and what the person values.'

'That's working at a different level, then?' Ronald said.

'Yes, although the goal is a behaviour change, we work at the level of feelings or values. If we can explore what's driving the behaviour and work with that, then the behaviour can change more easily.'

'How would that work for going to the gym?' asked Ronald.

'We'd look at how the person feels about it. If they don't feel motivated or don't really want to do it, then any change at the behavioural level might not last for long. I say "might" because sometimes the behavioural approach works. But more traction might be gained from exploring their drivers for going to the gym, why they want to do it and what their purpose is,' Rita said.

'I thought you said earlier that when someone says they want to be more motivated then that itself is the problem and helping them get motivated might not be what they need?' asked Ronald, puzzled.

'It might not,' said Rita, 'and it might.'

'That is not an answer!' Ronald exclaimed. 'My question is: when you start working with someone, how do you know what to explore?'

'I don't,' said Rita. 'I keep all these ideas in my mind and test them out as we progress. Essentially I'm trying to identify at what level the problem is. I might pursue one line of questioning to see what it brings, and if it's not fruitful I'll try another.'

'You three talk a lot,' interrupted Tad.

Alice had completely forgotten about the Frog who was sitting contentedly in the grass gently strumming his mandolin.

'What can I give you to say thank you for helping me find my mandolin?' asked Tad. 'Anything you like.'

'Anything we like?' queried Rita, 'I don't think ...'

'A space rocket,' interrupted Alice. 'I really want to go into space.'

'Done,' replied Tad. 'If that's what you want, you can have one.'

'Yes! YES! YEEESSS!' screamed Alice.

Rita rolled her eyes and looked at Ronald. 'Oh no. She's going to be very disappointed,' she whispered.

'Where can I find it?' Alice asked.

'In the park,' replied Tad.

'The park?' questioned Alice dubiously.

'Yes, the park, where the playground is,' he replied.

'Come on, then, let's go,' said Alice, setting off briskly.

Rita looked at Ronald. 'Let's go and find this alleged rocket then.'

'Yes,' replied Ronald, frowning at Tad. 'I don't think we're going to find very much.'

The duo saw that Alice was already far ahead of them, skipping along with excitement, so they set off in pursuit.

❧

'If only you'd known what was going to happen next, Alice, you might not have been so excited.'

'I know, Ben. I was really sad afterwards. I'm so excited right now because it's my favourite night of the year, though.'

'Alice, it's not your birthday ... is it?'

'*No*, Ben. Tonight is my other favourite night of the year.'

'You have two favourite nights of the year?'

'Actually, I have three.'

'Three! Which one is it tonight, Alice?'

'It's Firework Night! I love fireworks, although I'm not allowed to set them off on my own. My dad says I need supervision.'

'Well, I think he's very wise. And, talking of supervision, shall we do a quick recap?'

Supervision

The aim of supervision is to support and develop the coach and their coaching. It is typically an opportunity for a coach to share, in confidence, their work with a client or client(s) and may have three differing aspects. First, supervision provides the coach with space to reflect on their coaching work and process the experience of working with clients, exploring challenges and considering useful approaches and resources. Second, supervision offers development to the coach, enhancing skills, understanding and self-awareness. Third, supervision offers support in ethical dilemmas and sharing best practice.

'That's a lot of words, Ben. Can you put it a bit more simply?'

Very simply, I think anyone who is regularly coaching ought to have an experienced coach to speak to about the work they do. This is important both for new coaches and experienced coaches, and the supervision may focus on different areas for each.

'Much better, Ben!'

'Thanks, Alice.'

First- and second-order change

I also want to summarize the ideas of first- and second-order order change. This is a more advanced concept, so if you're new to coaching then take your time with it. Very simply:

First-order change is change within the problem as it is defined. It's doing more (or less) of the same thing.

Second-order change is changing the definition of the problem, shifting the paradigm to a different level of thinking about something. It might be considering what's really important, identifying drivers or values, and understanding the bigger purpose in trying to achieve something.

As a coach it is important to be mindful of when a first-order change will be effective and when a first-order change will just create another problem or perpetuate the existing one.

'Ben, I like to remember it like this. A first-order change is change within the situation as it is, like going faster by pedalling quicker. A second-order change is changing the definition of the problem or the construction of it – that's like changing into a new gear.'

'Yes, the cycling analogy is a good way of remembering the difference. By the way, I'm curious, you said you have *three* favourite nights of the year. What is the third, Alice?'

'It's Christmas Eve, of course, my favourite night of the year.'

'Along with your birthday and Firework Night?'

'Yes, they're all my favourite nights of the year. I don't know what you're confused about. Do you know my favourite fireworks are the rockets that have lots of different colours and look like a shower in the sky?'

'Is that right, Alice? Well, talking of rockets, we have a story to finish. Shall we get back to it?'

'Oh yes, I can't wait to talk about the rocket.'

CHAPTER 19

Rocket Girl

THE IMPACT OF THE BELIEFS AND PERCEPTION OF THE COACH

● ● ●

As the trio made their way towards the park, Rita began to talk. 'I think you're now ready to understand some more advanced ideas. First, I want to talk about perception, and to illustrate this I want you to think of someone you admire, someone you look up to.'

'Valentina Tereshkova, the first woman in space,' said Alice.

'Slash from Guns N' Roses,' said Ronald.

'You like Guns N' Roses?' said Alice incredulously. 'You do surprise me, Ronald.'

'I used to be a rockfish,' Ronald replied, 'always listening to GNR. "Paradise City" is my favourite.'

'I'm more of a Mötley Crüe fan myself,' said Rita. 'So, when you think about Valentina and Slash, I want you to identify exactly what it is that you admire about them, and I don't mean the things they've done. I'm talking about their strengths and character traits.'

'I think Valentina had a lot of determination and drive and didn't let herself be constrained by society. She said, "If women can be railroad workers in Russia, why can't they fly in space?" I admire those traits. I wish I was like that,' said Alice.

'I admire Slash because he followed his own path in life: guitar playing was his passion and he dedicated himself to it. In his early years he practised endlessly. I think he stayed true to himself and made the most of the talent he had,' said Ronald.

'Do you each think you have those traits?' asked Rita.

'I don't,' said Alice.

'Me neither,' said Ronald.

'And yet on some level you must do because otherwise you couldn't recognize them in someone else.'

'What do you mean?' asked Ronald.

'It's very hard to observe something if you don't already know it. Our perceptual filters tend to delete data that we can't compute or distort it to fit what we already know. We discussed that before.'

'Yes, you used the example of my father's new silver car,' said Alice.

'Right,' continued Rita, 'you tend to see silver cars once they exist in your world. The same thing is true when it comes to what we observe in others. We have to know something ourselves to see it in them.'

'So, are you saying that we already have some of these traits ourselves?' asked Ronald.

'That's exactly what I'm saying,' said Rita. 'I realize that they may not be as developed as you would like or they may be unexpressed in some way but they are there.'

'That's a reassuring thought,' said Ronald. 'I like to think that I have some dedication already and that I will make the most of the talents I have.'

'This is a recognized phenomenon,' said Rita. 'It's called projection and happens when we see attributes that we possess showing up in other people. We can only do so because, at some level, we possess these characteristics ourselves. If we did not, then we would be unable see them in others. What we perceive is what we project as being present in others.'

'Let me give you another example,' Rita said, handing them her notepad which was covered in writing.

'Look at the notes on this page and notice how many times the letter *t* occurs.'

Alice and Ronald began looking at the page and scanning for each occurrence of the letter *t*.

'Now, close your eyes and see how many letter *t*s you can remember,' Rita said.

'Thirteen,' said Alice.

'Eleven,' said Ronald.

'Keep your eyes closed and see how many letter *l*s you can remember.'

'I can't remember any,' said Alice. 'I know there must be some but I can't remember any specifically.'

'Me too, I count zero,' said Ronald.

'OK, open your eyes and look at the page again. How many of letter *l*s are there?' Rita asked.

'One, two, three, four ... There's a lot,' said Alice.

'And yet you couldn't remember any,' said Rita.

'That's because you told us to look for *t*s,' Alice replied.

'Exactly,' said Rita. 'If *t*s are your focus of attention, then that's what you'll observe on the page. And, while you do this, you don't observe any other letters that are present. Your perception is a projection of what's in your mind. The same thing happens with our experiences and interactions with others: often what we perceive is a reflection of what's inside us. However, unlike when you were reading my notes, most of the time you're not conscious that you're doing this. You're not conscious of what the letter is – that is, of the characteristic, belief, idea, emotion or attitude that you're projecting from your own unconscious.'

'How does this relate to coaching?' asked Ronald.

Rita continued: 'The famous psychologist Carl Jung said, "Projection is one of the commonest psychic phenomena ... Everything that is unconscious in ourselves we discover in our neighbour, and we treat him accordingly." In coaching we need to be mindful that the observations and answers our client gives are not projections from ourselves and are indeed what our client means. Otherwise we won't really be working with their map of the world and it will be our own instead.'

'Does this really happen?' Ronald asked doubtfully. 'Do we really project our own unconscious thoughts on to others?'

'Let's think back to your conversation with Victor. Do you remember how you described Simon?' asked Rita.

'I said he thinks he's better than he actually is,' said Ronald, wincing a little.

'That's right,' said Rita, 'and do you recall in your conversation with Victor that you said you didn't want to be an angry person.'

'I do,' said Ronald.

'You said it's not who you are and you'd like to think you're better than that, although, as you acknowledged later, you were actually very angry.'

'It's true but I don't get your point,' Ronald said.

'You said Simon thinks he's better than he actually is, and you think that you're better than you actually are at dealing with your anger.'

'But that's different,' said Ronald, shaking his head.

'How is it different?' Rita asked.

Ronald opened his mouth and closed it again. And opened it. And closed it. 'Well, even if it is the same, how do you know I'm projecting?'

'I don't,' said Rita. 'All I know is that the thing you didn't recognize in yourself is the thing you identified in Simon.'

'Argghhhh!' said Ronald, putting his head in his fins. 'You are so annoying sometimes.'

'In what way am I annoying?' asked Rita.

'In that way ... IN THAT WAY!' Ronald yelled. 'Always being right about everything.'

'Have I gone too far?' Rita asked. 'I'm sorry if I have, really I am.'

'No, you haven't,' said Ronald. 'I just don't like it when I discover things I don't know about myself. It makes me uncomfortable.'

Rita paused. 'I'm sorry if I pushed it too far. You don't have to discover anything about yourself, and I will refrain from that kind of conversation if you feel uncomfortable.'

'This has been such an amazing journey,' Ronald said, 'learning about coaching with you both ... I just feel a bit overwhelmed.'

'We've covered a lot in our conversations,' Rita said. 'You are both quick learners and you assimilate ideas very quickly.'

'Do you think so?' asked Ronald.

'I really do,' Rita said. 'You're still here, asking questions, exploring and learning. Some people would have stopped a long time ago. Maybe you're more like Slash with your dedication than you realize, and, Alice, maybe you're more like Valentina than you realize, too.'

'You haven't heard me play guitar yet,' said Ronald with a smirk. 'You'll discover I'm nothing like Slash then. I understand your point, though, and thank you.'

'Let me give you a couple of other examples. Remember the coaching with Hugo that you observed. Do you recall what he imagined others thinking when they saw him on his own?' asked Rita.

'He thought that other people would think he was boring or unlikeable,' said Ronald.

'Exactly. How did he know that?' asked Rita.

'He didn't,' said Alice. 'It's just what he imagined.'

'Exactly, he projected those ideas on to people. To my knowledge, no one ever said that; it was his own thought.'

'So, he projected this idea on to others and then responded to them as if it were really true?' Ronald asked.

'Indeed, our projection is unconscious. We're not aware of it and so we react as if the projections are really how the person is.'

'Wow,' said Ronald. 'I think the same thing was happening with Camilla, too, wasn't it?'

'Indeed. Camilla described her business partner, Clarissa, as refusing to listen and being stubborn. I think Camilla realized during the session that she herself had not been listening and had been very stubborn in her approach.'

'This makes more sense now,' Ronald said. 'So, what should we do with this?'

'It's something to be aware of, and, as a coach, it's a reminder to ensure you ask questions that really explore your client's map of the world without imposing your own ideas.'

'You said you wanted to share some advanced ideas with us,' Alice said. 'Perception is projection is one idea. What else is there?'

'I wanted to talk about beliefs,' said Rita, 'about how our beliefs and expectations as a coach can have an impact on the coaching.'

'Our beliefs and expectations about what?' asked Alice.

'Our beliefs about our clients and our expectations of them. I want to share an experiment with you that was conducted with schoolteachers. At the start of a school year, teachers were told that certain students in their class had high IQs and would make excellent progress in the year ahead. These students were chosen at random from a mixed class of students, whose IQs in reality were about average. The experimenters measured the progress of the students at the end of the year and it was found that the students who had been labelled as more intelligent showed greater increases in their IQ than students in the class not labelled as having a high IQ.'

'Wow,' said Ronald, 'what did they think was happening?'

'The researchers surmised that the effect was because teachers had higher expectations for the students labelled as more intelligent and responded differently to them. For example, the teachers may have asked more challenging questions to the students they believed were more intelligent or may have praised them more or given them more attention. The teachers weren't doing this intentionally. Good teachers would always treat their students equally, but the beliefs the teachers had about these students had an impact.'

'That is fascinating,' said Alice. 'Are you saying that as a coach our beliefs and expectations about our clients will make a difference?'

'That's exactly what I'm saying. Let's imagine someone comes to you for coaching and deep down you don't really think that they can resolve their issue. How might that affect your coaching?' Rita asked.

'I might give up more easily or not push them to explore certain possibilities,' said Ronald.

'The client might notice it in my body language,' Alice said.

'Either or both, and there are many more possibilities – your own beliefs and expectations would leak out of you,' Rita said.

'But what if you don't think a person can achieve something or resolve something?' Ronald asked.

'Maybe they can't. I'm probably never going to be world-class basketball player, for example. If you genuinely don't believe they can do something, then you aren't the right person to be coaching them,' said Rita.

'Yes, I see that,' said Ronald. 'So, what expectations and beliefs should I have of my clients?'

'An interesting question,' Rita said. 'Can I share a few ideas with you?'

'Yes, please,' said Alice.

'I'm not saying these ideas are actually true,' Rita began, 'I'm really not. What I am saying is that they can be useful things to believe, and that acting as if they are true will give you a greater range and flexibility within your coaching.'

'OK,' said Ronald, 'I get that. What are these ideas?'

'The first one is: *People make the best choice they can at the time.* Each of us makes the best choice we can, given the map of the world we have. Sometimes a choice may be self-defeating or hard to understand or have negative consequences but on some level it seems the best way forward.'

'That's quite a challenging thing to believe,' Ronald said. 'I see people doing some awful things.'

'Indeed,' said Rita. 'This idea doesn't mean people don't do bad things or deliberately hurt others, but let's consider how this idea would change your questioning if you hold it as a truth.'

'I suppose I would be more intent on understanding why a person does something and what is going on in their map of the world that would make it a good choice, so I would be less judgemental,' Ronald mused.

'Exactly, I would agree. You're more likely to explore their choice in a way that will bring insight and understanding. Through this may come other possibilities and different choices the person can make. If you assist someone in finding a better choice in their map of the world, then they will have other ways to act.'

'What else?' asked Alice.

'The second idea is: *People are not their behaviours*. It has been shown that we have a bias towards identifying people with the behaviours they display. In psychology, attribution theory is concerned with how we explain actions and behaviour. The most common attribution error is that we attribute the behaviour of other people to something about them whereas we attribute our own behaviour to the environment or situation we're in.'

'Really, I never knew that,' said Ronald.

'We must be mindful as a coach that we don't confuse who someone is and their traits with how they are behaving,' said Alice.

Rita continued: 'For me, I think the key idea in coaching is that people are more than their behaviours and people are more than their challenges or problems. Even though someone has a difficulty they are still fundamentally OK as a person. My goal is to see each client as good enough and resourceful. Which leads on to the next idea.

'*We already have all the resources we need, or we can create them.* This is the idea that there are no un-resourceful people, only un-resourceful states of mind. We are more than our problems and we have, within us, the answers and solutions to life's challenges *or* we can learn how to deal with them.'

'It's an idea of hope,' said Alice.

'I suppose it is,' Rita replied. 'I'd never really considered it like that before. It's more than hope actually; it's a belief that people are capable and resilient. It's also a separation between the things people experience and how they feel – the old Buddhist saying that pain is inevitable, suffering is optional.'

'Wow, some of this is really challenging for me,' Ronald said.

'I know and, like I said, I'm not saying these ideas are true. I'm inviting you to explore them for yourself and notice your own responses. If you have resistance to an idea, then I am not suggesting you try to override that; instead be curious about your resistance and get to know it. There may be something of deep value there for you.'

'Thank you,' Ronald said, 'I will.'

'I think this is the slowest walk ever to the park,' Alice said.

'Yes, we've been talking rather a lot,' Rita replied. 'Come on we're nearly there.'

As the trio arrived in the park, Alice saw a children's playground. In the middle of it was a magenta space rocket surrounded by a noisy group of people.

The three approached the rocket, and Alice recognized the Caterpillar, still dressed in his suit. Next to him was Hugo, the chimpanzee, deep in conversation with Reynard. Camilla was there, still dressed immaculately, looking at something, with Victor. As Alice got closer, she saw that they were talking to Christina the Ladybird. At the back of the group she heard a gentle strumming and saw Tad the Frog playing his mandolin.

'What a lovely farewell party,' said Rita.

'I'm going to miss you, both,' said Alice, giving each of them a hug. 'Thank you so much for everything.'

'It's been wonderful to learn alongside you,' said Ronald, 'and I've really enjoyed your company.'

'It's a been pleasure for an old turtle like me to remember what it's like to be young again,' said Rita. 'Thank you, Alice.'

Alice hugged them both again and moved over to the rest of the group.

'Hello, Victor,' she said.

'Alice! Brought me some cake, have you?' he asked with a twinkle in his eye.

'Next time,' Alice replied, 'I promise. It was a pleasure to meet you.'

'You, too,' Victor said. 'You have a great deal of potential, my dear. Don't be afraid to use it.'

'How are things?' Alice asked Camilla.

'Much improved,' Camilla replied. 'Clarissa and I had our first productive conversation in a long time. We made some real progress.'

'I'm pleased to hear it,' Alice replied.

'Aren't you going to say hello to me,' said a squeaky voice.

'Christina! It's lovely to see you again.'

'Thank you for the coaching, Alice. I've already started preparing for the interview. I'm actually looking forward to it,' said Christina.

Alice moved on to the next group.

'Hello, Hugo,' she said. 'We've never actually met in person.'

'Pleased to meet you,' the chimpanzee replied. 'Reynard has told me so much about you.'

'I was just telling Hugo how you got us out of The Doghouse,' Reynard said, 'and how you helped me personally. Thank you, Alice.'

'I wish you both well for the future,' she said, 'I really do.'

'Hello, Mr Caterpillar,' Alice said. She thought back to the first morning she had met Rita and Ronald and the Caterpillar. It seemed ages ago – so much had happened since then.

'Hello, Alice,' he said with a smile. 'Thank you again for our conversation. You really helped me out that morning, and I appreciate your expertise.'

'It's a pleasure,' she said. 'You know, I don't know anything about funnels or wine making. All I did was listen and ask you some questions.'

'You did more than that,' the Caterpillar replied. 'You gave me a whole idea for what I could do in the future.'

'I think you did that yourself,' Alice replied, 'but it's nice to know that it was useful.'

'Goodbye, Tad,' Alice said. 'Make sure you look after that mandolin, and thanks for the songs.'

'Thanks for the puzzles,' Tad replied, 'and for helping me find it.'

Alice turned to look at the space rocket and began to climb the steps to the door. As she reached the top, she turned around to say a final goodbye.

'I think it would be nice,' said Rita, 'if you could leave us with a thought before you say goodbye.'

Alice felt her eyes begin to moisten. 'Stop crying and think, Alice,' she said to herself. 'If you can remember everything, you've been taught and express gratitude to this crew, you can leave on a happy thought and it will make a nice thank you.'

Alice wiped a tear from her eye, cleared her throat and drew herself up to her full height:

> *'If you can listen to what's said when all about you*
> *Are thoughts and feelings that belong to you,*
> *If you can explore the map your client gives you*
> *And find the assumptions implicit in it, too;*

If you can question and not be tired of asking,
    Or observing words and feeding back,
Or noticing expressions that need unmasking,
    And yet maintain rapport and keep on track:

If you elicit client wants – and not the don't wants;
    If you support responsibility without assigning blame;
If you can meet Persecutor and Victim
    And treat those two impostors just the same;
If you can split content and process,
    See how the problem lives inside their map,
Probe, enquire and help clients express
    And not get caught in the logical trap:

If you can know it won't be plain sailing,
    And when it's hard, acknowledge and admit,
Ask for supervision when you feel you're failing,
    And own your role and part in it;
If you can observe your own projection,
    Explore and learn what's unconscious in you,
Subject your beliefs to thorough reflection,
    And work with that same client anew:

If you know the ways change can be reckoned,
    Recognize when a solution keeps the problem there,
Think about the order being first or second,
    And help your client be aware;
If you maintain your coaching endeavour,
    Practise, practise and persevere,
Yours are the skills and rewards for ever,
    And – which is more – you'll be a coach, my dear!'

The group broke out into applause and Alice waved a final goodbye as she entered the rocket. The door slid shut silently behind her and she looked around at the gleaming white interior. In front of her was a large comfortable armchair into which she settled herself. There was a thunderous noise from outside as the clapping continued, and she braced herself for the rocket to lift off.

CHAPTER 20

Awakening

A COACHING EXAMPLE OF THE SOLUTION BEING THE PROBLEM

● ● ●

The rocket began to toss Alice gently from side to side as the clapping died away. The intercom buzzed and she recognized her father's voice.

'Alice, Alice. Are you OK?'

How awfully strange, she thought to herself, I wonder how my father is speaking on the rocket's radio.

'Alice,' came her father's voice again, 'time to wake up.'

The rocket began to shake more and then faded away as Alice opened her eyes. Her father was bending over her looking concerned, and he was rocking the chair she was sitting in. Looking over her father's shoulder Alice saw a large room with a group of people exiting through some double doors.

'Alice, are you OK, dear?' her father asked.

'Yes, I think so,' she replied.

'You've been asleep all day. Every time I came to check on you, you were still dozing.'

'All day?' Alice queried. She looked around again and discovered she was at the back of a large conference room with lots of chairs and a screen at the front. She had no recollection of how she got there.

'I'm so sorry I had to bring you to work with me today. I know it hasn't been a good start to the school holidays for you. I could see you were still unwell this morning, but I couldn't stay at home today. You were half asleep when we arrived so I put you in the armchair at the back here.'

'Oh, I see,' said Alice, adjusting to her new environment. 'Have you been teaching a workshop today, Dad?'

'Yes, dear,' her father replied. 'I had lots of people booked so I really couldn't cancel it. I'm so sorry.'

'What was the workshop about?' Alice asked.

'It was about something called coaching, darling.'

'I see,' said Alice with a smile. 'Did it go well?'

'Really well,' her father replied. 'There were some really interesting people attending.'

'Oh yes, and who were they?' Alice asked.

'Well, there was Ronald who works for a bike manufacturer; a gymnast named Hugo; a lady named Christina who works for a clothing company; Camilla, the head of a charity; a guy who has been unemployed, and many more.'

'Did Christina want a promotion?' asked Alice.

'Yes, she did,' replied her father. 'You were awake! I thought you'd been asleep all day. Did you see her red-and-black dress? It was incredible.'

'Not exactly,' said Alice, smiling.

'And Ronald, the guy who cycled here?' asked her father. 'He was a real star today. Did you see him?'

'Were you working on your own today?' Alice asked.

'Most of the time. I had a colleague come in for an hour during the afternoon to help me with something.'

'Victor?' asked Alice.

'Yes!' said her father. 'You have been watching and listening. Victor came in to do a short talk about something. He's getting older now, so doesn't like to do a whole day.'

'Supervision,' said Alice. 'It was a fascinating conversation, although I felt a bit sorry for Ronald. Was Victor miffed that I ate all the cakes?'

'You ate all the cakes? You haven't eaten a thing today. I brought you some pizza and ice cream at lunchtime and left them next to you but you haven't touched them. Then I left some cake at one of the breaks but you haven't eaten that either. Look, they're all still sitting here.'

'Oh yes, of course, silly me,' Alice said, looking at a plate of pizza and cake.

'Shall we go home, then?' asked her, father picking up his bag.

As the two left the conference room Alice saw a sign that said 'Atrium' and they walked into a light and airy entrance foyer before exiting into the car park.

As they drove away, Alice thought her father looked pensive and preoccupied.

'What are you thinking about, Dad?' she asked.

'I've got a rehearsal tonight.'

'For the jazz band?' Alice asked.

'Yes, I'm feeling a bit stuck with it,' her father replied.

'What are you stuck with?' Alice asked.

'Well, you know I've told you that much of what we play is improvised and we don't know what's going to happen until we're performing. I just feel that I'm not doing it very well. I understand the theory but I'm unhappy with my performance.'

Alice could hear Rita's voice in her head explaining the difference between surface structure and the deep structure of someone's experience.

'What are you actually stuck with?' she said.

'I'm not sure how to improve. Don't get me wrong, my performances are really good but I want to take it to the next level.'

'And you're not sure how to improve?' Alice repeated.

'Yes, I've studied the theory and I really understand it. Musically, my skills are excellent, you know that. I practise my scales and my fourths and fifths, but it seems like the more I try to play along when we're improvising the worse I get,' Alice's father replied.

'The more you try, the worse you get?' Alice probed.

'That's not really the case. I'm not getting worse but I'm not improving either. I make mistakes, I miss things that the others are doing, and I know it could sound better.'

'What things are you missing?' Alice asked.

Her father looked across at her from the driver's seat. 'What's happening, Alice? You don't usually ask so many questions? Have you been awake all day and making notes on the workshop?'

'I think I must have been listening in my sleep, Dad,' said Alice with a fond smile. 'Tell me, though, what things are you missing when you're playing?'

'I'm missing some of the notes the lead plays, some of his riffs and melodies. I don't pick up on them quickly enough and then don't incorporate them into my own playing.'

'What's your goal?' Alice asked.

'Now I know you were listening today,' Alice's dad said, laughing.

'Maybe I was,' Alice replied, 'but tell me, what is it?'

'Well ...', said her father thoughtfully, 'I guess it's to improvise better in the band.'

'You or the other people in the band?' asked Alice, thinking back to Rita's criteria for a goal.

'Me. This is about me. It's about me responding better to the others.'

'OK,' said Alice, 'so it's in your control. How would you know if you were responding better?'

'Alice! Where have you got this from? You seem to have come out of your shell – you're asking really good coaching questions.'

'Thanks,' Alice said, smiling and wishing Rita and Ronald could see her now. 'How would you know if you were responding better?'

'A few ways,' her father replied. 'First, the music would flow more and would feel less effortful. Sometimes when I'm playing it's almost like it just happens on its own. Second, the others in the band would give me feedback. Sometimes we discuss how the performance went afterwards and I pick up on things I've missed. Ultimately, the audience would enjoy the performance more as well.'

'That sounds pretty clear to me,' Alice said. 'Tell me more about what happens when it doesn't go well. I'm interested.'

'When it doesn't go well?' her father queried.

'Yes,' replied Alice.

'Well, I'm playing and I hear the lead begin to change what we're playing. I'm wondering what he's going to do – there's quite a lot of theory in jazz improvisation so I'm thinking about some of the possibilities for where he might take it.'

'How are you feeling at this point?' Alice asked.

'A bit anxious perhaps.'

'Anxious about what?' Alice continued.

'Anxious about getting it right. I want the performance to be amazing and I'm trying really hard to get it right. It's a bit stressful.'

'So, you're feeling anxious because you want the performance to be amazing, you're trying hard to get it right and you're thinking about the possibilities for where the music might go to.'

'Yes, that's it exactly,' her father replied.

'How well is this approach working?' Alice asked.

'It's not. I'm playing OK, but I'm not improving and I know I could be better. If your next question is what ideas have I got to improve, then I have thought about this. I think sometimes I'm not focused enough when we're playing and I need to try harder to focus more and try to anticipate where the music is going.'

'Interesting,' said Alice. 'You're telling me that you're trying hard to perform well and that this approach isn't working, but your solution is to do more of the same and try harder.'

Alice's father looked at her in the same way as when he scolded her for eating too many cakes. 'I don't think you understand this, Alice, it's adult stuff. Trying hard is part of it.'

Alice took a deep breath. 'Is it OK that I'm asking you these questions, Dad. I'm only trying to help?'

Alice's father looked at her and his face softened. 'Of course, it's OK, dear. I'm just not used to you talking like this. It's surprising me.'

'You said that there have been times when the music seems to flow; it's less effortful and just seems to happen on its own. What's that like?'

'It doesn't happen very often. It's usually in rehearsal, not the performances. Sometimes I just feel that I'm in the zone. Some of my best improvisation happens then.'

'How do you feel at this time?'

Alice's father paused and took a breath. 'I feel relaxed. Calm, actually.'

'Relaxed and calm. And what are you paying attention to?' Alice asked.

'I'm listening,' her father said. 'I'm listening to the lead. I can hear every note and I can hear how they flow together and I can see the patterns.'

'You're listening,' repeated Alice. 'What are you thinking about?'

Her father paused. 'I'm not thinking anything, I'm just listening.' He looked at her. 'You're a clever girl. A very clever girl.'

Alice gulped. 'What do you mean?' she asked.

'You've just told me how to improve. Why did I not see this?'

Alice was sure she hadn't told her father how to improve, and she was pretty sure she wasn't seeing whatever it was. 'What are you seeing now, Dad?'

'Well, the harder I try to improve the more anxious I become, and the more anxious I become the more I worry about not getting the notes and riffs. Then, I try harder to anticipate what's coming based on the theory and the more I do that, the less I listen. I've just realized that when I don't try hard to get it right I feel more relaxed, and when I'm relaxed I listen better and that's when I'm at my best.'

'The less you try, the better you play,' said Alice.

'The less I try to get it right, the better I play,' corrected her father. 'Instead of trying to get it right, if I put my attention on what the lead is playing and I listen, then I play better.'

'You said earlier that trying hard is part of it?'

'I've always tried hard at things. Trying hard is how I get better.'

'What do you think about that now?' Alice asked.

'I still think it's true. Trying hard and putting effort into being successful is often required in life. But sometimes it's *not* true. I can see that trying hard to be successful or get it right is the very thing that can stop me achieving it. The more I relax about my performance and focus on listening, the more I will play better. It's so counter-intuitive. Even though my goal is to improve, the less I try to get it right, the better I do.'

'What's the first step to improving then?' Alice asked.

'To continue listening,' her father replied. 'I know I want to improve – that hasn't changed – but it's *how* I go about it. Instead of trying to get it right, I want to listen more and be relaxed when I'm playing because this will help me achieve it.'

'That sounds great, Dad.'

'Thank you, Alice, that was a great piece of coaching. You've obviously learned a lot today.'

Alice smiled. What an amazing few days – what an amazing *day*! She was so engrossed in her thoughts and the conversation that she had hardly noticed the car journey. As her father pulled up into the driveway, she looked up and saw her sister playing on the grass outside the house. Alice walked over and saw her sister was playing with her pet tortoise. Alice smiled to herself, and the tortoise seemed to look right at her with a knowing smile. Walking towards the front door, Alice glanced at the pond and saw a fish near the surface looking in her direction.

'Thank you,' she mouthed at the fish.

As her sister glanced away, Alice looked at the tortoise and mouthed another 'thank you', and she was sure the tortoise winked back at her.

CHAPTER 21

The End of the Beginning

SUMMARY AND QUESTIONS TO CONTINUE THE READER'S JOURNEY

● ● ●

'Alice, I want a short précis of the book to finish.'

'What's a pray-sea, Ben?'

'Haven't you learned that in French yet, Alice? Think summary.'

'Sunshine and blue sky and apple trees and picnics and freshly cut grass?'

'Not summery, Alice, a summ-a-ry. I want to write a summary.'

'Why didn't you say so? I'll help with that.'

'You will?'

'Ben! This whole story is about me. If anyone can write a pray-sea, I can.'

'Great, I want this to be a quick summary. There won't be an opportunity for poetry, Alice.'

'OK, Ben. I think we should start by remembering why a coaching approach is useful. The main thing I've discovered is that it's possible to help someone without solving something for them, and that, by helping them find their own solutions and ways forward and giving them ownership, I am empowering them and fostering self-reliance instead of dependence.'

'That's a great start, Alice. In a business context we might also consider that a coaching approach often leads to more engagement and "buy in" than a directive, "tell" approach. A coaching approach also has the potential to bring innovative ideas and solutions. Coaching unlocks potential, increases flexibility, gives options and develops the individual.

'So, Alice, what are some of the key coaching skills and ideas you've learned?'

'Well, Ben, let me see, there's tell versus ask, different levels of listening, asking open questions, the GROW model, separating content and process, rapport and maps of the world, surface structure and deep structure, relationship dynamics (Persecutor, Rescuer and Victim), giving feedback, supervision, different levels of change, perceptual positions, and my own beliefs and ideas as a coach. Phew! That's quite a lot.'

'It is.'

'I think it's time to say goodbye, but I have a final question.'

'What is it, Alice?'

'Sometimes when I'm having a conversation I hear Rita's voice in my head giving me advice or encouragement. I hear her say things like "Ask an open question" or "Make sure you've agreed the contract for this conversation." Sometimes I even ask myself, "What would Rita say?" to work out what to do. Do you think that's weird because, after all, it was only a dream, and she's not actually real?'

'Is it helpful having Rita give you advice or encouragement?'

'You know what, Ben, it is helpful. I'm able to take a step back and consider how to approach a conversation. But does it matter that it's not coming from me and I've got an imaginary turtle in my mind?'

'Let's be clear about something, Alice. The "Rita" is in your mind and is just a part of you. It's the part of you that has assimilated the coaching skills, knowledge and understanding. We all have parts of us that do different things and represent different skills. It's just that usually we don't give them a name.'

And, as you're reading this, I don't know if you will have your own Rita, Ronald or Alice who will help you remember the coaching ideas and skills that you've learned. You may have already begun to integrate the ideas from this book into your own internal coaching wonderland and have put them into practice or you may be looking forward to opportunities to do so.

It might be helpful to reflect right now on the following:

- What have been the most useful ideas for you in this book?

- What have you learned that will help you have better coaching conversations?

- Are there things you would like to practise and develop your skills in?

Next time you're in a coaching conversation you might be curious as to whether it is your own Rita, Ronald or Alice helping you listen and ask questions. You might remember that each of the clients you are coaching has their own internal wonderland, a map of the world which, metaphorically, is full of different characters, too. Your role as coach is to help your client explore this wonderland, to understand it better, find new perspectives, discover potential and guide them through a journey of learning and development. As you continue to practise and develop, the skills and ideas that were once new to you will become more automatic and you'll find yourself using them without thinking. At some point in the future you may look back on now and on your own adventures in coaching and reflect on how much you've learned.

For now it's time for Alice and I to say goodbye and to wish you well.

References and Further Reading

The following are either referred to in the text or suggested for further reading on the topics covered in this book:

Berne, Eric (2016). *Games People Play: The Psychology of Human Relationships*, London: Penguin.

Broadwell, Martin M. (20 February 1969). 'Teaching for learning (XVI)', *The Gospel Guardian*.

Covey, Stephen R. (2013). *The 7 Habits of Highly Effective People*, reissue edn, London: Simon & Schuster UK. First published 1989.

Knight, Sue (2009). *NLP at Work: The Essence of Excellence*, 3rd edn, London: Nicholas Brealey.

Korzybski, Alfred (2010). *Selections from Science and Sanity*, ed. Lance Strate and Bruce Kodish, 2nd edn, Forest Hills, NY: Institute of General Semantics.

Kostere, Kim M. and Malatesta, Linda K. (1992). *Maps, Models and the Structure of Reality: NLP Technology in Psychotherapy*. Portland, OR, USA: Metamorphous Press.

Starr, Julie (2016). *The Coaching Manual: The Definitive Guide to the Process, Principles and Skills of Personal Coaching*, 4th edn, London: Pearson Business. First published 2008.

Whitmore, John (2016). *Coaching for Performance: The Principles and Practice of Coaching and Leadership*, 4th edn, London: Nicholas Brealey.

Acknowledgements

I would like to thank many people who have been teachers and coaches to me and others from whom I have learned a great deal. I will name a few here and recognize that there are countless more in the fields of psychology, coaching, NLP and psychotherapy who have influenced my thinking and provided moments of insight. If I have omitted thanks or acknowledgement for any ideas in this book, I apologize and will happily rectify this upon notification.

First, I wish to thank each and every one of my coaching clients who have shared themselves and their challenges and who have enriched my own coaching experience. Second, I am grateful to everyone who has participated in my workshops and trainings and with whom I have been able to test material and discover the common questions that arise. Third, I wish to thank John Overdurf, Julie Silverthorn, Mark Stein, Ty Francis and Gillian Kelly for their direct input into my own journey.

Finally, a thank you to Jane Talbot, Jen Hodgins, Matt France, Nicky Hope, Penny Huggard and Ty Francis for reading an early draft of this book and for valuable feedback.

Index

Would you like your people to read this book?

If you would like to discuss how you could bring these ideas to your team, we would love to hear from you. Our titles are available at competitive discounts when purchased in bulk across both physical and digital formats. We can offer bespoke editions featuring corporate logos, customized covers, or letters from company directors in the front matter can also be created in line with your special requirements.

We work closely with leading experts and organizations to bring forward-thinking ideas to a global audience. Our books are designed to help you be more successful in work and life.

For further information, or to request a catalogue, please contact:
business@johnmurrays.co.uk
sales-US@nicholasbrealey.com (North America only)

Nicholas Brealey Publishing is an imprint of
John Murray Press.